AMERICA
MAGICA

AMERICA
MAGICA

When Renaissance Europe Thought
it had Conquered Paradise

Jorge Magasich-Airola &
Jean-Marc de Beer

Foreword by
David Abulafia

Translated by
Monica Sandor

SECOND EDITION

ANTHEM PRESS
LONDON · NEW YORK · DELHI

Anthem Press
An imprint of Wimbledon Publishing Company
www.anthempress.com

This edition first published in UK and USA 2007
First edition published by Anthem Press 2005
by ANTHEM PRESS
75-76 Blackfriars Road, London SE1 8HA, UK
or PO Box 9779, London SW19 7ZG, UK
and
244 Madison Ave. #116, New York, NY 10016, USA

British Library Cataloguing in Publication Data
A catalogue record for this book is available from the British Library.

Library of Congress Cataloging in Publication Data
Magasich-Airola, Jorge, 1952-
[América mágica, quand l'Europe de la Renaissance croyait conquérir la Paradis. English]
América mágica : when renaissance Europe thought it had conquered paradise / Jorge
Magasich-Airola & Jean-Marc de Beer; translated by Monica Sandor. — 2nd ed.
p. cm.
Includes bibliographical references.
ISBN-13: 978-1-84331-292-5 (pbk.)
ISBN-10: 1-84331-186-0 (pbk.)
1. American — Discovery and exploration — Spanish.
2. Geographical myths. I. Beer, Jean-Marc de, 1956- II. Sandor, Monica. III. Title.
E121.M2813 2007
970.01'6 — dc22
2007026384

ISBN-10: 1 84331 292 1 (Pbk)
ISBN-13: 978 1 84331 292 5 (Pbk)

1 3 5 7 9 10 8 6 4 2

Printed in the EU

CONTENTS

The Fabled Shores of the New World

The discovery of America was both a shock and a confirmation of existing expectations. Paradoxically, Europeans were both amazed by what they saw, and determined to apply preconceived notions about the peoples and lands that must lie on the opposite shores of the Ocean Sea. One reason for this was the assumption in the mind of Columbus and his contemporaries that what he had discovered was a series of islands off the shore of Asia or 'India', islands indicated in the travel narrative of Marco Polo two hundred years earlier. Even Amerigo Vespucci's insistence that the New World was not the outer edge of Asia but a new continent (which would soon be proved to be two continents) did not immediately deprive America of its 'Indian' character, for no one could be sure, until Magellan circumnavigated the globe, how vast was the distance separating its western shores from the real Indies, nor, until Bering discovered the straits dividing Asia from North America, was it clear that the landmass of the Americas was physically detached from that of Asia. In any case, the finding not just of lands but of peoples generated a great many difficult questions. If the New World was connected to Asia, if it was a vastly expanded Malayan peninsula, for instance, then one could understand how people arrived there. But if these new lands were separate from and enormously remote from Asia, if they were the southern continent postulated by some medieval writers, how had mankind reached these places? And what sort of mankind could this be? The New Testament, as well as St Augustine, seemed confident that the word of Christ had been sent to all the peoples of the world, and for Augustine that also included monstrous-looking peoples. There were plenty of tales of strange peoples whose appearance was markedly different from that of Europeans: headless people, one-legged people, massive giants, dog-headed people who consumed human flesh, and these tales had been recycled even by Marco Polo, who sometimes preferred to expose such legends as credulous misunderstandings.

It is the achievement of Jorge Magasich-Airola and of Jean-Marc de Beer to have exposed both the novelty and the antiquity of European ideas about the peoples and places discovered by Columbus and his rivals. They have brought together biblical and classical sources, medieval bestiaries, ethnographies and travellers' tales, and the narratives of those who actually explored the New World, to show that the New World was not always seen as something new, after all, but was reinterpreted in the light of received knowledge. A case in point was the idea that Paradise could be found in the lands discovered by Columbus; it was an idea that obsessed him more and more, so that he even claimed to have reached the outer edges of the Garden of Eden (which itself was inaccessible, as the Bible made plain), a place where the sea itself sloped upwards, forming a sort of nipple on the round surface of the earth, which, Columbus insisted, was in fact pear-shaped. And then the four great rivers described in the book of Genesis made sense; the Orinoco, with its deafening roar as it reached the Ocean, was evidently one of them; and further evidence of the proximity of Paradise could be found in the benign climate, far less oppressive than might be expected at this latitude, and in the lush vegetation, which was always a great source of wonder for Columbus. There was also the hope of discovering the Fountain of Youth, for which Juan Ponce de León searched in the northern Bahamas; his patron, King Ferdinand the Catholic, was possibly keen to acquire some precious liquid which would rejuvenate him and help him to father an heir by his second wife, Germaine de Foix. All the evidence seemed to indicate that the inhabitants of the New World lived very long lives and suffered few diseases (though this would change dramatically when Europeans unwittingly brought their own infections across the Atlantic, killing something like nine-tenths of the population). In fact, these notions of a Paradise in the west persisted even when the outer coasts of the Americas had been mapped; as Magasich-Airola and de Beer show, the idea that Paradise could be found in America was still articulated in the seventeenth-century.

This search for an earthly Paradise, whether the Garden of Eden or a place where the souls of the just might foregather, also inspired accounts of the Atlantic Ocean before it was regularly traversed. The Canary Islands were one of several candidates to be identified with the 'Fortunate' or 'Happy' islands of antiquity, a place where the souls of the just were supposed to dwell. These attempts to identify the

Happy Islands were sometimes unsatisfactory. The assumption that the Cape Verde Islands, several of which are salt desert, might be the Happy Islands not surprisingly did not secure a large following. But the mythical island of St Brendan and the vaguely named 'Antilia', meaning no more than 'the island over there', claimed their places on medieval maps. The colonisation of Madeira and the Azores in the early fifteenth century, all uninhabited, raised the question whether there were more islands out there in the Ocean Sea, including inhabited ones such as the island of the Seven Cities; this place was supposedly inhabited by the descendants of Christian refugees from the Moorish invasion of Spain in 711. So it is no real surprise that there were occasional attempts to explore the Atlantic further, as when Ferdinand van Olmen (Fernão Dulmo) obtained Portuguese permission to sail beyond the Azores, a few years before Columbus first sailed west. Still, there was a great gulf between expeditions in search of more islands like the Azores and Columbus' great project to reach Japan, China and India by sailing west.

The intensive search for gold was already under way before Columbus. Indeed, in the fifteenth century it led Portuguese ships down the coast of Africa, towards the supposed River of Gold; and before them there were Catalan navigators who shared the dream of finding limitless deposits in the lands warmed by the sun, for this was the sun's metal, radiant and incorruptible. Columbus was guided by his greed, to be sure; but he was also keen to show that there were supplies of gold in the New World sufficient to cover the costs of a great new crusade that would bring King Ferdinand dominion over Jerusalem and lead to the defeat of the Turks, masters since 1453 of Constantinople. Biblical tales of great ships that came from the far west laden with gold and spices fuelled the enthusiasm of Columbus and many successors, among whom were some who imagined, as Magasich-Airola and de Beer show, that the ancient land of Ophir lay in America. Others heard of Indian kings fabulously rich in gold (legends which had some basis in fact), and set off in search of the land of El Dorado. Headless men apparently lived near a mountain made of gold. In 1595, Walter Raleigh went in search of this land; but somehow his proceeds amounted to a few small nuggets of gold.

As for Columbus, his disappointment at not finding great amounts of gold had several results. One was that he magnified the wonders of the lands he visited in his reports to his paymasters back home – his letters to Ferdinand and Isabella, and to his patron the converso courtier Luís de Santángel. Here he spoke not just of his certainty that there was plenty of gold to be found just over the horizon, but of the natural wonders of the islands he explored, and of the gentleness and warmth of the native inhabitants, who were not monstrous peoples at all, but fully human, resembling if anything the native peoples of the Canary Islands (indeed, one of the names attached to the islands Columbus discovered was simply 'New Canaries'). However, his obsession with finding Cipangu, Japan, did not leave him. He knew from Marco Polo's book that the island of Cipangu was awash with gold, so much so that the inhabitants 'do not know what to do with it'. So he was somewhat disappointed to find that the Taíno Indians of the Bahamas had some gold, but not very much, and that all the Indians he met, even on the bigger islands, encouraged him to go just a little further over the horizon in the insatiable search for the inexhaustible gold mines of his imagination. This led to the second major result of his disappointment at finding rather little gold. As he established mastery over Hispaniola, he imposed tribute in gold, sending the native Indians into the interior to pan for gold in the riverbeds, and to scour the river banks for small nuggets. This became back-breaking work once the first layers of surface gold had been removed. Overwork destroyed the native communities; the imposition of a labour system, the *encomienda*, compromised the claim that the peoples of the islands where he had raised the standard of Ferdinand and Isabella were free subjects of the Crown of Castile. This was the beginning of the tragic history of ruthless exploitation which was reported in stark detail by Bartolomé de las Casas, the impassioned defender of Indian rights, and which continued virtually uncontrolled despite occasional legislation to protect the native population.

The Taíno Indians of the Caribbean were seen as rather weak and docile; against them the Spanish imagination generated other peoples, with the opposite characteristics: warlike, physically imposing, cannibalistic (as indeed the Caribs whom Columbus encountered certainly seem to have been). One opposition was that between the unimpressive male soldiery of the Taínos on Hispaniola and the formidable female archers of the island of women, the Amazons who were said to live in Matininó (possibly Martinique). Here, fascinatingly, European traditions, rooted in classical imagery, melded with American Indian tales of an island where women lived without men, apart from occasional meetings for the purpose of generation. The Europeans were intrigued by the gender reversal they seemed to observe (except that no one actually found any of these Amazons): tough women, feeble men. And, as Magasich-Airola and de Beer explain, the Amazons were great travellers, at least in the imagination of the Spaniards, for they migrated up and down the American continents, now appearing here, now there. Other gender confusions added to the wider confusion of the Europeans: Tupinambá women who lived among men and were accorded male roles, Tupinambá men who feminised themselves and joined the female community; there were even, though the evidence for this comes from the late nineteenth century, women's longhouses, whose residents combined a life of all-female orgies with expertise in bowmanship and warfare. Of course, one would like to know whether the Frenchman who claimed to have witnessed all this was another fantasist in the tradition of Vespucci, Orellana and other travellers in the first age of exploration.

Sometimes it was the Europeans who appeared to be small and feeble. Magellan's circumnavigation brought Iberian sailors into contact with the Patagonian Indians in southern South America. All the evidence suggests that Pigafetta, the diarist of Magellan's voyage, exaggerated the size of these Indians; but a long slender body is thought to serve as an effective natural adaptation to the cool climate, allowing these Indians to conserve heat while wearing little more than body paint. Once again, images drawn from classical antiquity and from medieval writers framed expectations of who or what would be discovered in the New World. The eyes through which the New World was seen were not those of sixteenth-century Renaissance men, but of men who had read and heard about strange peoples and places, and recognised them, or imagined that they did so, in the lands they explored. Indeed, as Magasich-Airola and de Beer show, these expectations lingered well into the eighteenth, even the nineteenth, century. Thus the New World was strangely new, and at the same time strangely familiar.

– DAVID ABULAFIA

PREFACE

The central characters in this book are the myths born of the European collective imagination about the lands beyond Europe and the beings that inhabit them. We have limited our field of study to the myths that bore directly or indirectly on the behaviour of the men – Spanish and Portuguese in the main, but occasionally English, French and Dutch – who embarked on the first American adventure. As a result, we have not taken into account certain beliefs that, though important and widespread in medieval Europe, had no evident link with the discovery of America. This is true, for instance, of the legendary southern continent known as *Terra australis incognita* as well as of the kingdom of 'Prester John', who was supposed to have been the king of a powerful Christian realm that the European imagination located somewhere in Asia or Africa.

Our starting point is the idea of an Earthly Paradise, that fundamental myth around which the geographical beliefs of the medieval world were organized and which we have adopted as a sort of golden thread. Each of the eight chapters addresses one particular myth or coherent set of beliefs and unveils its origins, developments and impact on reality during the period under consideration. This method allows us to emphasize the close relationship between the course of historical events and the shifts in the way those who took part in them perceived these imaginary worlds.

Work on this book began in 1983, when an architect friend asked for our help in gathering some illustrations of the imaginary landscape of the explorers. The subject turned out to be captivating, and so our project of writing a book was born. We burrowed away in libraries, both public and private, and bookshops until we had constituted a veritable archive of references and images that form the backbone of this work. The major part of the book was written in Spanish and immediately translated into French by the authors or their collaborators; in a few cases, the process was the other way around. We might say, therefore, that *America Magica* was written in two languages right from the start.

Three particularly brilliant studies were of enormous help to us in our research and deserve to be highlighted, namely, the *Historia crítica de los Mitos del Descubrimiento* by the Argentine Enrique de Gandía; *Mitos y Utopías del Descubrimiento* by the Spaniard Juan Gil and *L'Amérique espagnole vue et rêvée*, a Doctoral Thesis by the Frenchman Jean-Paul Duviols.

The first edition of the book was published in 1994 under the title *America Magica. Quand l'Europe de la Renaissance croyait conquérir le Paradis* (Paris: Autrement). In 1999, it was translated into Portuguese and published in Brazil by Paz et Terra as *América Mágica. Quando a Europa da Renascença pensou estar conquistando o Paraíso*. The first edition in Spanish, the original language, dates from 2001 by Lom Ediciones in Santiago de Chile, entitled *América Mágica. Mitos y creencias en tiempos del descubrimiento del Nuevo mundo*.

INTRODUCTION

The time will come
In a number of years, when Oceanus
Will unfasten the bounds, and a huge
Land will stretch out, and Tiphys the pilot
Will discover new worlds, so
*The remotest land will no longer be Thule.**

The great geographical discoveries of the fifteenth and sixteenth centuries represent a unique moment in history, not only on account of the technical and human feat involved but also because the protagonists came to believe that they had reached the land of legends. In fact, the European cultural traditions had located those myths in the East, and the Bible and other, secular sources confirmed that the Earthly Paradise, the Fountain of Youth, the impure hordes of Gog and Magog, King Solomon's mines, the kingdom of the Amazons and the fabulous golden-roofed palace of Cipango were to be found at the easternmost ends of the Asian continent, a region scarcely known and inaccessible to the inhabitants of the Christian world.

For centuries, the most sought-after spices, silks and precious stones came almost exclusively from the Far East, over a very long route along which they frequently changed hands until finally reaching various western markets. From the Hellenistic period onwards, these products reached Europe fairly regularly, either by means of the overland route – the famous Silk Road – or by the predominantly maritime route that involved coastal shipping from the Gulf of Bengal to the Red Sea or the Persian Gulf, and from there overland

*Seneca, *Medea*, Book 7, translated by August Kling and Delno C. West in their *The Libro de las Profecias of Christopher Columbus* (Gainesville, FL: University of Florida Press, 1991), p. 225.

by caravan to the Mediterranean. These commercial links would be maintained throughout the Roman Empire and until the end of our Middle Ages. However, at the beginning of the fourteenth century the situation changed with the formidable expansion of the Ottoman Empire. After conquering Anatolia and the Balkans, the Turks finished off the ailing Byzantine Empire with the capture of Constantinople in 1453. The Christian lands of the Near East did not withstand this onslaught much longer, and the last Genoese trading post on the Black Sea wound up its activities in 1475. The power of the Ottomans would serve as a powerful and ever more insurmountable barrier preventing trade between the Far East and the Christian kingdoms. Little by little, the latter would come to realize that they had no choice but to find new routes toward the land of spices.

On the Iberian Peninsula, however, and contrary to what was happening in Central Europe, Muslim domination was coming to an end. In 1415, Portugal, having completed the reconquest of its territory in the middle of the thirteenth century, crossed the Strait of Gibraltar to occupy Ceuta. In January 1492, only seven months before Christopher Columbus left for the Indies, Spain finished its own *Reconquista*. It seemed at the time that to reach the Orient there was no other way than the immeasurable expanse of the Ocean Sea, the 'Exterior Sea' of the ancients.

This was a time of great movement of population and capital. Lisbon, Sagres and a little later Seville were filled with cartographers and navigators, often of Genoese origin, who were summoned to put their knowledge at the service of the two flourishing kingdoms.

To succeed in this new undertaking, however, it was essential to unveil the mysteries covering these poorly known regions, venture across unexplored oceans, and visit countries both distant and enigmatic, where the imagination had located a world of marvels. The discovery of America seemed to open another path towards these worlds, and in Europe people began to believe that the myths were now close at hand. As a result, we see numerous fantasies that the imagination had hitherto placed in the Orient being transferred to the new continents, where falling on fertile ground, they gained a new vigour and even underwent some curious metamorphoses. These myths have exerted a constant influence on human behaviour, but at the time of the discoveries they served as a truly mobilizing force: the efforts to locate these mythical regions determined the activities of many of the conquerors. Treatises were composed, maps were drawn, dangerous and difficult expeditions by land and sea were undertaken, entire fortunes were invested and many lives were lost.

What do we mean by myth? Efforts to define the term have filled countless pages, yet the many schools of thought in the fields of philosophy, anthropology, sociology and psychology have failed to propose a single definition that could reconcile the opposing tendencies, and more importantly, to tell us exactly what it is. Acknowledging that it is extremely difficult to articulate a precise definition, we can say that, originating in prehistory as codified signs of a people's worldview, myths preserve the mystery of their origins, and determining their boundaries is undoubtedly as challenging as is defining the limits of the unconscious.

Let us limit ourselves, therefore, to affirming that what we are dealing with is the sentiments, aspirations, fears, desires or dreams of a people. The products of the collective imagination of a particular civilization in a specific era, they may take the form of legends, traditions or epics, often recorded in holy books. Born at the dawn of millennial civilizations, they endured through the centuries and various empires until reaching the age of exploration. The Freudian school has posited a seductive analogy between dreams and myths: the former is located on the individual level and corresponds to subconscious recollections of the psychic life of one's childhood, while the latter expresses vestiges of the psychic life of the childhood of a people and thus corresponds to the 'centuries-old dreams of youthful Humanity'.[1] On the other hand, for the Spanish philosopher Ortega y Gasset, myths act like hormones on the psyche, since they are forces that move one to act, unleashing patterns of behaviour, thought and sensibility.[2]

This is indeed what happened to the men who first headed for the New World and who have been called 'discoverers' and 'conquistadors'. In reality, these two words refer to the same category of individuals but in two different sets of circumstances: discovery and conquest were the results of expeditions that began with the same goal in mind: Cortés and Pizarro were the conquerors of Mexico and Peru because they found and subjugated two wealthy empires. By contrast, Orellana has been called the discoverer of the Amazon River, because it was as a result of a failed expedition in search of El Dorado that he became the first European to travel down the river to its mouth. These men were generally of low social status: impoverished noblemen, hidalgos, haunted by misery, they were all motivated by gold fever and the desire to gain social favour by conquering with blood and the sword the honour that Spain had refused them. Many of them came from Andalusia and Extremadura, and had begun their careers as sailors or soldiers of fortune in armies fighting the Muslims, and were trained in the absurd school of the *limpieza de sangre* (blood purity) that refused to recognize any rights of Jews and Moors to their own distinctiveness. Having completed the Spanish reconquest, they threw themselves into the assault on America, where some were rewarded by grants of land, while others continued to wander aimlessly with no specific destination. But all were consumed by the obsession to conquer the kingdom of fantastic wealth that would raise them to so great a social rank that they would be the envy of all powerful men.

Although the Spanish expeditions launched in quest of such kingdoms did not really cease until after the colonies became independent – half a century after their discovery – many of the conquistadors were transformed into colonists themselves, and in 1556, the Spanish crown prohibited anyone from even using the terms *conquista* or *conquistadores*, insisting they be replaced by *descubrimiento* (discovery) and *pobladores* (colonists).[3] The discovery of the mines of Zacatecas in Mexico and Potos' in Bolivia, as well as the establishment of sugar cane plantations in Cuba, Santo Domingo and Brazil, demonstrated the economic potential of the New World: the wealth and the manpower necessary for production seemed to the colonists to be a real gift of nature, without requiring payment either for the natural resources or for the labour force.

The effects on the indigenous population were disastrous. Epidemics, destruction of political, religious and social structures, the dismantling of the systems of production of the Aztec, Inca and other empires, which had made it possible to feed all their subjects adequately, as well as the imposition of forced labour annihilated the Native American people. There are, unfortunately, no precise estimates of the continent's population prior to the conquest; some speak of 40–45 million inhabitants, while others estimate as many as 110 million. The best-known region from this point of view is central Mexico, which was certainly the most populated area. In the 1960s the California school laboriously went through all the Spanish fiscal, administrative and religious records of the sixteenth century in order to produce subtle calculations of the decline of the native population in the region. From these findings, Cook and Borah have proposed the following figures: in 1519 (arrival of Cortés in Mexico), there were 25.3 million inhabitants; in 1523, 16.8 million; in 1568, 2.6 million and in 1605, only 1 million.

Although their reliability is now called into question, these figures send a chill down one's spine. The colonization of America in the sixteenth century, perpetrated by the Spanish, Portuguese, English, French, Dutch and some Germans, turned into the worst genocide in recorded history. Despite the few courageous voices that tried to defend the inhabitants of the New World, the latter were treated as sub-human, their beliefs banned, their temples razed to the ground, their writings burned. The Indians would lose even their lands, which would be granted – together with their inhabitants – to the new masters. The negation of the 'other' and his culture would lead to the annihilation of a whole branch of human civilization and the disappearance of approximately nine-tenths of the continent's population.

The discovery of America, as beneficial for human knowledge as it was disastrous for its inhabitants, was the result of an accumulation of knowledge in the realms of transportation, navigation and above all geography. If in Antiquity the geographers described with quite remarkable precision the lands they were familiar with, they often had recourse to the collective imagination to describe distant regions that were practically unknown to them. During the Middle Ages, efforts to understand the nature of the planet moved from the domain of science to that of faith, and for a millennium, it was through mythology that Europeans sought to grasp the world.

THE ROAD TO GEOGRAPHICAL KNOWLEDGE

The geographical information gathered by the Greeks is the most ancient that has come down to us. Situated as they were in the middle of the Mediterranean, the inhabitants of these islands were able to forge links with Asians, Africans and Europeans alike. Starting out from the Hellenic lands, many an illustrious traveller criss-crossed the world in search of information: in the fifth century B.C., Herodotus wrote no fewer than nine books to communicate his valuable observations; in his view, the earth was shaped like a disc at the centre of which were the continents, surrounded by a peripheral sea. Later, in the third and fourth centuries B.C., Ctesias of Cnidus* and

---

*Ctesias was a Greek physician at the court of the Persian king Artaxerxes II Mnemon from 404 to 398/397 B.C. He wrote several books about Persia and India, now lost but often cited by other ancient authors. Megasthenes was a Greek historian from Ionia, sent by the Macedonian king Seleucus I as an ambassador to the court of King Chandragupta Maurya in India. His accounts of the culture and history of India formed the basis of western knowledge about India in which he rails against the abominable heresy of the roundness of the earth and the existence of the antipodal regions. An attentive reading of Genesis, Exodus, the Prophets and the Letter to the Hebrews led him to assert that the earth and the firmament had the form of a tabernacle.[4] The Church Fathers confirmed this line of thought: St Augustine, St Basil, St Ambrose and St Boniface decreed that the earth was not spherical.

Megasthenes recounted what they had seen and especially heard in the Indies. In their accounts, as well as in those of other travellers, reality and legend are intertwined. They describe mysterious islands, marvellous beings, extraordinary animals and tribes of Amazons. Their writings conferred on the East the status of a land of mystery.

Yet the ancients also made some remarkable scientific discoveries. In the sixth century B.C., Anaximander, a disciple of the philosopher Thales, hypothesized that the earth was spherical, a theory that received approval from Plato and Aristotle and was then generally recognized as true in the Hellenic world. Eratosthenes tried to measure the earth's circumference, Hipparchus of Rhodes, the inventor of trigonometry, subdivided the globe into 360 degrees and Marinus of Tyre theorized that the Eurasian continent stretched across 225 of the 360 degrees of the earth's circumference (in fact it covers only 131 degrees). From such data, scientists concluded that the ocean that separated the Portuguese coast from China had to be relatively narrow. This theory would serve, 1500 years later, as the basis for Columbus's project.

Under the Roman Empire, the emphasis was less on making new discoveries than on gathering together the geographical knowledge of the period. This was the time when the great encyclopaedic works were composed, such as Strabo's *Geography* and the *Natural History* of Pliny the Elder. Following the example of their Greek colleagues, these authors painted a fabulous image of these far-flung territories which they referred to as India and Ethiopia.

The following centuries witnessed the inexorable decline of the Empire and its rational spirit. Julius Solinus's *Collection of Marvels*, a third-century treatise, prefigured a new mindset: he reproduced Pliny's work but in such a way that mythology occupied pride of place, with its jumble of magical lands, monsters and fantastical beings. His influence on geography was as decisive as it was harmful: his work was to influence St Augustine and other Fathers of the Church.

In this new Europe that was now Christian, knowledge was to be gained by intuitively grasping the divine plan. The Bible made its influence felt in all branches of knowledge, and its precepts were considered to be the source and ultimate expression of science. Any description of the earth and of the beings that inhabit it had to conform to the scriptural view of the heavens and the earth, the sea and the continents. From that time on, the little geographical knowledge about Asia and Africa that was available was structured around the assertions of the Book. Thus, for a millennium, the Europeans thought they lived in a world crowned, at its summit, by an Earthly Paradise with its four rivers, and contaminated by the presence of the hordes of the Antichrist.

The vision of the planet underwent a radical shift, one of the most remarkable examples of which is to be found in the theories of Cosmas Indicopleustes, an Alexandrian merchant who had been to India and who converted to Christianity around 548 and became a monk. In his monastery on Mount Sinai he composed at least three books, of which only the *Christian Topography* is extant. In returning to the Roman tradition, the scholar of the high Middle Ages tried to gather into a single work the totality of human knowledge, including ancient learning now subjected to Christian precepts. The Etymologies of St Isidore of Seville, written between 622 and 633, constituted a most remarkable 'Medieval encyclopaedia'. The holy man revived the views of Herodotus: he imagined the earth as a wheel, with at its centre the three continents – corresponding to the three sons of Noah: Shem, Ham and Japheth – surrounded by an exterior ocean. The maps that reflect this tradition place Asia at the top of the wheel, surmounted by the Earthly Paradise.

In thirteenth-century France, Vincent of Beauvais produced a similar work. His *Speculum Maius* gave prominence to the various marvels – be they imaginary or real – describing warm springs, bitter waters, thunderbolts and darkness. Around the same time, the monk John of Sacrobosco, who lived in Oxford and then Paris, wrote the *Treatise on the Sphere*, relying on a few of Ptolemy's ideas that he had encountered thanks to his contacts in Spain and with the Arabs. His work would serve as a handbook for countless travellers and navigators during several centuries.

While Vincent and Sacrobosco were preparing their compendia, on the other side of the world important political changes were taking place: in the Far East the Mongols, heirs to Genghis Khan, conquered all of Central Asia, giving rise to the Yuan dynasty. Until its replacement a hundred years later by the Chinese Ming dynasty, it would maintain the political unity of most of Asia, guarantee a certain degree of security along the roads and open up its empire to foreign contacts, including with the West. The Khan's court was relatively tolerant in matters of religion: the sovereign listened to the disquisitions of Muslim, Buddhist, Eastern Christian (Nestorian) theologians and others who tried, clearly in vain, to win him over to their faith. The European kings, among them Louis IX (St Louis) of France, aspired to nothing more nor less than to convert the Great Khan and his people to Christianity, in the hope of establishing a military alliance that would squeeze the Muslims in a giant pair of pincers.

Nurturing this illusion, kings and popes sent their ambassadors, mainly itinerant monks, to the court of the Great Khan. Among them were Jean de Pian Carpin (1245), André de Longjumeau (1250), Guillaume de Rubrouk (1253) and Odoric de Pordenone (1330), who crossed hills and valleys, steppes and deserts, never reaching their destination but leaving behind valuable accounts of the people inhabiting the far reaches of the earth. Similar descriptions were made by a few travelling merchants such as Marco Polo (1298) and Niccolò dei Conti (1419). All offered fantastical descriptions of India, recounting the existence of monstrous animals, giant birds, islands inhabited by women and palaces with golden roofs.

BOOKS

At the time when a few monks were preaching the Gospel at the court of Genghis Khan, interest in reading and in good libraries was gaining ground among the nobility. Little by little, they developed a certain intellectual curiosity about nature, the physiognomy of the earth and humanity's history. The collections that claimed to include the totality of human knowledge still held pride of place, but other types of treatises appeared as well: between 1100 and 1200 many beautiful manuscripts on minerals (*Lapidaries*), plants (*Herbals*) and animals (*Bestiaries*) were produced.

The most widely translated and diffused text after the Bible, however, was the *Alexander Romance*, a so-called history of the exploits of Alexander of Macedonia, written in the third century of our era, highly distorted by the fantastic fictions that had been spun over the six centuries that separated them from the feats of Alexander the Great. Although the quality of the work is certainly questionable, its success was impressive and lasting. Most people had to content themselves with listening to these stories being told on the church steps or public squares, while others had the privilege of being able to read them in splendid manuscripts, but all were captivated by the adventures of the great conqueror.

Asia, referred to as India, was an almost unknown and unimaginable world for the inhabitants of the Old World, and let us not forget that it was in these distant regions that the marvellous world imagined by the West were situated. Alexander the Great was the paladin of a European civilization that was considered the model for a large part of the Middle Ages and the Renaissance. As he was the only western monarch to have been able to penetrate the mysterious East with his armies, he represented a symbolic link between the known world and the lands of their dreams. Those who found pleasure in the reading of his peregrinations imbibed the foreign landscapes and discovered extravagant people and new wonders of nature. They were thus persuaded, all in all, that they had come to know better the world they inhabited.

Written in French, English and Latin in the second half of the fourteenth century, the fantastic voyages of Sir John Mandeville also appear among the most widely read books of their day. Despite the numerous losses and destructions to which it fell victim, there remain more than 250 original manuscripts and 180 editions in ten

Frontispiece of the Spanish edition of The Voyages of John Mandeville.

languages, including Gaelic. In 1530 alone, three editions of this work were produced.[5] Along with this enthusiasm for travel narratives, literary fictions fantasizing about the same subject began to appear. Thus, Christine de Pisan in 1402 wrote a long poem entitled *Le chemin de longue estude*. In it, she undertook an imaginary voyage to Constantinople, the Holy Land and Cairo; then, having crossed deserts infested with ferocious beasts, she arrived in the lands of the Great Khan, whence she left for Ethiopia, the mysterious land of Prester John.[6]

Another genre came to be all the rage as well, especially in Spain: chivalric romances. Combats and duels alternated with amazed descriptions of monsters, strange creatures and enchanted islands. These tales had something of the flavour of actual history: a lost manuscript, a hero who, ignorant at first of his noble origins, succeeds in reestablishing his prerogatives thanks to his valour and his ultraheroic deeds. An example of these was a collection entitled *Palmerin de Oliva*, but it was undoubtedly the three volumes of the romance known as *Amadís de Gaula* that had the greatest impact on the tastes of the age of the explorers. The work had its origins in the sixteenth century; its first edition was dated 1508, corrected, apparently, by the 'Regidor' Garcia Rodríguez de Montalvo. It is certainly the latter who was the author of a fourth volume, entitled *Les Prouesses du tris mystérieux et vaillant chevalier Esplandián, fils d'Amadís** and of the subsequent ones. In the fourth volume he describes an island known as California, situated near the Earthly Paradise, inhabited by black women living almost like the Amazons. Indeed, Bernal Diaz del Castillo, chronicler of the conquest of Mexico, would recount how the splendours of the Aztec civilization reminded him of the 'enchanted things' described in *Amadís*.[7]

From the fourteenth century onwards, private libraries of great value were established, evidence of the ardent desire to know the world. One of them belonged to Jean, duke of Berry, who was also well known for his misappropriation of funds from the royal treasury, which he used to support his patronage of the arts as well as for his own prestige. His collection was made up of more than 300 volumes,

---

**Las Sergas del muy misterioso y esforzado caballero Esplandián, hijo de Amadís.* The day came when millennial dreams and fantastic voyages seemed to become reality: the Portuguese made their way inexorably towards India, while in several scientific circles people cherished the idea of reaching it by sailing along the coast. Regardless of the route taken, the sailing ships made for the most secret and hidden places on earth, those they hoped would reveal its riches and its mysteries.

among which were 40 historical collections, numerous scientific books, astronomical treatises and adventure romances, not to mention the irreplaceable edition of the *Book of Marvels* by Marco Polo which is now in the Bibliothèque Nationale in Paris.[8]

THE RENAISSANCE

In the fifteenth century, the modern European nations began to take shape and gradually Latin gave way to the national languages. From Italy, notably Florence, there came a torrent of new ideas. At the very time when Portuguese caravels were navigating for the first time beyond the world known to the Romans, there was a passion for knowledge and a hitherto unseen flowering of artistic energy, accompanied by the exaltation of classical art: ancient statues were dug up, and Greek and Latin writings were read and translated. The patrons of this veritable cultural revolution were first and foremost the humanists, ardently convinced that there was nothing on earth quite as admirable as Man.

The encounter with Ptolemy's *Geography* was a significant event for the humanists. Its contributions were the subject of a controversy within a circle of erudite Florentines who between 1410 and 1440 gathered together the most prestigious humanists of the Republic: Strozzi (who introduced Ptolemy's *Geography* to Europe), Bruni, Vespucci (uncle of Amerigo), Toscanelli (intellectual initiator of Columbus's project), Niccoli and Piccolomini (the future Pope Pius II).[9] They were influenced by three sources of information: the biblical geography of the Middle Ages, the writings of the ancients in full revival and the recent discoveries of sailors who pushed ever farther the boundaries of the known world.

Yet these scholars did not dare openly contradict the Scriptures. Those who organized the discoveries still adhered to the medieval traditions, but were no longer satisfied simply with reaffirming a dogma. To evoke the Earthly Paradise no longer sufficed, they wanted to know on which longitude and latitude it was to be found, and to determine the characteristics of the planet on that spot. The same principle was applied to the legendary islands: their location had to be identified. The explorers of the Renaissance were not content simply to believe, they wanted to verify, explain, prove: that is the great difference between their mindset and the dogmatic spirit of the Middle Ages.

In 1492, Columbus thought he had reached the coast of that rich and famous land of India; around 1504, Amerigo Vespucci announced that this land mass was not India but a fourth continent, hitherto unknown. In 1522, the *Victoria* (the only remaining ship from Magellan's expedition) put into port at Seville, having sailed steadily westward until it returned to its point of departure. History and geography seemed to have come full circle. The essential mystery and age-old myths were now transplanted to America: it is there that Paradise, the Fountain of Youth, the headless men and the armies of Amazons must be found. But above all, it is there that gold no doubt gushes forth in waves, the very same gold that King Solomon had used to build the Temple of Jerusalem. It seemed as though everything was now within reach of the inhabitants of the Iberian Peninsula; all they had to do was to sail for the New World.

A new cycle was about to begin, in the course of which mysteries would mingle with the noise of war, monstrous machines would devour entire people, forests and the bowels of the earth itself. In the ports of Spain, old troubadours consoled the dispossessed by announcing imminent departure:

> *Come on, courage, good sires,*
> *Courage, poor hidalgos,*
> *Miserable folk, good tidings,*
> *Rejoice, you unfortunates!*
>
> *Whoever wishes to leave*
> *See this new marvel*
> *Ten ships setting sail together*
> *From Seville this very year!*...[10]

CHAPTER 1:

In Search of the Earthly Paradise

The discoverers of the New World lived in an age characterized by the confrontation between two visions of the world. The first was still dominated by the medieval idea that one could interpret the world, and in particular the vast expanses of land and sea hitherto unexplored by Europeans, in light of the affirmations found in the Holy Scriptures. The second view, by contrast, already exhibited the first signs of an empirical and rational mentality typical of the Renaissance. These two perceptions came together in men such as Christopher Columbus, Amerigo Vespucci, André Thevet and Antonio Pigafetta. Each of them strove to uncover unknown regions of the globe, but at the same time they were moved by the centuries-old desire to locate the place where Divine Providence had 'planted' the Earthly Paradise, foundational myth and doctrinal basis of the Judaeo-Christian and Muslim worlds, the original site where the Creator had decided to bring humanity into existence.

I completed a new navigation towards the south, where
I found infinite lands and the waters of a freshwater sea.
I believed and I believe what so many saintly and holy theologians
believed and believe, that there, in that region,
is the Earthly Paradise.[1]

Letter by Christopher Columbus to Pope Alexander VI, February 1502.

At the dawn of a new era, a great burst of energy impelled the explorers to undertake innovative scientific endeavours: they devoted themselves to understanding the logic of winds and ocean currents, to be initiated into the sciences of sailing, shipbuilding and astronomy and to use any and all sources that could provide them with new information on the geography of the planet. Well versed in the earth sciences, Columbus had the brilliant idea of using its spherical shape for commercial purposes.

Parallel to this extraordinary modernism, there remained a medieval vision of the world, permeated by the myths concerning the existence of fabulous creatures and extraordinary places: around the notion of an Earthly Paradise, there had grown up a world of fantasy in which people believed for over a millennium. Columbus's theories are the meeting point between this medieval mythical geography and the more scientific one of classical antiquity that had recently been re-discovered.

The ancient philosophers had succeeded in sketching an image of the planet that was quite close to reality. In one of his dialogues, Plato had posited that the earth was round.[2] Through a series of logical deductions, Aristotle arrived at the same conclusion: the earth constituted the centre of the Universe, and thus, its only possible shape was that of a sphere, which moreover was visible during lunar eclipses. But it is to Eratosthenes, a geographer and librarian of Alexandria, that we owe the first exact calculation of the earth's circumference, a calculation of extraordinary precision for his day. He had observed that at midday on 21 June, the day of the summer solstice, the sun was exactly vertically overhead at a well located in Syene (present-day Aswan) near the Tropic of Cancer, whereas at the same moment in Alexandria, 800 km to the north, the sun was no longer exactly vertically overhead. Taking into account the difference in angles and the distance between the two villages, the scientist calculated the perimeter of the planet: the result, translated into present-day measurements, was about 45,000 km or scarcely 10 per cent more than the actual figure. Finally, around A.D. 160, Claudius Ptolemy described the physiognomy of the known continents, and his

Geography included the most advanced scientific knowledge of his day in this field.

This fund of knowledge could not survive the collapse of the western Roman Empire. After the extinction of the great centres of ancient learning, a new culture arose, nourished by the remnants of ancient civilizations, Germanic elements and medieval Christianity; the perception of the cosmos was shifting. Europe experienced a veritable phenomenon of 'scientific amnesia'[3] that saw geography lose its status as a pure science: a large part of the Greco-Roman achievement was replaced by the illusions of mythology. Society no longer recognized the boundary between reality and the imaginary, which thus came to be mingled in a mystical vision in conformity with the teachings of the new faith.

With the advent of the Middle Ages, then, the science of geography fell into a thousand-year slumber. Culture became the preserve of a few religious orders, that was accepted without criticism or discussion any event or place described in the Scriptures. In this milieu, the locating of the Garden of Eden was regarded as an undertaking of the highest priority.

THE GARDEN OF EDEN

There is no doubt that there resides in some far-flung corner of humankind's cultural unconscious the myth of a return to a distant Paradise lost. The Greeks had the notion, emerging from the mists of time, of a Golden Age when everything grew without effort, when domestic and wild animals coexisted without conflict and human beings lived together in friendship, peace and mutual sharing. In their view, after a series of troubled aeons, human beings would return to this initial age. They also believed that the souls of the dead travelled to the Underworld, described by Homer as a vast cavern traversed by four rivers separating them from the land of the living.

In a sense, the Judaeo-Christian civilization adopted the idea of the Golden Age, which it turned into the Earthly Paradise. Obsessed with the desert that surrounded them, the authors of the first books of the Bible described this ideal place as a well-protected garden with abundant water, where everything grew spontaneously. Later, it would be situated at the summit of a mountain that was inaccessible to humans, the height of which meant that it had escaped the ravages of the Flood.

This human aspiration is clearly found in Genesis:

And the LORD God planted a garden in Eden, in the east; and there he put the man whom he had formed. Out of the ground the LORD God

God uniting Adam and Eve. Paradise is represented as a walled garden with four openings from which flow four rivers. Numerous animals graze peacefully. At the summit, God the Father, the great architect of the Universe, manipulates a compass with which He seems to direct the course of the sun. Illumination by Jean Fouquet, fifteenth century, taken from The Antiquities of the Jews *by Flavius Josephus, Bibliothèque nationale de France (BnF) Ms. Fr. 247.*

made to grow every tree that is pleasant to the sight and good for food, the tree of life also in the midst of the garden, and the tree of the knowledge of good and evil.

A river flows out of Eden to water the garden, and from there it divides and becomes four branches. The name of the first is Pishon; it is the one that flows around the whole land of Havilah, where there is gold; and the gold of that land is good; bdellium and onyx stone are there. The name of the second river is Gihon; it is the one that flows around the whole land of Cush. The name of the third river is Tigris, which flows east of Assyria. And the fourth river is the Euphrates. (Genesis 2.8–14)

He drove out the man; and at the east of the Garden of Eden he placed the cherubim, and a sword flaming and turning to guard the way to the tree of life. (Genesis 3.24)

The prophet Ezekiel situated Eden on a mountain:

You were in Eden, the garden of God; every precious stone was your covering, carnelian, chrysolite, and moonstone, beryl, onyx, and jasper, sapphire, turquoise, and emerald; and worked in gold were your settings and your engravings. On the day that you were created they were prepared.

With an anointed cherub as guardian I placed you; you were on the holy mountain of God; you walked among the stones of fire. (Ezekiel 28.13–14)

The word Eden, used in the Bible, takes its origins from the Akkadian word *Edinu* meaning valley and the Sumerian *Edin*, translated as fertile ground. The same ardent desire for abundance may be found in Islam as well: for the Bedouin, desert nomads, Paradise is a garden (*djanna*) that offers its tasty fruit, a perpetual freshness and unfailing rivers of milk and honey.[4] In the Zoroastrian story of Gayomart, the first man lived in a garden at the centre of which was a stone circle. Later, in Christian Europe, the term 'Paradise' would be used, taken from the Greek *paradeisos*, which in turn derives from the Persian *pairi-daēza*, the original meaning of which is 'boundary surrounding a garden'.[5]

The first Christians thus saw in Paradise, the place where they were freed from their earthly sufferings, but they were not yet concerned with finding its precise location. Access was postponed to the afterlife, linked to the symbolism of the Ascension and to a change in physical state.

One of the first Christian mentions of Paradise is found in the visions of St Perpetua and her young companion Saturus who had converted her to the Christian faith*. Both died as martyrs at Carthage in the year 203, and a few hours before her execution, Perpetua had a famous vision of Paradise. In a dream, she saw a ladder ascending to heaven, so narrow that only one person could climb it at a time. Swords, pitchforks and knives were swinging from both left and right, slashing her feet and hands. Beneath the ladder, a terrifying dragon kept watch, ready to strike.

Saturus ascended first, and from the summit stretched his hand out to Perpetua who, trusting in God, began the ascent. After placing her foot on the first rung, she crushed the head of the monster. Slowly she continued to climb until she arrived at an immense garden, where she saw a shepherd with white hair milking his sheep, surrounded by the 'blessed'. The shepherd stretched out his hand to offer her a piece of cheese, and when Perpetua put it in her mouth, the blessed cried 'Amen'.

In a parallel vision, Saturus was contemplating a vast garden adorned with roses and all sorts of flowers; the trees were as tall as cypresses and their leaves were falling continually. In the middle, was a palace whose walls appeared to be made of light, the dwelling place of God, where the two future martyrs were received according to the ceremonial reserved for Roman imperial audiences.[6]

These two visions heralded the beginning of a new worldview.

THE CENTRE OF THE GEOGRAPHY OF THE IMAGINARY

St Isidore of Seville (c. 560–636) is the author of a magisterial work, the *Etymologies*, a veritable encyclopaedia of knowledge in the early Middle Ages. Suffused with Roman culture, Seville was an important cultural centre at the time thanks to its ongoing contacts with North Africa. The writings of St Isidore date from a time when the episodes

*The *Passio Perpetuae et Felicitatis* is one of the most valuable extant documents concerning the persecution of Christians in the Roman empire. The work is made up of three parts: according to tradition, the first part is attributed to Perpetua (Chapters 3–10), the second to Saturus and the prologue and the epilogue to the person who edited the entire work, probably Tertullian. Tertullian mentions the text (*De animo* 55, 4) as does St Augustine (*Sermones* 280, 282; *De natura et origine animae* 1–10, 12…).

and places described in the Scriptures were common currency, and it was here that the Garden of Eden made its entry into geography. In Book XIV of the *Etymologies*, entitled *De Terra et partibus* (On the earth and its parts), the venerable bishop took it upon himself to locate the lands of Adam and Eve on the earth's surface.

> Paradise is a place lying in the parts of the Orient, whose name is translated out of the Greek into the Latin as *hortus*. In the Hebrew it is called Eden, which in our tongue means delight. And the two being joined mean garden of delight; for it is planted with every kind of wood and fruit-bearing tree, having also the tree of life; there is neither cold nor heat there, but a continual spring temperature.

> And a spring, bursting forth from its centre, waters the whole grove, and divides into four rivers that take their rise there. Approach to this place was closed after man's sin. For it is hedged in on every side by sword-like flame, that is, girt by a wall of fire whose burning almost reaches the heaven.[7]

As soon as the Garden of Eden had been situated on earth, it began to appear on geographical maps, which became in a sense 'guides of the faith'.[8] St Isidore himself was credited with having designed the model of a map engraved in wood and printed in Augsburg in 1472, which seems to have been the oldest map printed in the western hemisphere. It belongs to a very particular type of map known as the 'T–O' maps because they show the three known continents separated by two arms of a sea that form the letter T, surrounded by an external ocean in the form of an O. The centre is always Jerusalem, held by the Bible to be the centre of the world (Ezekiel 5.5); north is to the left and the Asian continent is in the upper part, often crowned by Paradise. This model would inspire a significant number of medieval cartographers*.[9]

The voyages to the far reaches of Paradise fed the popular imagination throughout the Middle Ages, the prototype of these narratives being the *Life of Alexander the Great* written in Alexandria in the

---

*To cite only a few: the aforementioned T–O map of St Isidore (seventh century) and the *mappamundi* found in three manuscripts of the Apocalypse of the Asturian monk Beatus of Liébana, which are those of Burgo de Osma (eleventh century), the abbey of Saint-Sévère (eleventh century) and Altamira (twelfth century). In the course of the following centuries, the land of Adam and Eve appeared on the world maps of the Benedictine monastery of Ebstorf (c. 1235), Hereford Cathedral (c. 1275), the oval map of Ranulph Higden (1350), the circular map of the world by Hans Rust (c. 1490) as well as on a 1492 map attributed to Columbus himself.

third century of our era, nearly six hundred years after his death. Its anonymous author was erroneously identified as Callisthenes, a young nephew of Aristotle who had accompanied Alexander the Great on his campaigns. The young man was implicated in a plot against the king and was later executed but his name remained attached to the work; by tradition, this 'biography' and its author are referred to as the Pseudo-Callisthenes.

In fact, the author was someone singularly lacking in erudition and with little inclination to historical rigour. His sources are dubious: many of them date from several centuries after Alexander's expeditions to Persia. Moreover, he added fables that were widely known during the reign of Caracalla, the emperor who brought the cult of the greatest of antiquity's conquerors back into fashion.

Despite its mediocrity, or perhaps because of it, the work had a surprisingly wide distribution: it was translated from Greek into Latin, Armenian, Georgian, Persian, Syriac, Arabic, Turkish, Amharic, Coptic and Hebrew. It even reached India and Indonesia. After the Bible, it was the most widely translated work until the Renaissance,

Representation of the Garden of Eden. At the centre, the Fountain of Life from where spring the four rivers. Adam and Eve are about to eat the forbidden fruit. Death, the consequence of sin, is represented in the form of a corpse. Engraving by François, son of Jean Fouquet? for The City of God, *c. 1473. (BnF).*

for there were editions in no fewer than 30 different languages. Over the centuries, new versions of this veritable *Roman d'Alexandre* would see the light of day, incorporating a large number of medieval legends. In the twelfth- and thirteenth-century poems by Alberic of Trois-Fontaines, Lambert le Tort and Alexander of Paris, as in many others, the voyages to Paradise have pride of place. These fantastic stories nourished the popular imagination until the dawn of the contemporary era.

According to several medieval narratives, when Alexander the Great conquered India, he reached an immense river, the 'Ganges', and with 500 men sailed down the river. A month later, they came across a great walled city, where the souls of the righteous awaited the last judgment: this was, of course, considered the Earthly Paradise.

The T–O map of St Isidore of Seville, seventh century, is from the first printing of the Etymologies *made in Augsburg in 1472. This engraving is the first printed map in the western world.*

According to another legend, Seth, the third son of Adam and Eve, had kept seeds from the tree of knowledge of Good and Evil. Upon the death of his father, he placed them in his mouth, and from the tomb, there grew a tree out of which would be made the cross of Christ. It was also widely believed that Adam's remains were buried under Mount Golgotha, the site of the crucifixion, thus forming a symbolic link between the redeemer and the first sinner.

No less surprising is the tale of the adventures of three itinerant monks who set out from their monastery on the Tigris and Euphrates to find the place 'where the earth meets the sky'. They crossed the deserts of India populated by dog-headed men, pygmies and terrifying dragons, discovered the altars built by Alexander the Great to mark the limits of his peregrinations and found a lake filled with the souls of the damned and a giant chained to two mountains. Then they crossed a land of incomparable beauty and 20 leagues from Paradise met St Macarius living in a grotto together with two lions. The venerable old man described in vivid detail the marvels of Paradise but ordered them to turn back, reminding them that 'no one can enter the Garden of Eden'.[10]

Around the year 1000, the Christian world, filled with anguish, and convinced that the end of the world was imminent, revived the ancient tradition of millennial cycles. This mysticism became so widespread that it became a way of seeing and understanding reality. Here too, biblical images fed philosophical demonstrations, and one of the few extant manuscripts from the period uses the image of the four rivers of Paradise to expound on the vices and virtues.

Shortly after 1000, the Burgundian monk Raoul (Radulphus) Glaber wrote his *Five Books of the Histories* of the world using analogies to demonstrate that the physical world can help us learn something of the divine. The source that springs from the Garden of Eden – affirms Glaber – divides into four well-known rivers: the first, the Pishon, the name of which means opening the mouth, evokes prudence, the finest of all the virtues, for it is on account of his thoughtlessness that man lost Paradise, and it is by practising prudence that he shall be able to recover it. The second river is the Gihon, which means opening the earth. It symbolizes temperance, the basis for chastity and roots out the vices. The third, the Tigris, along the shores of which live the Assyrians, that is, the masters, represents the force that makes it possible to expel vices and leads human beings, with the grace of God, towards eternal bliss. As for the fourth river, the Euphrates, the name of which evokes abundance, it undoubtedly stands for the justice that nourishes and comforts all souls who ardently beg for it.

Thus, the monk concludes, just as the name of each of the four rivers symbolizes the image of the four virtues and the four Gospels, so each of the four virtues is contained in each of the four epochs of world history.[11]

For medieval Europe, the Far East – where Paradise was believed to be – was a world as full of marvels as it was inaccessible, and the few travellers who succeeded in reaching the mysterious Indies observed them through the distorting lens of mythological fantasies. Travel narratives all describe places and creatures born of the inexhaustible imagination that characterized this mystical era: one such account of a trip from the fourteenth century even placed Paradise at the southern part of Africa.

In 1877, the Spanish historian Marcos Jiménez de la Espada, a man of remarkable erudition, discovered and published under the title *Libro del conosçimiento de todos los reynos y tierras y señoríos que son por el mondo...*, the tale of the voyage of a Franciscan friar from Castile, who was said to have left Seville in 1304 for a trip around the world. The itinerant friar – the book tells us – crossed the African continent until he reached the Empire of Abdeselib, who had defended the churches of Nubia and Abyssinia. The country was prosperous and irrigated by an excellent body of water coming from the South Pole, where the Earthly Paradise was to be found.

Continuing his travels, the Franciscan reached the city of Malsa (Melea), believed to be the seat of the kingdom of Prester John. When the friar enquired after the whereabouts of Paradise, he was told that it was made up of high mountains near the circle of the moon and surrounded by very deep seas, and that from its peaks sprang the greatest rivers on earth, namely the Tigris, the Euphrates, the Gihon and the Ficxion (Pishon). These mountains were inaccessible, illumined day and night by the sun, and their summits knew neither cold nor heat, neither aridity nor humidity, for their temperature was constant. Plants there never withered, and animals never died. The noise of the four rivers rushing down them was so loud that it could be heard at a distance of two days' walking and caused the inhabitants of the neighbouring villages to lose their hearing. The Greeks – the monk concluded – had named this place Orthodoxis, the Jews Ganheden and the Latins Earthly Paradise, since its temperature was constantly agreeable.[12]

The *Libro del conosçimiento* is one of the many medieval descriptions whose authors did not worry about drawing a line between the real and the imaginary. For the valorous explorers who succeeded in reaching this mysterious India observed the East through the prism of their own beliefs. Neither Marco Polo nor the itinerant monks could free themselves from the prevailing medieval imagination; when they returned home, they recounted having seen or heard tell of monsters and fabled lands. Their accounts could not help but confirm the faith of credulous Europe in the existence of extravagant worlds.

However, in the fourteenth century, changes began to appear. Spices, considered a great luxury item at the time, were brought to Europe from the Far East and sold at exorbitant prices. After the failure of the crusades, the routes along which merchants had to transport these precious delicacies were not only long and dangerous but necessarily crossed Muslim territories where they were taxed heavily on their wares. As for precious metals, they were the veritable touchstone

Circular map of the world by Hans Rust, pyrograph c. 1490 (Augsburg). From a walled Paradise spring forth the four rivers, and at the top left we can see the mountains of Gog and Magog, enclosed in the middle of a mountainous circle.

of the economy of the day, Europe's tragedy was that it did not produce any at all.

THE RENAISSANCE: MEDIEVAL TRADITIONS AND ANCIENT WISDOM

Having decided to seek direct access to the very source of all the spices and precious metals, Portugal was the first European state to launch a systematic exploration of new commercial routes. However, the geographical knowledge that was indispensable to the success of such a massive endeavour was lacking in the Middle Ages. In search of more precise information, European scholars turned to the Greek classics for enlightenment and in particular to Claudius Ptolemy and his *Geography*.

It was in 1295 that the Byzantine monk Maximos Planudes discovered the *Geography* in an old bookstall at Constantinople, and this treasure of ancient science thus emerged from its thousand-year slumber. Around 1400, the work began to spread through Europe; it met with such enormous success that in 1468, only 15 years after the invention of printing, it was printed in Ulm.

This influx of new information acted as a stimulus for scientists and navigators, who sought to understand the shape of the continents. Thus, it was that the French cardinal and theologian Pierre d'Ailly wrote his *Ymago mundi* in 1410, a compilation of medieval ideas about geography. Legendary beings and lands did indeed abound within its pages but the author also included details found in Ptolemy's *Geography*. The work of the cardinal likewise took into account the intellectual developments of the time: he wished to buttress biblical affirmations with solid scientific foundations, though protecting himself with a series of caveats and precautions and carefully citing his sources. Even though the scientific value of the work is only relative, it made its mark in history because it would be one of the most influential books read by the future discoverer of America.

During the time he spent in Portugal, Christopher Columbus did indeed study the cardinal's writings with such assiduity that he wrote almost a thousand annotations in the margins of his copy of the work. There he found the assertion – which would prove erroneous – that the distance from Europe to Asia, if heading westwards, was quite short: this was the scientific backing he needed in order to show that his mission was possible.

Pierre d'Ailly conceived of the world as divided into three climatic zones. A cold zone lay at the Arctic and the Antarctic, followed by a temperate zone in the north and the south, and finally, a hot zone along the equator. However, the cardinal claimed, there might be a temperate zone within the Torrid Zone and that is where the Paradise would be found. Impressed, Columbus took note and turned d'Ailly's prudent hypotheses into categorical affirmations.

Ymago Mundi	Notes by Columbus
Various opinions on the earth's habitation:	
There are various opinions respecting the habitation of the above-named regions of the earth. As was said before, some say that the third region is uninhabitable. Others declare on the contrary, that it is quite temperate, especially towards the middle under the equator. This was the opinion of Avicenna, for whom there seemed to be some reason, namely the heat that exists there because of the proximity of the sun can be tempered by other factors. Indeed, some affirm that an Earthly Paradise is there on a mountain towards the east.	*Avicenna and others say that the region below the equator is quite temperate. Earthly Paradise is there.*[13]

On the subject of exceptional geographical locations, influenced probably by the legend of the Irish monk St Brendan*, the cardinal placed Paradise in the 'Fortunate Islands' (the Canaries), something that Columbus did not doubt for an instant.

Ymago Mundi	Notes by Columbus
...if the special causes of a pleasant habitation concur with the general cause, that is, if the ground is quite fertile and well situated towards the sun with favourable exposure to the sky, then such a region would be delectably temperate and most certainly prove to be a terrestrial Paradise. Perhaps it is such a place that the authors call the Fortunate Isles.	*Earthly Paradise is certainly the place which writers refer to as the Fortunate Isles.*[14]

*This theme is developed in Chapter Six, 'The Fabulous Islands of the Ocean Sea'.

When d'Ailly goes on to describe the rivers of the world, he
unhesitatingly follows the tradition that had situated the Earthly
Paradise in the East. The future Admiral of the Ocean Sea shared this
belief. It is in this passage that d'Ailly mentions a myth told already
by the itinerant monk of the *Libro del conosçimiento*: the roar of
the torrents of Paradise is responsible for deafening the inhabitants of
the surrounding areas.

Ymago Mundi	Notes by Columbus
Paradise, according to Isidore, John of Damascus, Bede, Strabo and the Master of History [Petrus Comestor] is very delightful, situated in the regions of the Orient and separated from our habitations by a wide expanse of land and sea. It is so high that it reaches the orb of the moon, where the waters of the Deluge did not intrude. However, we are not to understand that it actually reaches the sphere of the moon: but that, speaking hyperbolically, its altitude is prolonged incomparably with respect to the inferior earth; also that it attains to the calm air beyond the boisterous atmosphere, where there is an end of the exhalations and humid vapours whose ebb and flow approach the lunar body, as Alexander explains. Consequently, the waters falling from that extreme elevation form an immense lake, and by their fall create such a roar that all the inhabitants become deaf because the loud noise destroys the sense of hearing in little children – so say Basil and Ambrose. From the single source of that lake, four rivers of Paradise are believed to issue, although their sources appear to be discovered in different places: Pishon which is also the Ganges, the Gihon which is also the Nile, the Tigris and the Euphrates	*A fountain in the Earthly Paradise. The Earthly Paradise is the most agreeable spot in the East, far removed by earth and sea from our habitable world. The Earthly Paradise. Lake... The Ganges, the Nile, the Tigris and the Euphrates.*[15]

During the years of preparation, Columbus systematically examined
all the descriptions of distant worlds that he could find. The
Columbine Library in Seville possesses four works that had belonged

to the Admiral: the above-mentioned *Ymago mundi* by cardinal Pierre d'Ailly, the *Historia rerum ubique gestarum* by Pope Pius II Piccolomini published in Venice in 1453, the *Natural History* of Pliny the Elder translated into Italian and a copy of the *Travels of Marco Polo*.

Thanks to this reading material, during a Renaissance filled with technical innovations and ideological convulsions, Christopher Columbus forged a curious image of the world, one that was a sort of projection of the Middle Ages with its fantastical geography. As his famous biographer Salvador de Madariaga tells it, Columbus was an 'inextricable mixture of an empirical, truly scientific spirit of observation and of a medieval faith in tradition and authority.'[16] When he set off in search of new routes to the Orient, he did not for an instant doubt that he was heading for the mysterious Indies, where medieval Europe had situated the great myths it had imagined.

COLUMBUS AT THE THRESHOLD OF PARADISE

The Admiral made four voyages to the New World: on the first, he discovered it; but it was during the second that he colonized it. From that moment on, as a neophyte in the subject, he had to be initiated into the delicate art of governing. The spot on which Isabela was built, the first European town in America, was a poor choice: swarms of insects, torrential rains, indomitable vegetation and a population of Indians reluctant to collect gold on behalf of the kings of Spain made life difficult for the conquerors who, in a hurry to make their fortune, avidly accumulated significant wealth and thus ensured that conflict was not long in coming.

Columbus then returned to Spain in order to organize a new expedition, in the course of which he would discover the regions where gold was abundant and would establish contacts with the kingdom of the Great Khan of Cathay.

In May 1498, the Admiral sailed from San Lúcar with a fleet of six ships. After they reached the Canary Islands, three of these took the usual route towards Santo Domingo while Columbus himself continued with the other three towards an unknown destination: from the island of Gomera, he sailed to the Portuguese islands of Cape Verde and then headed southwest until he found himself in a zone of stifling heat. He then changed course slightly towards the northeast in order to reach, as he believed, the shores of the Far East. When his flotilla approached the American coast near present-day Venezuela, the caravels were swept along by the enormous outflow of fresh water from the Orinoco River into the Atlantic Ocean.

This conjunction of strange circumstances led Columbus to draw some surprising conclusions. The inhabitants of these regions, the Admiral noted, are less black than those of Africa at the same latitude. Moreover, the climate is temperate, whereas in the East it is torrid: this must mean that the ships had 'climbed' to a latitude where temperatures are more moderate. As further proof of this, he argued that only waters flowing down mountains could have such force. The earth, Columbus thus concluded, was not round. Instead it was pear-shaped, or rather, in the western hemisphere south of the equinox (the equator), it presented a protuberance 'like a woman's nipple on a round ball':[17] it was precisely there, on the peak, that Providence had 'planted' the Earthly Paradise.

The myth thus took on its full significance, for the great discoverer believed fervently that he had reached the outskirts of the Garden of Delights. He wrote:

> I do not hold that the Earthly Paradise is in the form of a rugged mountain as some descriptions declare, but that it is at the summit, there where I have said that the shape of the stalk of the pear is, and that, going towards it from a distance, there is a gradual ascent to it. And I believe that no one could reach the summit as I have said, and I believe that this water may originate from there, though it be far away and may come to collect there where I was and form this lake. These are important signs of the Earthly Paradise, for the situation agrees with the opinion of those holy and wise theologians, and the signs are also very much in accord with this idea, for I have never read or heard of so great a quantity of fresh water coming into and near the salt. And the very mild climate also supports this view; and if it does not come from Paradise it would appear to be a still greater marvel, for I do not believe that there is known in the world a river so great and so deep.[18]

In his view, the New World combined all the characteristics of Paradise: the temperate climate, a mountain peak, the need to climb in order to reach it; he even identified one of the four mythological rivers, referring always and inevitably to the Scriptures.

This desire to be seen as a 'messenger'[19] of Providence may also be explained in terms of his particularly difficult personal circumstances after the third voyage. If he undoubtedly deserved the title of Admiral of the Ocean Sea, he was nevertheless far from having the political astuteness needed to be a viceroy, and his inability to manage conflicts proved disastrous. In addition, the much sought-after gold reached Spain in such small quantities that the kings decided to summon him to the royal court. Arrested by Francisco de Bobadilla in 1500, he was brought back in chains.

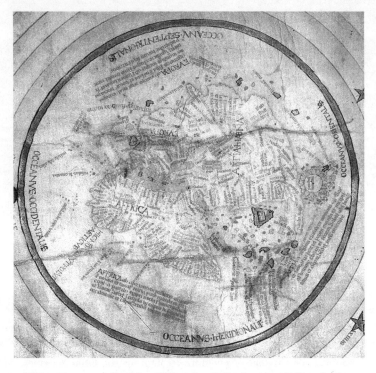

The 1492 map attributed to Christopher Columbus himself. Paradise is on the left at the summit of a cluster of mountains. BnF, maps and charts, Res. Ge. AA 562.

After such great humiliation, the Admiral complained of the ingratitude of Christendom, which sought only to amass gold and engage in vile conflicts, whereas Divine Providence had permitted him to reach the very edge of the Garden of Eden. To attain his goal, he did not limit himself to reproaches but used other arguments as well: he was sure, he said, that he was very close to discovering the much vaunted source of gold and spices. As a result, he finally gained authorization to undertake his fourth and final voyage: this time, he would have to limit himself to exploration and discovery.

Paradise and the First Discoverers

Like Columbus, all the first discoverers were committed to the mission of confirming the accounts handed down by tradition; however, they did not necessarily pursue this goal with the same ardour.

At least three times Amerigo Vespucci claimed to have come near the Garden of Delights. Thus, in 1500, while sailing along the equatorial regions of the continent that would bear his name, he noted:

> The trees were so beautiful and so fragrant that we thought we were in a terrestrial Paradise. Not one of those trees or its fruit was like those in our part of the globe.[20]

Two years later, the delightful scenery evoked for him once again the place of his dreams:

> This land is most agreeable and is covered with an vast quantity of very large green trees that never lose their leaves, give off a mellow and aromatic scent and produce an infinite variety of fruits that have a very pleasant flavour and are very good for one's health. The fields yield many herbs, flowers and delicious, sweet-tasting roots. I sometimes was so amazed by the sweet odour of the herbs and flowers and the flavour of the fruits and roots that I thought perhaps I was near the Earthly Paradise.[21]

The same idea appears even more strongly in the famous letter to Lorenzo di Pierfrancesco de Medici, in which Vespucci speaks for the first time of the 'New World'.

> It is certain that if the Earthly Paradise is to be found somewhere on earth, I believe it cannot be far from this land, which, as I have told you, is in the south and enjoys such a temperate climate that it knows neither freezing winters nor torrid summers.[22]

The sailors on Magellan's expedition, who made the first circumnavigation of the earth (1519–21), associated the beauty of a hitherto unknown bird with the environs of the Garden of Eden. During the crossing, Antonio Pigafetta faithfully fulfilled his role of chronicler and conscientiously noted the details of the adventure, overcoming hunger, thirst, battles and disease. In southeast Asia, he described the gifts offered by the king of Bachian – a kingdom situated near Malaysia – to the king of Spain:

> He offered the king of Spain a slave, two "bahar" of cloves (he gave us ten but given the excess weight on board, we could not load them

onto the caravels) and two very beautiful dead birds. These birds resemble thrushes, with small heads and large beaks, and thin and pointy feet like a quill pen. They have no wings but instead two bumps of long multicoloured feathers. The tail is also like that of the thrush, and all their other feathers are brown. They only fly when the wind blows.

They told us that this type of bird came from the Earthly Paradise, which is why they called them *bolon dinata*, that is, "birds of God".[23]

Even in 1575, the famous French traveller André Thevet, who held the honourable title of cosmographer to the King, mentioned Paradise albeit without sharing the enthusiasm of his predecessors:

Although it would be a most execrable impiety to abandon faith in what is written in the Sacred Scriptures, as many have done, no matter how impossible some things may appear, one must seek to discover where Paradise was located... It is said that it was in the East... Some said it was between the two tropics, below the equator, on a high mountain rising up near the clouds, never reached by the waters of the Flood... We confess therefore that there is such a place created for the pleasure and nourishment of man: but where it is, no one can say.[24]

Throughout the centuries, there were thus many who strove to identify the spot where Paradise lost may be found.

The jurist Antonio de León Pinelo, royal councillor of Spain, principal chronicler and compiler of the laws of the 'Indies', enjoyed enormous prestige in the viceroyalty of Peru, despite the fact that his Portuguese grandparents had been burned at the stake by the Inquisition. The lawyer devoted a large chunk of time between 1645 and 1650 to composing no less than 838 handwritten pages to demonstrate that Paradise had been planted in America. There is only one complete edition, published in Peru in 1943, in a modest print-run that is now out of print. The Brazilian historian Sérgio Buarque de Holanda succeeded, however, after much effort in reading a copy.

To persuade others of the truth of his message, Pinelo begins by arguing against 17 opinions, unfounded in his view, concerning the place where our first parents had lived. The Garden of Eden was in fact located in the centre of South America, he said, and he put all his energy into proving that this was the case. Since the Bible said that

Eden was to the east of the land where Adam lived after his expulsion, Pinelo argued, and since to the east of Asia lies America, it is obvious that Paradise is in the New World. The four biblical rivers correspond to the four American ones: the Pishon is the Rio de la Plata, the Tigris is the Magdalena, the Gihon is the Amazon and the Euphrates can only be the Orinoco. The tree of knowledge of Good and Evil did not produce apples, as was wrongly believed, but the *maracuyá* or passion fruit, which because of its appearance, colour and flavour led Eve to perdition. His exegesis allowed him to determine that humanity was born in South America – and that hence its heart-like shape was no coincidence – and lived there until the Flood. After having established a very complicated equivalence between the Hebrew and the Julian calendars, Pinelo determined that Noah had built the Ark on the western range of the Peruvian Andes just before the Flood, which he reckoned began on 28 November 1636 after the creation of the world and ended on 27 November 1657. During this period, Noah sailed as far as Asia, populated it and then returned immediately to his point of departure.[25]

Nor did the following centuries escape from this enigma. The Spanish the Spanish *Enciclopedia Universal Illustrada* published in 1920 still states the question in similar terms:

> What did become of Paradise? We don't know. Some think that Enoch and later Elijah were taken there, and that this righteous place was spared by the waters of the Flood that covered the sinful earth.

> Others, by contrast, think that Paradise disappeared during an earthquake or tremor, or that it was wiped out by the waters of the Flood, the latter scenario being the most likely.

The encyclopaedia comments on the fact that there have been numerous debates concerning the location of Paradise. Some situated it in Mesopotamia, Armenia, India, China, Ceylon, Peru, the Canary Islands and other regions of Europe and America, and some even claimed it was at the North Pole. However, according to biblical teaching, Paradise was in the East, and four rivers flowed out of it. In his *Treatise on the Situation of the Earthly Paradise*, Calvin had located Paradise in Babylon, and the four rivers were in fact only two. This was the view defended by eminent Assyriologists even in the twentieth century.

THE 'DISCOVERY' OF 1881

A hero of the British Empire, General Charles Gordon*, made a short visit to the Seychelles in 1881 to report on the condition of its defences. Upon arriving in the exuberant Indian Ocean colony, this keen observer and brilliant cartographer, author of a map of Central Africa was so inspired by the idyllic landscapes of these islands that he found there the answer to the age-old question. Good fundamentalist Christian that he was, Gordon took the biblical texts literally and declared that in his opinion, Providence had placed the Garden of Eden on these islands and proceeded to prove it!

Besides the delightful climate, there were abundant cascades of crystalline water, and in the opulent forest, he observed bizarre vegetation unknown in Europe, in particular a great palm tree, the *coco de mer*. In fact, there were two: the male with strange protuberances similar to 'certain parts of Adam's body', and the female tree, the fruit of which is an enormous coconut weighing 20 kg and whose shape is reminiscent of Eve's belly and hips.

Gordon, who seems never to have seen a female body from up close, did not doubt for a moment that this was the tree of the knowledge of Good and Evil. Another tree, the 'bread tree', became for him the tree of life of which the Bible speaks. Better still, he saw a serpent with his own eyes and observed that a local inhabitant was named Adam, as was his entire family.

The mystery had been cleared up. Filled with enthusiasm, Gordon sent all his friends maps and drawings of the Garden of Eden.[26]

Though less intense, certainly, than in the days of the first discoverers of the New World, the quest has never really ended. If Paradise is no longer to be found on the face of the earth – as some concede – it did exist in the past or better yet is somewhere in outer space where humans cannot venture. For there is no doubt that in some distant corner of their unconscious, people want this place of eternal bliss to exist.

---

*Charles Gordon became famous under the name Gordon of Khartoum after his intervention alongside Egypt fighting against the Mahdi's rebels in Sudan. In 1881, he was sent to the British colonies of the Indian Ocean as 'Commanding Royal Engineer'. He reached Mauritius in June. From there, he arranged his brief visit to the Seychelles. He died in Sudan in 1883.

CHAPTER 2:

On the Threshold of Paradise

The overburdened imagination of the discoverers was fed by still other mythical places and peoples mentioned by the Bible. Thus they identified the Native American 'Indians' with the ten scattered tribes of Israel, whom Christian folklore linked to the peoples of Gog and Magog in the Book of Revelation. The explorers likewise transplanted to the American continent the millennial myth of the Fountain of Youth, and they thought they had found traces of the apostle Thomas, who tradition said had died in the Indies.

> The Spaniards did not set out in order to gain new information but rather to verify ancient legends: the prophecies of the Old Testament, the Greco-Latin myths such as those of Atlantis and the Amazons. To this Judaeo-Latin heritage, they added medieval legends such as that of the empire of Prester John and the Indian contribution: El Dorado and the Fountain of Youth.
>
> *Claude Lévi-Strauss*

A late, Christianized version of the *Romance of Alexander*, written in the seventh century and known under the title of the Pseudo-Methodius (and published as an appendix to the Pseudo-Callisthenes) describes an episode – the imprisonment of the unclean people – of which certain elements would recur throughout the Middle Ages and would even reach America. According to the text, when the armies of Alexander the Great reached the eastern limits of Asia, they found themselves face to face with unclean people:

> They all ate disgusting, repulsive things: dogs, flies, cats, snakes, corpses, offal, foetuses and embryos that were not yet fully formed and were of indeterminate shape and not only domestic animals but also all manner of unclean beasts. As for the dead, they did not bury them but devoured them.

Faced with such ignominy, Alexander with God's help gathered the people together, women and children included, and drove them back to the far North, penning them up between a circle of mountains and a mythical Northern ocean. The Macedonian king repelled every attack by these depraved people and sealed his victory by closing off the only existing passage with a bronze door, which he covered with an indestructible substance, 'asceton, which prevented iron from smashing through it or fire from altering it.'[1]

THE PEOPLE OF GOG AND MAGOG AND THE LOST TRIBES

Beyond the Caspian Gates built by Alexander, there were thus 22 imprisoned nations that would be summoned to invade the earth in the apocalyptic age of the Antichrist. At the top of the list were Gog and Magog, followed by bands of dog-men – the Cynocephali – as well as Sarmatians and Alans*.

---

*The 22 unclean people are as follows: Gog and Magog, Anug and Aneg, Eshkenaz and Diphar, the Photinians, Libyans, Eunians, Pharisees, Declemes, Sarmats, Tebleans, Sarmatians, Canonians, Amatarzes, Garmiades, Cannibals, Cynocephali, Tarbians, Alans, Phisolonicians, Arneans and Asalterians.

This terrible story can doubtless be traced back to a text by Pliny the Elder who, in his *Natural History*, told of the existence of the 'gates of the Caucasus', which some have interpreted as an allusion to the Great Wall of China: '[It was an] immense force of nature that, in one fell swoop, split the mountain. A gate was placed before it, made of iron-covered beams, a river of nauseating waters was made to flow through it and a fortress was built on the rocks. All this in order to stop innumerable people from getting through…'[2]

The book of Ezekiel, dating from the sixth century before the Common Era, contains the first biblical reference to people who would become 'the cursed hordes'. When Ezekiel prophesies divine punishment for sinful humans, he evokes King 'Gog' and his people 'Magog':

> The word of the Lord came to me: Son of man, set your face against Gog, of the land of Magog, the chief prince of Meshech and Tubal, and prophesy against him! (Ezekiel 38.1–2)

But it is in the last book of the Bible that we find the prophecy of the final assault of the satanic hordes:

> And when a thousand years are ended, Satan will be loosed from his prison and will come out to deceive the nations which are at the four corners of the earth, that is, Gog and Magog, to gather them for battle; their number is like the sand of the sea. (Revelation 20.7–8)

The belief in the existence of these people thus rested on biblical references and became so widespread that it spilled over the frontiers of the Christian world. Al Idrisi, an Arab geographer, noted that an expedition had set out to find them, and Muhammad himself spoke of them in the Qur'an.

This idea of a last battle became such an obsession that it was even invoked to explain the invasions that ravaged Europe. Attila's Huns in the fifth century, the Magyars thereafter in the 900s and the Tartars of the twelfth century were seen as infiltrators or as the hordes of perverted people, imprisoned by Alexander bursting their bonds as if to announce the inexorable final invasion.

Around 1165, the famous letter from Prester John made its appearance, attributed to a mythical king of a no less mythical land and also referred to the people of Gog and Magog. The missive, sent to the Emperor at Constantinople and the king of France, is one of the masterpieces of the medieval imagination. The true author and the original language are unknown. It is undoubtedly a fake, but it became so famous that it was translated into several European languages. In it, Prester John warned his colleagues against the allies of Antichrist:

> This nation is accursed by God; it is called Gog and Magog and its people are more numerous than all other people. When Antichrist comes, they will overrun the entire world, for they are his friends and allies.[3]

The accounts told by the monks, who had been sent to the East by the kings of Europe to find Prester John, are yet another source of information on these famous people of the Book of Revelation. Thus, André de Longjumeau, ambassador of Louis IX (Saint Louis), had been entrusted with the mission of concluding a pact with the Tartars against the Arabs. Upon his return, he explained that the Tartars originated from a great sandy desert that began at the easternmost end of the world, and that they had crossed the mountain wall – the Great Wall of China – that held the people captive.[4]

Marco Polo, one of the only medieval travellers who had a relatively rational outlook, posited that the people of Gog and Magog lived in the province of Tenduch (Georgia) on the lands of Prester John. In these lands gold, silver and lapis lazuli were abundant, and the inhabitants manufactured extremely fine armaments. Christopher Columbus, upon reading this paragraph, noted laconically: 'Gog, Magog', 'lapis lazuli', 'armaments', 'silver mines'.[5]

Steeped in mysticism, governed by biblical precepts, Europe began nevertheless to show the first signs of a rationalist mentality. A new form of thought was born that without wishing to deny the dogmas of faith, sought to explain them. There was a desire to be better informed about these people who were believed to threaten the West.

The English Franciscan philosopher Roger Bacon, who was one of the first to defend experimental science against scholasticism, took an interest in the problem. He undertook a serious study of geography in order to determine, among other things, the precise spot, where the people of Gog and Magog were to be found. Once aware of their location, people would be able to defend themselves properly and prepare to meet the final attack that was felt to be imminent.[6]

The debates surrounding the people of the end times continued over several centuries: they were situated at various places, according to the political contingencies and the state of geographical knowledge of the day. From the Derbend gorge in the Caucasus, they were shifted all the way to the Caspian Sea, until finally they were situated beyond the Great Wall of China that held back the Tartars.

At the dawn of the thirteenth century, the belief in Gog and Magog underwent a profound change. At the third and fourth Lateran Councils, the Church adopted a resolutely hostile attitude to the Jews. Members of the mendicant orders delivered violent sermons that awakened the latent anti-Semitism of a considerable segment of the European population. The sons of Judah were made to wear a distinctive mark. They were obliged to live in segregated neighbourhoods* and were accused of committing ritual crimes, profaning Eucharistic hosts and poisoning wells. The connection to the savage hordes and the ten dispersed tribes of Israel was one that Christendom was quick to make.

According to the First Book of Kings, upon the death of King Solomon, his kingdom was divided into two: the kingdom of Judah, faithful to his son Rehoboam and made up of the tribes of Judah and Benjamin, and the kingdom of Israel, led by Jeroboam who gained the allegiance of the ten other tribes**. The division of the kingdom was followed by a long period of captivity in Assyrian Babylon, from which only the two tribes of Judah returned to settle in the Promised Land. Deported en masse to the eastern part of the empire, the other ten tribes of the kingdom of Israel disappeared without a trace.

Following its merciless logic, the Middle Ages would decree that the ten dispersed tribes of Israel were no more than the people of Satan themselves. This would be affirmed by Peter Comestor in his *Historia scholastica* and by Petrus Brutus in his *Tractatus contra Iudeos*.[7] Certain cartographers also supported this new version of the legend: in the *mappamundi* of Contarini-Roselle (1506), J. Ruysch (1508) and Waldseemüller (1513), the 'Iudei Clausi' (enclosed Jews) are represented as being surrounded on all sides by mountains.[8]

Scarcely had the New World been discovered when certain observers unhesitatingly identified its inhabitants with the people of the East. The first chroniclers did indeed note that many Indians had a morphological resemblance to the Mongols. Michele di Cuneo observed that the Indians had 'flattened heads and Mongol faces'.[9] Amerigo Vespucci wrote that 'Their features are not very handsome, because they have broad cheek-bones like the Tartars.'[10]

Fray Diego Durán (1537–88) goes even further, taking a decisive leap in his *Historia de las Indias de la Nueva España* (History of the Indies of New Spain) and launching into a long disquisition to prove that the Indians are well and truly the remnants of the ten dispersed tribes.

---

*The term *ghetto* was used for the first time in Venice in 1516.

**Reuben, Simeon, Levi, Issachar, Zebulun, Joseph, Dan, Naphthali, Gad and Asher.

The Dominican Gregorio García in 1729 agreed: he thought that the Hebrews had crossed the legendary Strait of Anian to reach the New World, and he claimed to recognize in the Indians all the characteristics that the Christian Middle Ages had attributed to the Jews: 'they are timid and fearful, highly ceremonial, sly, liars and inclined to idolatry.'[11]

Making a connection between the Amerindian people and the people of Israel may seem preposterous if we fail to take into account the historical context and the logic of colonialism. After their victory, the conquistadors sought quickly to make a colossal fortune; to this end, they began to extract minerals and appropriate the lands. The Indians, under the *encomiendas* system*, were thus reduced to serfdom or worked in the mine pits under inhuman conditions. As for the Jews, considered to be dangerous enemies of the Church, they were expelled from Spain the very same year as Columbus's discovery. In this atmosphere of colonial expansion, associating the inhabitants of the New World with the perfidious Jews would permit the colonizers to rid themselves of the few scruples they might have had with regard to the fate of those they had vanquished.

The conquest of the New World complete, another sort of war was about to begin: a complex and multifaceted war that pitted the beliefs of the indigenous people and their views of the world against the ideas and beliefs of the conquistadors. None of them doubted the words of the apostle Mark when he said that Christian doctrine had been preached throughout the whole world to all living creatures. This idea was picked up by St Augustine in his *City of God*, where he affirmed that 'the Word of God was spread throughout the whole universe.' Given this certainty, people imagined that the new continent had already been Christianized in the past.

THE PREACHING OF ST THOMAS IN AMERICA

The encounter between the Iberian and the American cultures provoked a confrontation between radically different images, traditions and ideas. In order to 'extirpate idolatry', and following a well-known method, the Church would Christianize the indigenous deities. Such strange hybrid divinities are still to be found today – half-Christian, half-Indian, the products of this sordid war. There are numerous such representations of saints, of the Virgin or of Christ endowed with bizarre traits that are the vestiges of ancient Inca or Aztec cults, and

---

*A feudal arrangement introduced by the Spanish in the New World whereby colonists received grants of land along with the native people living on it.

who received the homage that the Indians formerly rendered to their Gods. One episode in this conflict was the identification of one of the founding divinities of the tribes of the Tupí-Guaraní, Zomé or Zumé, with the apostle Thomas, conceived by the missionaries of the Society of Jesus.

The Gospels stigmatized St Thomas as the disciple who doubted the resurrection of Christ. When the twelve apostles dispersed throughout the world, Thomas was supposed to have taken the road to the Orient: St Eusebius affirms that he went to preach the Gospel among the Parthians, according to St Jerome, he went to Persia, and Gregory of Tours in the sixth century mentioned his presence in India. The tradition gradually consolidated itself in the Middle Ages when certain chroniclers situated the apostle's tomb on the territory of Prester John. As for the Christians of Malabar, whose ties were with the Syrian Church, they considered St Thomas to be that Church's founder.

It is important to remember that in the age of the explorers, there were no precise boundaries in people's minds, whether geographical or cultural, separating the East from the West Indies. The legendary worlds that the European imagination located in the Indies were thus extended all the way to the New World, and the accounts of the incredulous apostle's travels followed suit.

The first known written mention of his stay on the shores of Brazil appeared in the chronicle of a voyage in 1514 entitled *Nova Gazeta Alemã*. The author informs a friend in Antwerp of the existence of a 'very good race' that bows to no king or law other than that of honouring the ancestors. Yet 'they mention St Thomas… They wanted to show the Portuguese the traces of St Thomas in the interior of their land. They also said that they had crosses there. And when they spoke of St Thomas they called him "the little God", for there is another, much greater God.'[12]

The Jesuit Manoel da Nóbrega, who settled in Brazil in 1549, investigated the rumours that St Thomas had once preached the Gospel there.[13] The phonetic resemblance between the name of the God *Zomé* and *Tomé* (Thomas in Portuguese) as well as the traces of the apostle's footsteps on the ground seemed to him to be decisive proof:

> In Brazil, the Indians know St Thomas, and call him Pay Zomé. If we are to believe the tradition handed down by their ancestors, he had crossed this region and his footsteps were still visible on the edge of a river. I personally went to see them and saw with my own eyes, four extremely deep traces of the feet and fingers of a human being; sometimes they are flooded when the level of the river rises, and it is said that the traces were

imprinted on the ground when people tried to kill him with arrows, and that when he tried to escape his aggressors, the river stopped flowing to let him pass. He crossed it without getting his feet wet and was able to return to India. They also say that the arrows flung at him by the Indians turned back against them, and that the vegetation opened up before him to let him through; some people say this mockingly. They also say that he promised to return one day.[14]

Simão de Vasconcelos, also a Jesuit, claimed to have found traces of the saint at five different sites along the Brazilian coast, namely São Vicente and Toqué–Toqué (along the São Paulo coast), Itapoã (a beach 30 km from Salvador), Todos os Santos Bay (a beach on the Gulf of Salvador) and Itajuru (near Rio de Janeiro). In the last spot, a miraculous spring of healing waters was supposed to have appeared.[15] Moreover, he apparently heard tell of white men who had once come and preached sermons on God and eternal life. These strangers had not been well received and soon left, but not before teaching the Indians to sow and reap manioc: 'One of these preachers was named Zumé', said Vasconcelos, 'which means Thomas.'[16]

By appropriating the image of the God Zumé and transferring it into the Christian world, the religion of the conquerors began to penetrate the Tupí-Guaraní universe. The Church hierarchy did not spare its efforts to locate the footsteps the apostle was believed to have left behind and to consecrate certain places to Christian worship by turning them into pilgrimage centres. Their efforts to prove that one of Jesus' companions had passed this way did not have only a doctrinal aim but also a political one, for if the apostles had indeed reached America before the conquistadors, the Church could lay claim to more rights over these lands than the kings of Spain or Portugal.

The Spanish missionary and linguist Antonio Ruiz de Montoya, who in 1639 wrote *La conquista espiritual hecha por los religiosos de la Compañia de Jesús* (The spiritual conquest by the religious of the Society of Jesus)[17], thus strove to find signs proving that there had been an ancient Christian presence in these distant regions. Thomas was believed to have reached America on 'Roman ships that sailed from the African coast, went as far as America or else he got there by a miracle, which is much more likely.'[18] The traces of his preaching tours were so numerous that they made it possible to retrace the paths taken by the apostle. From the coast of Brazil to the city of Asunción in Paraguay, the evidence of the saint's sermons multiplied: the imprints of his sandaled feet and of the paws of the animals who stopped to listen to him, traces of stones that he had used as altars.

From Paraguay, he was alleged to have gone to Peru by way of Santa Cruz in Bolivia, where he would leave the most important traces.

For Montoya, the first signs of his voyage were to be found on the island of São Vicente near São Paulo. Two hundred leagues from the coast, he discovered a trail the width of eight palm trees, where the grass was very short and always grew back exactly the same way even after a fire. In Asunción, Montoya continued, one could see the imprints of sandals on a rock: the left foot was slightly forward and more visible than the right, making it possible to confirm the position of an orator; it was evident that this had been the saint in the process of delivering his sermons.

The itinerant apostle was also credited with punishing native people who were hostile to his preaching. According to the Jesuit, the Indians recalled him with fear, for to punish the insolence of their ancestors, he had extended the time it took for manioc to ripen.

In Peru, the miracles proliferated. The deeper the saint penetrated into Peruvian land, the more significant were the traces of his passage, and this in spite of the fact that St Thomas was competing there with St Bartholomew who, according to certain authors, had also been to America.[19] In the Peruvian province of Chachapoyas, such remarkable traces were found that the Church authorities decided to erect a chapel in his honour.

> In this province of Chachapoyas, where I have been, two leagues from a village named San Antonio, there is a great stone slab more than a stadion in length and more than six paces wide, on the surface of which are deep imprints of two feet... In front of the imprints, there are two indentations for the knees, proving that it was there that the saint had knelt, and this is what everyone believes... The holy archbishop of Los Reyes, Mgr Toribio Alonso Mongrobejo, went in person to see them and gave thanks to the Lord on his knees. The archbishop had a chapel built on the stone in order to preserve this relic in a worthy manner.[20]

The miraculous cross that the apostle carried in memory of Jesus' sufferings also enjoyed great honour. According to the priest Nicolás del Techo, the inhabitants of the region had tried to destroy it: they threw it into the water but it would not float away; they then tried to burn it, also unsuccessfully, and finally buried it at the edge of Lake Titicaca. The relic was recovered and became the object of special veneration because of the miracles attributed to it.[21]

The preaching of St Thomas was one of the few myths of Luso-Brazilian origin, and we would not be wrong to think that the account of his presence corresponded to the needs of the Portuguese colonizers. For the enslavement of the Tupinamba Indians and of Africans met with less resistance among Portuguese intellectuals than among the Spanish: if indeed one of Christ's disciples had preached the Gospel in America, the native people were no longer sinning out of sheer ignorance of revealed truth, but were in fact apostates, and their reduction to captivity and slavery was done in the name of the faith.

In America – as in Sri Lanka, where other traces of the Apostle had been found – the legend of St Thomas aroused a great deal of emotion right up to the beginning of the twentieth century, when a less passionate vision of the story relegated it to the rank of an anecdote.

Still other legends, of great antiquity, were transplanted from the distant and mysterious Indies to the young America, nearer but no less mysterious. The first generation of conquerors also dreamt of finding marvellous springs, the waters of which could restore youth to anyone who drank it or bathed in it.

THE FOUNTAIN OF YOUTH

Recovering lost youth and returning to a golden age are ultimately the same sorts of aspiration, whereas the former is limited to the individual, the latter extends to all humanity. Numerous civilizations since the beginning of human history have dreamt of enjoying perfect health in a supple and vigorous body, and of trumping the fate that inexorably leads to death by escaping decline and old age.

A Sumerian myth over four thousand years old recounts the extraordinary adventures of Gilgamesh, who set out in search of immortality. He reached the island of Utnapishtim, where he met the sole survivor of the great Flood. The latter taught him how to attain his goal: he would have to get a hold of a marine plant the thorns of which have the particular ability of inducing unbearable pain... Gilgamesh dived down to harvest some from the bottom of the ocean and returned to the surface with his priceless bounty. But while he was sleeping exhausted on the beach, a snake appeared who, to his great misfortune, took the precious plant from him and ate it.

Another legendary hero of antiquity, Odysseus, resisted the charms of the beautiful Calypso who offered him eternal life on condition that he stayed with her.

The longing for eternal life manifested itself in the symbolism of water. Since the dawn of time, numerous cultures have attributed a quasi-magical value to certain springs and fountains. Contact with water, whether by drinking, bathing or sprinkling, is linked to rites that lead to recovering health, purifying the body or spirit, fertilizing the land and reproducing life.

The Bible certainly considers water a symbol of life when it speaks of the existence of a spring that predates the creation of human beings and is thus older even than Paradise:

> In the day that God made the earth and the heavens, when no plant of the field was yet in the earth and no herb of the field had yet sprung up – for the Lord God had not caused it to rain upon the earth, and there was no man to till the ground; but a mist went up from the earth and watered the whole face of the ground. (Genesis 2.5–6)

The waters from this source fed a region, where suffering, labour and death were unknown: they must, therefore, have had extraordinary properties. In keeping with this logic, the waters flowing from Paradise held pride of place in the medieval imagination, symbolizing the continuity of life and victory over death.

The *Roman d'Alexandre* says Alexander the Great approached the fount of life but, to his great misfortune, it was not he but his cook who succeeded in drinking its waters. With 360 men, he entered a strange land called the Land of the Blessed (*Pays des Bienheureux*), where the sun never shone. Crossing a flat territory covered with fog and shadows, he suddenly found himself in a place

> Where there was a stunning fountain, the waters of which twinkled like lightning, and many other springs. The air in this place was perfumed and completely pure.

> I was starving and wanted to have my meal, and so I summoned my cook Andreas and said to him: "Make me something to eat!"

> The cook took a dried fish and, to prepare it for my meal, went to wash it in the glistening water of the source. Scarcely had he touched the water when the fish sprang back to life and escaped from his hands. The cook collected himself and, troubled, did not tell me what had happened. But he took some water from the fountain and drank, keeping a small amount in a silver receptacle. Since the entire place abounded with springs, we were all drinking the water from the other ones. Oh what misfortune is mine, not to have been destined to drink of this fount of immortality that brings the dead back to life, while my cook had tasted of it!

The cook – growing very bold – decided to seduce one of the daughters of Alexander, Neraira, by promising to give her water from the

How Alexander found the Fountain of Youth. Fifteenth-/sixteenth-century miniature taken from the Histoire du roi Alexandre *manuscript from the library of the dukes of Burgundy. The fountain of life, at the centre of the garden, is guarded by lions, dragons and griffins. Its waters fill a bathing-pool, in which the inhabitants of Paradise are immersing themselves. Dutuit collection, Petit Palais Museum, Paris.*

miraculous fountain to drink; and so he did. The king, jealous of the immortality that they had thus obtained, banished his daughter and had the cook thrown into the sea with a millstone attached to his neck. Tradition has it that the couple are wandering eternally at the bottom of the sea. Of the happy fish that was brought back to life, nothing further was ever heard.[22]

The medieval English writer Sir John Mandeville likewise mentioned the existence of a miraculous spring. Something of a braggart, he claimed to have travelled to the Near East. Back in Europe, between 1356 and 1390 at Liège, he wrote the story of his adventures liberally spiced with his prodigious imagination. This work enjoyed extraordinary success and became one of the most widely read works of his time.

The author tells of having landed on an island, which he named Lomba, where he claims to have found the Fountain of Youth and drank of its waters:

> Also towards the head of that forest is the city of Polombe. And above the city is a great mountain that also is called Polombe. And of that mount, the city takes his name.

And at the foot of that mount is a fair well and a great, that hath odour and savour of all spices. And at every hour of the day, it changeth his odour and his savour diversely. And whoso drinketh three times fasting of that water of that well, he is healed of all manner of sickness. And they that dwell there and drink often of that well never have sickness; and they seem always young. I have drunken thereof three or four times, and yet, methinketh, I fare the better. Some men call it the well of youth. For they that often drink thereof seem always young-like, and live without sickness. And men say that that well cometh out of Paradise, and therefore, it is so virtuous.[23]

Carried along by the imagination of the conquistadors, the myth of the Fountain of Youth crossed the ocean. The Europeans were fascinated by the lush vegetation, the idyllic landscapes and, curiously, the physical beauty and youth of the native people. When Columbus took possession of the new territories in the name of the Catholic sovereigns, he noted at once in his journal his first impressions of the people who lived there:

All go as naked as when their mothers bore them, and so do the women, although I did not see more than one and she was quite young. And all the men I saw were young, none over thirty. They were all very well made, with very handsome bodies, and very good countenances, with hair as thick as that of a horse's mane, and short.[24]

Thirty years was then considered the perfect age; according to an ancient Jewish tradition continued by Christianity, Adam had the physique of a thirty-year-old man when God created him. It was at about the same age that Christ rose from the dead and that the dead will be resurrected on the Day of Judgement. Columbus was impressed by the great generosity of nature; for him, the new territories and their inhabitants were part of this world of perfection that old age could never destroy.[25]

Columbus's idyllic vision of the New World and its inhabitants were quickly abandoned by the explorers who followed him to America, but many did believe that the 'savages' enjoyed unusual longevity.

According to the historian E. de Gandía, the Indians, who practised natural medicine, knew of trees whose wood endowed water with extraordinary curative powers that impressed the explorers greatly.[26] Thus, in 1502, Amerigo Vespucci thought that if the Indians lived as long as they did, it was thanks to the powers of their medicinal plants and the mild climate:

> They are a people of great longevity, for according to their way of attributing issue, they had known many men who had four generations of descendants. They do not know how to compute time in days, months and years, but reckon time by lunar months. When they wished to demonstrate something involving time, they did it by placing pebbles, one for each lunar month. I found a man of advanced age who indicated to me with pebbles that he had seen 1,700 lunar months, which I judged to be 132 years, counting 13 months to the year.[27]

A year later, Vespucci returned to the subject:

> They live for 150 years and are rarely sick. If they are attacked by a disease, they cure themselves with the roots of some herbs. These are the most noteworthy things I know about them. The air in this country is temperate and good, as we were able to learn from their accounts that there are never any pestilences or epidemics caused by bad air. Unless they meet with violent deaths, their lives are long.[28]

In the sixteenth century, a multitude of narratives flourished about men and women who lived a very long time, spending their lives in the countryside in harmony with nature. Pigafetta noted that some people lived to be a hundred and thirty. The French captain Jean Ribault told how during his visit to the fledgling colony of Florida, he met old people of surprising agility. René de Laudonnière, the lord of Ottigny, even claimed to have seen people who were 200 years old. Even in the seventeenth century, Claude d'Abbeville marvelled at the fact that at the mission of Marañón in Brazil, some women of 80 or 100 were nursing their grandchildren.[29]

There had to be an explanation for this prodigious longevity. The idea of a miraculous spring, able to restore one's failing strength, was firmly implanted in the minds of the first conquistadors, and some of them set off to find it.

Juan Ponce de León, illegitimate son of the ancient noble house of Arcos, was educated at the court of Aragon and became a page to the future King Ferdinand V. He probably took part in Columbus's second voyage and settled in Santo Domingo in 1502. As captain and the collector, he succeeded in obtaining the necessary authorization to go in search of gold on the neighbouring island of Borinquén (Puerto Rico). In 1508, he founded a town that the king named

Cibdad de Puertorrico but, a short time later, he found himself facing a general revolt of the Indians of the island, unhappy with the encomiendas system. His little army found itself in a very tight spot, and the defeats they suffered cost him his post as governor.

During his brief time as governor, Ponce de León formed solid ties of friendship with Agueybana (supreme chief of the Tainos), who probably told him about the island of Bimini – actually a small archipelago across from present-day Miami – where a fountain of marvellous waters was alleged to be able to restore one's youth. Enthused by this revelation, Ponce gained permission from King Ferdinand to discover and colonize Bimini.

The chronicler Antonio de Herrera, who knew the original documents, revealed the true objectives of the expedition:

> It is certain that the main object of Juan Ponce de León's setting out to sea…was to discover new lands…he went in search of the Spring of Bimini and, in Florida, of a river, putting his trust in the stories told by the Indians of Cuba and of Hispaniola, who said that by bathing in the spring old men regained their youth.[30]

In March 1513, Ponce and his companions left the harbour of San Germán, in Puerto Rico, heading north. On the twenty-seventh of the same month, they caught sight of land, which they took for an island, and since this was the Easter season (known in Spanish as *Pascua Florida* or 'flowery Easter'), they named it Florida. After having spent several weeks exploring the land and capturing a few Indians, they returned to Puerto Rico still stunned by the splendour of the vegetation of the land.

From there Ponce set sail for Spain, where he received the title of Adelantado of the islands of Florida and Bimini. He then returned to America crowned with glory. His short stay in Spain allowed him to divulge the existence of this miraculous spring[31] to the Spanish nobility who, with touching credulity, grew even more enthusiastic about the marvels of the New World.

Mortally wounded by an Indian's arrow on the coast of Florida, Ponce died in Havana in 1521. His remains are buried in the cathedral of Puerto Rico, where an imposing monument was erected to his memory.

During this period, the rumours Ponce had spread in Spain gave rise to serious historical and theological controversies, the intelligentsia of the Peninsula wondering whether this bold explorer might not indeed have discovered the fountain so desired by humankind since the dawn of time. The Italian chronicler Peter Martyr, as well as Dr Diego Álvarez Chanca, who as a physician had accompanied Columbus on his second voyage, confirmed that there were rumours that the famous source had been found. For theological reasons, however, they could not believe this possible: to restore a human being to youth was an exclusively divine prerogative.[32] These criticisms did not, however, stop people from continuing to believe for decades in the existence of the Fountain of Youth.

During the 1520s, the sailors on board two caravels charged with capturing and enslaving Indians met north of Florida. There they discovered new inhabited territories as well as a river they named San Juan Bautista (St John the Baptist).

The news reached the jurist Vázquez d'Aillon, one of the first judges in Santo Domingo who was a slave trader as well. This cultivated merchant, once back in Spain, looked for the necessary support for continuing his exploration of the recently discovered lands. He held meetings with several notables, including Peter Martyr, ever keen on news from the New World. From one meeting to the next, Aillon changed the name of the river from San Juan Bautista to Jordán, thus connecting the crystal-clear waters discovered in Florida with those of the fount of eternal life in which Christ had been baptized and lepers healed.[33]

The rumours spread by Ponce and the stories told by Aillon succeeded in giving credence to the myth of the Fountain of Youth and in arousing the enthusiasm of the first generation of conquerors. According to the chronicler Herrera, the Indians and the Spanish alike so often went to Florida in search of miraculous waters that soon 'there was no longer a river or a stream in all of Florida, nor even a laguna or a swamp in which they had not bathed.'[34]

A highly colourful tale told by a Spaniard who had spent 17 years among the Indians made a deep impression on this first wave of colonists, ready to believe almost anything. It was in 1551, after the sinking of their galleon, that Hernando de Escalante Fontaneda, then only 13 years old, arrived on the shores of Florida, where he would live until he was 30; through all those years, the young man searched unceasingly for the spring that was supposed to be able to renew one's declining energies. His account tells of the Indians of Cuba going on pilgrimage to these lands in order 'thus to accomplish the duty imposed by their law'.

A notable, Dean Castro, affirmed that the very elderly father of one of his servants, having set out to find the source, bathed in it and drank its waters for several days. Upon his return, the old man had such energy and vigour that he soon re-married and had several children.

If in 1514 Peter Martyr rejected the affirmations of Ponce de León, ten years later he wavered and, relying on the statements of medieval zoological treatises, asked himself: since the eagle can regenerate itself, the snake change its skin and the stag become youthful once again, thanks to an asp's poison, why would providence not have granted the same faculties to humans?[35]

Even though several generations shared the doubts expressed by Peter Martyr, the myth of the Fountain of Youth did not last long in America. A belief in the existence of these miraculous waters capable of making humans, if not immortal, at least renewed in vigour, stood in direct opposition to the precepts of the Church. For the latter, the immortality of the body was reserved, in a future existence, for the souls of the just, and thus it was inconceivable that there might exist on earth waters that could rival the promises of a glorious existence in the next life.

Many centuries have passed, and yet, despite the prevailing rationalism, the old myth still lurks at the back of our minds. Are not the walls of our cities papered with tantalizing images of products with marvellous properties that supposedly erase our wrinkles, return our skin to its original firmness and mask the signs of age? The regenerative power of the purest water from still untainted natural springs is sold in plastic bottles. Presented as a miraculous antidote to all the stresses of modern life, these waters are supposed to help you lose weight, purify the body by eliminating toxins and turn back the clock to erase the ravages of time... Do not the idyllic images used to sell these products prove that, in a sense, the dream of Juan Ponce de León and the legend of the Fountain of Youth are still well and truly alive?

CHAPTER 3:

King Solomon's Mines in America

More than the exploration of new lands and the search for the spice route, even more than the extension of the domains of the Catholic Sovereigns and of Christendom, far more than the evangelization of the pagans and the struggle against idolatry, it was gold that drove the conquistadors. The motive for their discoveries, this precious metal drew the adventurers like a magnet, in their obsession with getting rich quick. Even as the gold fever rose, two age-old traditions resurfaced: that of the fabulous mines where King Solomon had found the precious metal to build the first Temple of Jerusalem, and the Golden Chersonese, which the geographer Claudius Ptolemy had situated on the fringes of the Orient.

> Gold is most excellent. Gold constitutes treasure, and he who possesses it may do what he will in the world, and may so attain as to bring souls to Paradise.[1]

Christopher Columbus, Journal of the Fourth Voyage (1503).

A FASCINATING METAL

Gold was the first metal known to humanity, for it is found in its pure form in nature, and since the beginning of time its exceptional qualities held a mysteriously seductive power. The serenity of its splendid brilliance and warmth bewitched people; malleable, it lent itself to the production of extremely fine leaves and the most delicate objects, and above all, it is incorruptible. This noble quality, resisting the ravages of the centuries, has endowed it with an immortal value. But it is very rare and is to be found dispersed in the form of tiny grains. It is the precious metal par excellence: universally appreciated and desired, the very symbol of abundance and wealth, it naturally became a medium of exchange in commercial activities.

It was in the sixth century B.C., when King Croesus of Lydia first minted gold coins, that this metal began to fulfil its monetary function. After the political structures of the Roman Empire began to weaken, gold lost some of its importance and almost disappeared completely from circulation, accumulating in church treasuries and reliquaries and in jewellery made for the nobility. The decline of the monetary role of gold was at once both cause and effect of the diminution of trade.

It was not until the thirteenth century, after a significant revival of economic activity, and in order to help cope with the growth in commercial transactions, that Christian Europe felt the need once again to acquire a steady source of high quality gold pieces. While the lack of precious metals was keenly felt on the old continent, the relations between the latter and its Muslim suppliers deteriorated steadily each year. The authorities found themselves obliged to strike coins out of an alloy of gold, silver and other metals. Over the years, the proportion of gold diminished gradually in favour of the other elements, causing the coinage to depreciate.

During these years of penury, rumours began to circulate of an abundant supply of gold in other parts of the world. In western Sudan, it was said, dust with a considerably high gold content was being extracted from shallow trenches and sold or traded by weight: the Arabs called it *tiber* and the Mediterranean merchants *auris tiberi*. The term also appeared on a map dating from 1492 attributed to Columbus: on it we see an *insula tiberi*, or an island of gold dust.

Certain Arab chronicles describe the splendour of the pilgrimage made by the court of the king of Mali to Mecca in 1324. The king passed through Cairo, accompanied by 500 slaves, each bearing a magnificent rod with a pure gold handle that weighed about 3 kg. The caravan also transported 80 bags of gold dust, and the same sources speak of rocks of solid gold that were so large that '20 men together could scarcely move them'.[2]

THE SOURCES OF GOLD

Such an account could not but arouse the imagination and whet the appetite of the Europeans, for whom commercial success was worthless without a means of exchange, a credible form of currency that was universally accepted. The Old World felt an urgent and cruel need for gold, but the source of this metal, it was thought, lay far away in foreign lands, where the imagination constructed fabulous worlds.

The Europeans of the fifteenth century ascribed the most outlandish qualities to the precious metal. Gold could not be found just anywhere, but in distant, extraordinary countries with a paradisiacal climate, the natives of which were eternally young and enjoyed incomparably good health. These lands must therefore be situated near the Garden of Eden, and in these enchanting regions gold sprang forth or issued from the earth, the product of a mysterious alchemy resulting from the power of the sun and the erosion of minerals. In these remote and inaccessible places, the gold was closely guarded by enormous griffins and the giant ants mentioned by Homer.[3] The great voyages in search of gold thus took on an almost mystical dimension: the reward would be obtained only after boundless perseverance, risking all dangers and overcoming all obstacles over the long and tortuous road.

It was with such images in his mind that Columbus reached America. In his first notes following the discovery, dated 13 October 1492, he states: 'And also the gold that they wear hung in their noses originates here; but in order not to lose time I want to go to see if I can find the island of Cipango.'[4] The Admiral had examined the ancient documents in search of information on these lands where gold 'grew', and had garnered very precise directions on how to get there. The first set of clues was to be found in the Scriptures, which mention 'Ophir' and 'Tarshish' as two extremely wealthy regions where King Solomon had sent his ships in search of immense treasure. The geographer Ptolemy had offered a second hint: there was in the Far East a rich and auriferous peninsula called the 'Golden Chersonese'.

Among the dozen references to Ophir in the Bible, not one of them made it possible to locate the spot. The most detailed descriptions are to be found in the Books of Kings and of Chronicles, which tell of the wisdom, grandeur and sins of King Solomon who reigned around 1000 B.C.

The Hebrew king maintained excellent relations with his Phoenician counterpart, Hiram, who commanded one of the most remarkable navies in history. It was to Phoenician sailors that Solomon entrusted the mission of going to find the precious materials needed to construct the first Temple of Jerusalem:

> King Solomon built a fleet of ships at Ezion-geber, which is near Eloth on the shore of the Red Sea, in the land of Edom. And Hiram sent with the fleet his servants, seamen who were familiar with the sea, together with the servants of Solomon; and they went to Ophir, and brought from there gold, to the amount of four hundred and twenty talents; and they brought it to King Solomon. (1 Kings 9. 26–8)

And while Solomon committed extravagant sins with exotic foreign beauties including, according to popular tradition, the stunning and very wealthy queen of Sheba, Hiram's navy, bearing the treasures, reached the ports of the Red Sea:

> Moreover the fleet of Hiram, which brought gold from Ophir, brought from Ophir a very great amount of sandalwood and precious stones. (1 Kings 10.11)

> For the king had a fleet of ships of Tarshish at sea with the fleet of Hiram. Once in every three years, the fleet of ships of Tarshish used to come bringing gold, silver, ivory, apes and peacocks. Thus, King Solomon excelled all the kings of the earth in riches and in wisdom. (1 Kings 10.22–3)

The controversy regarding the exact location of the rich lands of Ophir and Tarshish kept exegetes busy for centuries and caused vast quantities of ink to be spilled. Consensus on the matter was elusive, and understandably so! Cardinal Pierre d'Ailly affirmed in his *Ymago mundi* that Ophir was located on the eastern frontier of Cathay (China), a remark that elicited one of Columbus's most famous annotations:

> It is in this land (Cathay) at the spot named Ophir that Solomon and Jehoshaphat had sent their fleets to bring back gold, silver and ivory.

The ships from Ezion-geber went through the Red Sea, reaching Ophir in a year and a half and returning in the same length of time.[5]

Thanks to this clear indication of the length of the voyage from the Red Sea to Ophir, Columbus could launch his project. According to the Scriptures, the king's fleet went to Tarshish every three years. Columbus concluded that three years were thus needed to sail from the Red Sea to the Far East and back. But in the fifteenth century, both this sea and the eastern Mediterranean were under Muslim control and thus difficult for Christians to cross. Columbus most probably imagined that to go from Europe to the Far East, one would have to add to the year and a half mentioned in the Bible the time needed to circumnavigate Africa, a voyage he believed to be impossible. On the other hand, by heading west the route would be shorter.

The existence of auriferous regions also received some support from Ptolemy's geography. The Alexandrian librarian had studied Herodotus, Hipparchus, Eratosthenes, Strabo and Marinus of Tyre and consulted numerous other travel narratives. As we have seen in Chapter 1, it was around the year 160 that he gathered together the fruits of his research in his *Introduction to Geography*, known simply as the *Geography*; this work gives more than 8,000 topographical indications. The oldest surviving manuscripts date from the final centuries of the Byzantine Empire, some of them including copies of the *mappamundi* drawn by Ptolemy himself.

Given the knowledge available at the time, this is a remarkable work. But two important errors ought to be noted. First, Africa and Asia are linked together by a *terra australis*, so that the Indian Ocean is no more than a big lake. Second, when Ptolemy calculated the circumference of the equator, repeating the error made by the mathematician Hipparchus, he set the zero meridian at Iron Island in the Canaries, and starting from there measured the perimeter of the earth as being 32,000 km,[6] whereas in fact it is 40,000 km. It was based on this imprecise calculation, repeated by Pierre d'Ailly in his *Ymago mundi*, that Columbus concluded that only a few days of navigation separated the Spanish coast from that of the Orient.

Yet another detail on the famous map caught the attention of the explorers: in the southern part of the Far East, around the spot where Malaysia lies today, we see the inscription *Aurea Chersonesus*, that is, 'Golden Peninsula'. Like the Bible, Ptolemy said that gold comes from unknown lands that he situated at the easternmost confines of his world map. On his globe dated 1492, Martin Behaim inscribed the following legend: 'In this region there are numerous gold mines.'

The book of Marco Polo, one of the favourite readings of Columbus, seems to support the idea that gold comes from the Levant. When he went on to describe the wealth found on the Island of Cipango (Japan), Marco Polo spoke with eloquence of gold objects and a famous palace with roof tiles of fine gold. It is understandable that such accounts entranced the navigators and princes avid for the precious metal.

Book of Marco Polo	Columbus's notes
Chapter II. On the Isle of Ciampagu: We will begin first with an island, which is called Cipingu. Cipingu is an island to the sun rising which is on the high sea 1,500 miles distant from the land of Mangi. It is an exceedingly great island. The people of it are white, fair fashioned, and beautiful, and of good manners. They are idolaters and keep themselves by themselves, that is they are ruled by their own king, but pay tribute to no other, and have no lordship of any other men but of themselves. Moreover I tell you that they have gold in very great abundance, because gold is found there beyond measure. Moreover I tell you that no man takes gold out from that island, because the king does not easily allow it to be taken from the island and therefore no merchant as it were nor other man goes there from the mainland, because it is so far, and ships are rarely brought there from other regions, for it abounds in all things; and therefore I tell you that they have so much gold that it is a wonderful thing, as I have told you, so that they do not know what to do with it… I tell you quite truly that (the chief ruler) has a very great palace which is all covered with sheets of fine gold. Just in such a way as we cover our house with lead and our church, just in such a way is this palace covered with fine gold…and the windows are likewise	*Gold is very abundant*

adorned with gold, all the pavements of
the hall of the said palace and of some
of his rooms, which golden tiles have a
measurement of more indeed than two
fingers thick... And they have large
white pearls in this island in infinite
abundance; and even if they are red, yet   *Red pearls*[7]
they are very beautiful and round and large
and of great value... They also have
many other precious stones enough there.

The references mutually reinforce each other. The Scriptures affirm that gold comes from Ophir and Tarshish, Ptolemy situates the Golden Peninsula in the Far East, and according to Marco Polo there is an abundance of gold in Cipango. Columbus was careful to gather all this information together in the hope that, sailing west with his caravels, he would find more than a new spice route: he was determined to be the first to reach these mythical lands where sun and nature so generously pour forth the marvellous metal that is the key to power, glory and fortune.

Towards King Solomon's Mines and the Golden Chersonese

In 1434, an unprecedented event took place: Portuguese ships headed south and rounded Cape Bojador, which since the most ancient times had been the southern boundary of the world known to Europeans. Under the orders of Prince Henry, the sailors sought to find a new route to India and its riches, hoping to meet Prester John and conclude a treaty with him against the Arabs. Their more immediate goal, however, was to reach the gold deposits of Sudan. This desire was so great that they would give the region just south of Cape Bojador the name Río de Ouro (Golden River)*, although there was in fact no river there and they found only insignificant quantities of gold. To finance this massive undertaking, they turned to a tried and true form of trade, and sent to Lisbon the first contingent of African slaves to be sold in Europe.

The Lusitanian navigators then continued to head south. In 1445, a Genoese sailor in Portugal's service, Antoniotto Usodimare, explored

---

*The region referred to as the 'Río de Ouro' would later be known as the Spanish Sahara and is now called Western Sahara; it is a region disputed between Morocco and the Popular Front for the Liberation of the Saguia el Hamra and Río de Oro (Polisario Front).

the coasts of Gambia because, he wrote, 'I knew that we would find gold and pearls in the region.'[8] Diego Gómez, one of the first Portuguese to penetrate the interior of Africa, affirmed in 1444 that the natives 'said that quite often 300 camels returned from Timbuctu laden with gold. This was the first time we heard mention of gold and its place of origin.'[9]

Exploration continued systematically along the African coasts until the arrival of Vasco da Gama in India in 1498. Two years later, Sancho de Tovar, a Portuguese spy, was entrusted with the mission of investigating a rich African port on the Indian Ocean, known as Sofala, where Africans, Arabs, Turks and Chinese crossed paths. He observed that great quantities of gold were circulating through the port, being brought there from the interior, more specifically from the empire of Monomopata, which was known to have trade relations with the coastal towns. These territories had been renowned for their gold since the earliest times. The Moors had said that this was where Ophir was located, and it was also believed to be the native land of

Engraving taken from André Thevet's Cosmographie universelle, *evoking the rich empire of Monomopata in southeastern Africa. Bibliothèque Royale de Belgique.*

the queen of Sheba.[10] Several Portuguese maps indicate mysterious 'lunar mountains' on this spot where the Nile was believed to have its source.

Meanwhile, Columbus's caravels had discovered lands to the west. For the Admiral, this discovery confirmed his ideas about the dimensions of the earth: he thought that by sailing west he had reached the eastern shores of Asia, the site of the realms of gold, and he did not hesitate to identify the island of Hispaniola with the biblical lands of Tarshish and Ophir and with the isle of Cipango mentioned by Marco Polo. One of his great dreams seemed thus to have been fulfilled: he would soon be able to lay the treasures of Solomon at the feet of the Catholic Sovereigns.

In his account of the third voyage, Columbus commented:

> As of Solomon who sent (his ships) from Jerusalem to the end of the East to visit Mount Ophir, in which the ships were engaged for 3 years, which mountain Your Highnesses today possess in the island of Española (Hispaniola).[11]

In February 1502, he wrote a letter to Alexander VI, one of the Borgia popes, describing his discoveries:

> Mines of all sorts of metals are to be found here, especially of gold and copper; there is (wood known as) brazil, sandalwood, lignum aloes and many other species, and there is incense; the tree it comes from is the myrobalan. This island is Tarshish, Cethia, Ophir and Ophaz and Cipango, and we have named it Hispaniola.[12]

From his very first voyage, Columbus had been exploring the Caribbean Sea looking for the island and the gold. The Indians explained to him, using signs, that on the beaches of an island called Babeque, people collected gold at night by torchlight and hammered it into ingots. This island, which so obsessed Columbus on all his voyages, was never found. In November 1492, the caravel of Martín Alonzo de Pinzón left the fleet for an unknown destination. Outraged, the Admiral assumed that Pinzón was being guided towards Babeque by an Indian hostage, and that they would find the gold before he did. In January 1493, the ships of Pinzón and Columbus met accidentally. But of the gold of Babeque nothing further was heard.

It was not until 1501, nine years after Columbus's first voyage, that a modest gold seam was found on the island of Hispaniola, but its production was far less significant than the Crown had hoped. At this point, Columbus fell into disgrace: the colonists, disappointed at not having found precious metals, rebelled; the Admiral was arrested and brought back to Spain in chains. On arrival, he was set free; his titles were restored to him – even that of governor of Hispaniola – and a tacit agreement was made. The Crown wanted gold, and Columbus wanted to preserve his honour: the monarchs therefore entrusted him with a fourth expedition, the object of which was to reach the sources of the precious metal by the western route before the Portuguese could get there via the East. A fleet of four ships left the port of Cádiz in 1502 with gold as their target.

When he sighted land, the Admiral once again thought he had reached the shores of Asia, for his notion of that continent's physiognomy was based on the globe of Behaim, on which the Far East extended southwards by a peninsula known as Cittigara, beyond which, slightly to the west, was the Golden Chersonese.

In search of a passage to the peninsula, the fleet explored the lands that the Admiral would name Veragua: in fact, these were the shores of Central America, between Honduras and Panama. During the

Black slaves working in the gold mines of America. Engraving by Théodore de Bry. Bibliothèque Royale de Belgique.

voyage, he modified his view of the lands he had discovered: contrary to what he had previously affirmed, notably in a letter to the Pope, he now believed that the mines of Solomon were not on Hispaniola but rather at Veragua.[13]

From the gesticulations of the Indians he encountered, Columbus thought that there was gold in the province of Ciamba – the name given by Marco Polo to Indochina – and heard of 'infinite quantities of gold' in the province of Ciguare (probably the land of the Mayas). He even specified that 'ten days from there was the river Ganges'.[14] The landscape Columbus described was filled with references to the world depicted by Marco Polo. Certain sailors, believing they were approaching the gold, secretly collected sand from the beaches they believed to be those of Ophir; they hoped that by melting it down, they would obtain pure gold.[15]

The Admiral, basing himself on the Jewish historian Flavius Josephus, author of *The Antiquities of the Jews* in the first century of the Common Era, announced grandiloquently what he considered the most wonderful result of his venture: that the mines of King Solomon and the land of Veragua he had just discovered were one and the same thing, and therefore could proudly announce that he had placed the source of gold – free of charge – at the disposal of the Catholic Sovereigns:

> To Solomon on one journey they brought six hundred and sixty-six quintals of gold, besides that which the merchants and the sailors brought, and besides that which was paid in Arabia. From this gold, he made two hundred lances and three hundred shields,… Josephus writes this in his chronicle of the *Antiquitatibus*; in the book of Chronicles, and in the book of Kings, there is an account of this… Josephus holds that this gold was found obtained in the Aurea. If it were so, I declare that those mines of the Aurea are one and the same as those of Veragua… Solomon bought all that gold, precious stones, and silver, and you may command it to be collected there, if you wish.[16]

The expedition had lost two ships, however, and the remaining two were rotting away; the Admiral, whose health was declining, decided to begin the journey home. It would be the last time that he would see the lands he had discovered, and he left them convinced that he had reached the edges of the realms of gold. Until the end of his life, he had hoped to put the precious metal to the same use as the legendary biblical king had done: to rebuild the Temple of Jerusalem, for the completion of that task was regarded as the sign that the end of the world was at hand.

Central American Indians placing their precious objects at the feet of the conquistadors. Engraving by Théodore de Bry. Bibliothèque Royale de Belgique.

The Admiral of the Ocean Sea died on 20 May 1506 in an inn at Valladolid. A year later, Martin Waldseemüller printed his *mappamundi*, on which we can see a narrow strip of land, separate from Asia, where the word America first appears, in homage to the navigator Amerigo Vespucci. The latter had suggested to the cartographer that the lands Columbus had discovered were a fourth continent, distinct from the other three known at the time. But the gold of America was still nowhere to be found.

AN EXERCISE IN EXEGESIS

Around the year 1508, the Portuguese heard for the first time of the empire of the Incas; the inhabitants of the Brazilian coast had told them that there lay, to the west, 'so much gold and silver that they would barely be able to load it onto their ships.' Three years later, at Panama, a *cacique* (chief) revealed to Vasco Núñez de Balboa the existence of a land beyond the sea where there were 'vast gold treasures, and large golden vases from which they ate and drank'.[17] These sorts of rumours could not leave the inhabitants of the Iberian Peninsula indifferent. Diego García and Sebastian Cabot soon obtained the necessary permission to go to the Spice Islands, but the two navigators soon changed course and headed for Tarshish, Ophir, Cathay and Cipango. Their fleets passed the waters of the Río de la Plata (La Plata River), where hunger and privations of all sorts awaited them. And yet they were so close to their destination.

In 1521, the armies of Hernán Cortés occupied Tenochtitlán, capital of the Aztec Empire. In 1532, an expeditionary force under the command of Francisco Pizarro captured emperor Atahualpa and took possession of the fabulous empire of Tahuantinsuyu, which means 'the four directions', and that would later be called the Inca Empire. The war booty was enormous. The victorious conquistadors completely emptied Tenochtitlán and Cuzco, so avid were they to lay their hands on the apparently inexhaustible treasure trove they found there.

Just as Columbus had predicted, no payment was required in exchange for these precious metals. After the discovery of the mines of Zacatecas in Mexico and of Potosí in Bolivia, the Indians were reduced to servitude and, forced to endure horrific conditions, were compelled to extract the treasures hidden within their own lands.

The legend seemed to have become reality. The galleons crossed the ocean with their holds filled with resplendent treasures destined for the Iberian ports. The inhabitants of the Peninsula, who had long yearned for the precious metals, now contemplated in amazement, the vast quantities of gold and silver in the form of ingots, vases, statues, rocks and fine dust that flooded Spain and Portugal.

At the same time, in the viceroyalty of Peru, a rumour circulated about the existence of very wealthy islands in the Pacific off the coast of the ancient Inca Empire, and in 1567, an expedition – in which a certain Sarmiento de Gamboa took part – set off to look for them. They would discover a group of islands in Melanesia, on which popular tradition, in the hope of finding the famous biblical mines, would immediately bestow their present name of 'the Solomon Islands'.[18]

These events triggered a revival of the theological debate around the origin of the mines of King Solomon, flavoured this time by a rampant nationalism. In the following paragraphs, we will review the broad outlines of the argumentation given by the Spanish philosopher Juan Gil.

As far as Tarshish was concerned, several theologians seemed to agree. They took their cue from the exegesis of St Jerome, who knew Hebrew: Tarshish means 'sea' and the expression 'ship of Tarshish' often used in the Bible, should be understood to mean an 'ocean-going merchant ship'.[19]

Locating Ophir proved to be more complicated. At the beginning of the sixteenth century, the sense of national belonging began to take shape in the two Iberian countries, giving additional impetus to biblical exegetes of both lands to seek to identify the realms of gold within the new boundaries of their respective territories.

The Lusitanians initially claimed that Ophir was located on the African coast near the port of Sofala,[20] in present-day Mozambique, but later they would change their minds and assert that they had discovered that the descendants of the inhabitants of Ophir had emigrated to Braga[21] in Portugal. The Hispanic world had a different interpretation: Benito Arias Montano (1527–98), the Spanish theologian who, in the context of the counter-reformation, was charged with the task of editing the polyglot Bible, believed he had discovered an etymological link between the words 'Pirù' and 'Ophir'. He concluded from this that the Peruvian gold that flowed into the Christian kingdoms was the same as the gold used by Solomon to build the Temple of Jerusalem.[22] A variant of this interpretation would be introduced a century or so later by the priest Ferdinand Montesinos, who thought Ophir was El Dorado and Paitití, while Tarshish was identified with the silver mountains of Potosí.[23]

In this context, the writings of Hippolytus, the Greek bishop who died a martyr in 240, were once again pertinent, since the saint had claimed that Tarshish was Tartessos, an ancient Iberian kingdom controlled for a time by the Phoenicians. This theory, still defended today, was interpreted in a rather unusual way by the Flemish doctor Joannes van Gorp (1518–72), known as Goropius Becanus, who proclaimed in his great treatise *Origines antverpianae* (published in 1569) that the Flemish language is the oldest in the world and therefore the mother of all the others born after the scattering of the nations at the time of the tower of Babel. Therefore, with the help of Flemish phonetics, it was possible to solve the problem of identifying certain biblical sites that had hitherto eluded the exegetes. Drawing on the etymology of words, he confirmed the earlier statements of St Hippolytus: Tarshish is indeed Tartessos, and Ophir comes from 'over' or 'ober', meaning 'what is above'. In conclusion, he postulated that Solomon's ships had gone to Tartessos and then continued until they reached Ophir in America, which explains why the journey lasted three years.[24]

The polemic soon turned into hyperbole, and the theologians gave themselves over to extravagant explanations intended to glorify the Spanish blood and soil: before being swallowed by the whale, Jonah was supposed to have travelled by a ship chartered in Cádiz; the Elysian Fields were alleged to have been in Seville; the names of several cities of Spain were given biblical origins; the three wise men were believed to have been Spaniards living in the Middle East; and finally, Cádiz was said to be the home town of Mattathias, one of the ancestors of Christ.[25]

The ghosts of Tarshish and Ophir would continue to torment the conquistadors for three centuries, even beyond the historical boundaries of the Spanish empire: a certain Onffroy de Thoron published a book entitled *Voyage des vaisseaux d'Hiram et de Salomon au fleuve des Amazones* (Voyage of Solomon's and Hiram's Ships to the Amazon River), printed in Genoa in 1876 and in Manaus a few years later. In it, he claimed to have found on the shores of that river inscriptions that pointed to survivors of one of the expeditions sent by Hiram, the Phoenician king and ally of Solomon. In his view, Ophir was located in the Amazon Forest. His theories were accepted by a great Brazilian landowner, Colonel Bernardo da Silva Ramos, who in 1930 published an enormous work, funded by the State, in which he affirmed that all the inscriptions he had come across in the Amazon Forest had Greek, Hebrew, Phoenician, Egyptian and in some cases Chinese names.[26]

Whereas in the metropolis exegetes were composing impressive treatises on the location of King Solomon's mines, in America the most far-fetched dreams seemed to be within reach. Rumours of the existence of kingdoms as rich as they were fabulous spread throughout the New World.

The successors of Cortés and of Pizarro would organize innumerable expeditions in the hope of replicating their achievements.

CHAPTER 4:

The Realms of Gold

After the seizure of the immense Aztec treasure in 1521 and that of the Incas in 1532, it became obvious that the New World was neither Cathay, nor Cipango, nor the Golden Chersonese, much the less Ophir or Tarshish, but that nevertheless there was indeed gold there in abundance. The biblical and Greco-Roman myths were relegated to second place, yielding to new legends; born of the ignorance of the territory and of native traditions, the stories were above all the products of the imagination of the adventurers, whose sole aim was to make their fortune. The imaginative landscape became Americanized. The conquistadors assumed that if Cortés and Pizarro had found the realms of gold, then the immense continent was no doubt the home of still others. These bore the mysterious names of Quivira, Cíbola, the land of the Amazons, Omagua, the land of Cinnamon, Meta, El Dorado, Manoa, Parime, Guayapó, Jungulo, Paitití or Mojos, Enim, the Gran Parú, Trapalanda and the Caesars.[1]

The Lord, our God permits this passionate search for El Dorado
because it opens up new paths for the Holy Gospel.[2]

Reverend Joseph Gumilla (1715)

El Dorado, Omagua, Paitití, Trapalanda, Cíbola...the names of these
legendary realms spread like wildfire and in infinite variation, giving
rise to still others in people's imaginations. Since precise descriptions
were not easy to come by, the mythical toponymy and location of
these sites were often confused. It is nevertheless generally possible to
locate four great kingdoms endowed with all that humans could possibly desire: in northern Mexico, the seven cities of Cíbola; in South
America, El Dorado and the Great Paitití and in the southern
regions, the enchanted city of the Caesars.

During the fifteenth century, the Portuguese and the Spanish
progressively occupied all of what would become Latin America.
Portugal at that time had no more than a million inhabitants, which
was insufficient for undertaking an intensive colonization of the new
territories. It therefore, limited itself to founding trading posts along
the Brazilian coast and engaging in commerce – initially peaceful –
with the Tupinamba Indians.

Spain, however, with its seven million inhabitants, had a surplus
population for whom America represented the only hope of making
their fortune. The waves of migration grew so large that in 1525, the
ambassador of Venice, impressed, stated that the city of Seville was
now populated largely by women.[3]

In the early days, the Spanish founded European-style cities along
the coast of the Caribbean Sea, such as Cartagena and Panama; then
they pushed west and south, settling in the great Aztec cities such as
Mexico and the Inca cities of Quito, Jauja and Cuzco, or erecting new
ones such as Ciudad de los Reyes (the future Lima) and Arequipa.
They continued their southward expansion, building Santiago de
Chile, and undertook the crossing of the La Plata estuary that would
culminate in the foundation of Buenos Aires and Asunción. The
Hispanic settlements were generally located near the coast, along the
edges of central South America.

At the heart of that continent was the majestic Selva (forest). The
conquistadors, for the most part, natives of the arid regions of
Andalusia and Estremadura, discovered the tropical forest, exuberant
and impenetrable, that began on the eastern slopes of the Andes
Cordillera. To reach it from Peru or Colombia, they had to cross the
Cordillera; from Chile there was a desert to cross as well; from the

Río de la Plata, the route went through the inhospitable Chaco plain. The vegetation quickly became extremely dense, making all progress difficult; the route was further impeded by innumerable marshes and torrents that often turned into waterfalls and rapids. The heat, the humidity and the insects were veritable plagues, the rivers infested with caimans, piranhas and anacondas up to 10 m in length. The chronicles tell of a snake that wrapped itself around the hammock, where an unfortunate explorer was sleeping, squeezing and suffocating him in order to swallow him up.

Thrown into an unfamiliar universe, the adventurers had enormous difficulty finding food and often survived only by sacking native villages, inevitably provoking the hostility of the forest dwellers who were so adroit in fighting river battles with their easily manoeuvrable canoes and so deft with their bows and slingshots armed with poison arrows.

Did not all these dangers evoke the mythological obstacles that were said to lie along the road leading to gold? After all, tradition had it that access to the precious metal is difficult, the gold being a reward for the sufferings endured along a mystical voyage strewn with terrible obstacles: only after having overcome them will a seeker reach the marvellous places, where it was reputed that gold could be gathered into fishing nets or, even better, sown and harvested*.[4]

THE GOLDEN KINGDOMS

The desire to find new empires bursting with gold became an obsession. Among the conquistadors, rumours began to circulate about marvellous kingdoms, inexhaustible riches and fantastic cities located at the heart of a natural environment that was as grandiose as it was wild.

El Dorado

It was from the city of San Francisco de Quito, in Ecuador, that the first echoes came, in 1534, of a fabulous kingdom. An Indian appeared there seeking the aid of the Spanish in his people's war against the Muiscas. He stated that in his land there was abundant gold, and described the ceremony of the gilded man that would tantalize people's imaginations for centuries.

---

*Bartolomé de Las Casas tells how the colonists arrived in America and asked 'where and how can we fish for gold with our nets.'

Engraving by Théodore de Bry showing the naked body of an Indian cacique being covered with an ointment onto which gold dust is blown through a tube. Bibliothèque Royale de Belgique.

The story turned out to be a sad one: in the village of Guatavitá in what is now Colombia, there once lived a *cacique* (chief) whose wife had cheated on him. When he discovered the betrayal, he forced her during a banquet to eat 'the organs by which her lover had sinned' and ordered the Indians to recount the crime before the whole village during their drinking party. Desperate and unable to bear such humiliation, the woman took her little daughter in her arms and threw herself along with the child into Lake Guatavitá. The chief was overcome with remorse, and his great sorrow did not diminish when the priests explained to him that his wife now lived in a hidden palace at the bottom of the lake, and that one could honour her by presenting her with gold offerings. The penitent chief made it a habit to navigate to the middle of the lake and throw in golden objects and emeralds; he went there stripped naked, his body completely covered with mud and powdered with gold dust.[5]

According to another version, the candidates to succeed the chief were locked up in a grotto for six years, eating neither meat, nor salt, nor peppers; they were forbidden contact with women or to see daylight. The day of the enthronement, their first act was to enter the lake offer sacrifices to the gods. Lighting fires all around the lake, the Indians undressed the chosen heir and anointed his body with a mixture of mud and gold dust. The new chief, thus adorned and bearing 'a great heap of gold and emeralds' set out on a raft made of rushes on which a bonfire had been lit, its smoke visible from a great distance. At the moment of the offering, total silence reigned. The music and chanting stopped, and the chief threw the treasure into the waters of Lake Guatavitá.[6]

The famous ceremony of El Dorado, described by an Indian from Quito, was recounted by the sixteenth-century historian and poet Juan de Castellanos in his work *Elegías para varones ilustres de las Indias* (Elegies for the Illustrious Men of the Indies). Singing an elegy for the conquistador Sebastián Moyano de Benalcázar and his lieutenant Pedro de Añasco, he wrote:

> *Añasco and Benalcázar were interrogating*
> *An itinerant Indian from foreign parts,*
> *Who lived in the town of Quito*
> *And claimed to be from around Bogotá –*
> *How he got there, I don't know.*
> *He spoke with them and asserted,*
> *'I know a land rich in emeralds and gold.'*
>
> *And along with the things he brought with him*
> *Was a tale of a certain king with no clothes:*
> *Floating on a raft in a lake*
> *To make offerings, according to what he saw,*
> *All covered in resin*
> *And gold dust*
> *From the bottom of his feet to the top of his head,*
> *Shining like a ray of the sun.*
>
> *His visits to the lake were frequent – said he –*
> *To make offerings there*
> *Of fine jewels of gold and emerald*
> *And other ornaments.*
> *And he affirmed that all this was true.*[7]

The account of the ceremony appears to be historically accurate. The Muiscas were skilled goldsmiths and their lakes were the objects of a special cult. The information provided by the 'pilgrim Indian' aroused the imagination of the Spanish. Though the most famous, El Dorado was neither the first nor the only fantasy kingdom that dotted the landscape of the New World.

Chroniclers recount that when in 1534, the impulsive Sebastián de Benalcázar heard the story of the Indian chief covered in gold, he exclaimed: 'Let's go find this gilded Indian!' ('Indio dorado' in Spanish). This expression inspired the name of the most famous American myth, and marks the starting point for innumerable mad expeditions to find the imaginary realm, where the precious metal – as seductive as it was diabolical – was reputed to abound.[8]

El Paitití

A few years earlier, in 1515, an expedition led by Juan Díaz de Solís in search of a passage to the Pacific Ocean began to explore the Río de la Plata, which they named 'Mar Dulce' (Sweet Sea). When Solís and seven of his men went ashore in what is now Uruguay, they were attacked by the native people; all but one sailor perished. Demoralized, the expedition began the return journey to Spain, now under the command of Francisco de Torres, Solís's son-in-law. Near Santa Caterina island one of the ships sank. There was no room on the two remaining vessels for all the survivors, and those that remained behind, intrigued by what they had heard from the Guaraní Indians, penetrated deep into the forests of Brazil in search of a white king who was supposed to reign over the Sierra de la Plata (Silver Mountains). Just over a decade later, in 1526, some of the survivors were picked up by Sebastian Cabot's ships. They spoke with eloquence of the fabulous Sierra de la Plata, and told Cabot's party that if they went upriver they would be able to load their ships with gold and silver. Cabot did not hesitate: in contravention of his agreement with the Crown, which had ordered him to sail to the Spice Islands in Asia, he decided to change course and sail up the river in search of the mountains from which Argentina and its principal river would take their name.[9] This fantasy was at the origin of the belief in the existence of a great empire hidden at the heart of the continent.

New reports would soon come of a *Noticia Rica* (rich news) in the same region, namely eastern Peru. This was probably not so much a myth, simply a misinterpretation of information provided by Indians referring undoubtedly to the splendour of the Inca Empire. All rumours of gold were met with avid interest, and so belief in the Noticia Rica quickly gathered the force of an avalanche, took on a life of its own and survived the destruction of the Quechua Indians' civilization.

Nevertheless, the Sierra de la Plata and the Noticia Rica would soon be relegated to second place, in favour of a new imagined kingdom, that of Paitití. The legend began in Peru, on the Cajamarca highlands, when Francisco Pizarro captured Emperor Atahualpa by surprise. The hostage proposed a compromise. On the wall of the room that served as his prison, he drew a line as high as he could reach, and offered to exchange his liberty for a chamber filled with gold up to the mark he had drawn. Pizarro agreed. From then on, endless llama caravans, laden with sparkling objects, would make their way across the 15,200 km of roads that linked the empire. If the emperor respected his commitment, Pizarro for his part did not keep his word, and Atahualpa was garrotted by the conquistadors on 3 August 1533, though only after having first been baptized and given the name 'Juan'. The story is told that when his subjects were informed of the Inca emperor's death, they diverted the caravans with their gold and silver wares to an unknown place, where they hid what they had been able to save of the ransom.

The legend of hidden gold was soon joined by rumours of a secret empire. The Incas gave the name *Antisuyo* to the territories stretching to the east of the Cordillera.[10] There the Inca dignitaries known as *orejones* ('long ears') were supposed to have withdrawn with all the treasures they were able to carry and to have built an immense empire named Mojos or Gran Paitití, governed by the younger brother of Atahualpa and Huáscar and dotted with the most fabulously rich cities, where gold shone from every nook and cranny.[11]

It is possible and even probable that parts of the Inca Empire survived the execution of Atahualpa; the fortress city of Machu Picchu, discovered only in 1912, reveals traces of human activity later than 1533. Moreover, the last three Inca emperors – Manco, his son Titu Cusi and his brother and successor Tupac Amaru – tried to restore the empire and continued their resistance until the capture and execution of Tupac Amaru by the conquerors in 1572. From this moment on, the various accounts of the realms of gold in upper Peru blended together with the myth of Paitití.

A lovely, image-filled description of the hidden empire is provided by the Spanish priest Martín del Barco Centenera, who arrived in 1572 on the territory of present-day Paraguay, where he was appointed archdeacon. He would share the life of the conquistadors for 24 years, recounting his experience in a very beautiful poem called *Argentina y Conquista del Río de la Plata, Tucumán y Otros Sucesos del Perú* (Argentina and the Conquest of the Río de la Plata, Tucumán and Other Successes in Peru). In the fifth verse, he talks about the Gran Moxo, lord of El Paytite, who lived in a lake:

> *In the middle of the lake was formed*
> *An Isle made up of buildings*

Of such great beauty and grace
That it surpasses all human imagination.
The Lord of all these people had a house
Set on that Isle; this of white stone was built
Up to the roof, and there two towers were set
Close each to the other, and between the two
A grade was placed, and in the midst,
A strong post fixed, with two live lions
Tethered thereto with chains of solid gold,
Locked fast with stout and cunning fastenings.

Upon the summit of this column stout
That in its loftiness did a score of feet
And another five surpass, was fixed
A moon of massive silver which o'er all
The lagoon shone...[12]

Further details are given by the sailor and writer Pedro Sarmiento de Gamboa, who accompanied the viceroy of Peru on a visit to the new provinces. Based on the information he had gathered, he described the connections between the Incas and the regions to the east of present-day Bolivia: a 'great captain' of the Incas was supposed to have reached 'a river of which we have recently heard, known as Paitite, where Inga Topa (the great Inca emperor Tupac Inca) had placed his stone markers.'[13] In addition to what Sarmiento de Gamboa was able to find out, there is an account by the priest Diego Felipe de Alcaya, written around 1635. In his version, after the defeat of Peru by the Spanish, the monarch of the fugitive Incas, 'taking into account the configuration of the site, populated the back side of the hill known as Paitití... And just as he had been the leader of the Kingdom of Cuzco, he now became the head of this great Kingdom of Paytití, known as Mojos.'[14] The news crossed the ocean and reached the court of Philip II in a letter from the viceroy of Peru informing the king that 'in the province of Paitití, there are gold and silver mines and amber in great quantity.'[15]

The priest Andrés Ortiz also alluded to the secret empire in a letter dated 1595, in which he expressed his desire to go to 'Paitití, so famous and greatly desired'. In general, the writings of the sixteenth century were agreed that the empire was located on an island in the middle of a great lake.

The most reasonable explanation of the belief in this fantastic kingdom has been proposed by the Argentine historian Enrique de

Gandía, who claimed that Paitití was essentially a mirage caused by the magnificent temple of the Island of the Sun on Lake Titicaca and by the impressive Inca cities. De Gandía analysed different etymologies of the word Paitití: the most likely one is that pai means monarch, and tití is a contraction of the word Titicaca, so that Paitití designates the monarch of Lake Titicaca.[16]

The City of the Caesars

During these years, rumours of another fabulous city situated further to the south of the continent reached the ears of the colonists. Curiously enough, information regarding marvellous treasures and stories of shipwrecked survivors living at the far reaches of the continent, though initially appearing to have nothing to do with each other, blended into a single fantastic amalgam under the name 'Enchanted city of the Caesars', allegedly built on the pampas of Patagonia.[17]

The first element of the legend came from the expedition led by Cabot between 1526 and 1530. While his fleet lay at anchor in the Río de la Plata he sent a detachment of fifteen men, led by Captain Francisco César, overland to 'discover the gold and silver mines along with other riches'. Two or three months[18] later, only 'six or seven people…telling of such great riches that it seemed a miracle' returned to the fleet. Captain César's men had most likely obtained information about the brilliant Peruvian civilization, the echoes of which reached as far as the Atlantic coast.

This expedition prompted the chronicler Ruy Díaz de Guzmán (around 1563–1629), author of *La Argentina*, to recount a fable based on an embellishment of Francisco César's adventure: when the latter's party returned laden with riches and smartly dressed, they found the fort abandoned and had to undertake a long march that took them up a mountain from which one could see both oceans. From there they continued to Cuzco, reaching the city just when Pizarro had captured the Inca emperor Atahualpa.[19]

Other facts without any obvious connection to the above incident also contributed to fashioning the myth. Thus, five years later, in 1535, a squadron led by the Portuguese cosmographer Simón de Alcazaba crossed the Strait of Magellan. Part of the crew mutinied and Alcazaba was assassinated. The sailors who remained loyal succeeded eventually in gaining the upper hand, and abandoned the surviving mutineers on the icy beaches of the Strait.

The series of shipwrecks in these difficult waters had only begun. In 1540, a new flotilla of four ships, equipped by the bishop of

Plasencia, arrived at the Strait in the vain hope of finding 'gold, silver, (precious) stones or pearls'; the flagship sank but the crew managed to escape, while the second ship returned to Spain, the third reached Peru and the fourth disappeared without a trace.[20]

In 1584, a fleet of 200 men under the command of Sarmiento de Gamboa (to whom we owe the earlier account of Paitití) was shipwrecked in the Strait of Magellan. The expedition's mission had been to fortify the two shores, where the strait was at its narrowest, in order to secure Spanish domination over this strategic zone that had already been much used by Drake and other English buccanneers. The survivors founded two settlements, Nombre de Jesús and Ciudad Real de San Felipe, while the remaining ship went vainly in search of assistance. Four years later, Tomé Hernández was found; he described before a notary the horrible famine that had wiped out the other victims of the shipwreck, and declared that he was the sole survivor of what would henceforth be called Puerto del Hambre (Hunger Port). Hernández also stated, when questioned about the language spoken by the Indians of the region, that one heard them constantly saying 'Jesus!' and 'Holy Mary' with their eyes turned toward heaven, and that they indicated that inland there were bearded and boot-clad men as well as other young people resembling Spanish sailors.[21] And indeed there were cities founded by the Europeans located further north. But since in those days rationality was not always the order of the day, it was the fantastical interpretation that prevailed: there must have been unknown cities in this region, populated by Europeans.[22]

It was the destiny of other survivors, very different from those shipwrecked in the Strait of Magellan that sealed the formation of the myth: that of the first Spanish colonists of southern Chile. The conquistador Pedro de Valdivia, the first governor of Chile, founded the towns of Villarrica and Imperial more than 1,000 km north of the Strait. His successor, García Hurtado de Mendoza, would add those of Angol and Osorno. These towns enjoyed extraordinary prosperity during the first years: the colonists cultivated vineyards, apple trees, cereals and vegetables and bred cows and sheep. But this enviable situation did not last long. In 1599, the Mapuche Indians launched a violent attack to regain their lands; the few colonists who were able to escape fled to the south. It was said that from the island of Chiloé they entered Argentinian Patagonia, where all trace of them was lost. It was then that legend took over.[23]

The myth of the enchanted city of the Caesars was thus based on four elements: the riches seen by Captain Francisco César's detachment; the survivors of the shipwreck of the fleets of Alcazaba, the bishop of Plasencia and of Sarmiento; the rumours of wealthy cities created by the fugitive Inca nobility; and the mysterious residence of the unfortunate Chilean colonists.

The collective imagination would forge a link between all these events, and turn their protagonists into the happy and powerful inhabitants of an enchanted city, thus creating a new myth peculiar to Argentina and Chile, quite different in many respects from the fabulous land of El Dorado or the secret empire of the Incas.

The Jesuit Diego de Rosales (Madrid 1605 – Santiago de Chile, 1677), in his *Historia general del reino de Chile* (General History of the Kingdom of Chile), basing himself on the testimony of two survivors of the bishop of Plasencia's fleet, would go so far as to name a head of state of this fantastic realm: a certain Sebastián de Argüello, alleged commander of the crew shipwrecked in the Strait. His fellow chronicler Antonio de Guevara would limit himself to an affirmation that 'Trapalanda is an apparently imaginary province, situated near the Strait of Magellan, or at least in the "magellanic" province, and which according to some people was none other than the city or cities of the Caesars, also known as Patagons.'[24]

At the beginning of the seventeenth century, the popularity of the Caesars enjoyed a veritable crescendo. Distinguished religious figures and the governor of Chile himself, drawn by the mystery of the wealthy city, organized search parties.

Four prodigious kingdoms would thus continue to nurture the dreams of the conquistadors over the centuries: the Seven Cities of Cíbola in northern Mexico (a theme developed in Chapter Six), El Dorado in Colombia and southern Venezuela, Paitití on the edge of Brazil and Bolivia, and finally the city of the Caesars on the southern pampas.

THE PARIAHS OF THE 'CONQUISTA'

The conquerors of Peru were unable to govern the lands they had conquered. It was not long before they split up into rival bands that would fight each other for 15 years. It was during the episode known as the *Guerra de las Salinas* that Francisco Pizarro and practically all the leaders of the expedition that had defeated the Incas met their deaths. The Spanish Crown then decided to send a new viceroy, in the person of the marquis of Cañete, whose iron hand imposed upon the New World, the social stratification of medieval Spain. Thus ended the brief period during which soldiers of modest background were transformed into rich and powerful men. Henceforth, the most interesting posts and the enormous territories – including those of the native people – known as *encomiendas*, would be given to notables often appointed directly by the metropolis.

Around 1560, approximately 8,000 Spaniards were living in Peru, of whom only between 450 and 500 had received sizeable tracts of land along with their native inhabitants; about 1,000 enjoyed some high position or at least a good salary. The rest had to scramble to survive, and were no more than vagabond soldiers, disinherited adventurers: the pariahs of the conquest.[25] They had invested their meagre resources and their youth and risked their lives in campaigns that flooded Spain with a sea of wealth. Many veterans were reduced to living off the charity of the wealthy, in the ever more distant hope of receiving an encomienda in a future distribution of lands.

There was only one sure way to make a quick fortune: to repeat history by discovering new empires bursting with gold and getting there in time for a share in the spoils. Despite the administrative and geographical obstacles, these impoverished soldiers hurried to enlist in the innumerable expeditions that were launched in quest of these hypothetical realms: the illusory hope of finding and plundering them was the only thing that helped them survive, and hence, their critical sense became more and more shaky.

It was this state of mind that can explain the ease with which the Spanish – and others – lent a more than sympathetic ear to the tales carried to the four corners of the continent by all sorts of visionary mythmakers who claimed to have information from the most reliable sources, often from the Indians, about this or that kingdom of unfathomable wealth. Yet as it turns out, the native people often referred in their 'testimonies' to empires that had already been conquered and of which they had heard from other Indians, to European colonies or settlements sometimes located at the other end of the continent, to previous Spanish or Portuguese expeditions, or even to the quasi-clandestine presence of English or Dutch pirates. Moreover, certain Guaraní or Tupí chiefs did not fail to point to a land much richer than their own located beyond the mountains or several days downriver in order to send the intruders on their way as quickly as possible.

Expeditions to El Dorado

One of the first great explorations of the South American continent was entrusted to Diego de Ordaz, who had been one of the best captains in Cortés's expedition to conquer Mexico. He set sail from Seville in 1531 accompanied by 400 men. Near the mouth of the Orinoco the better part of the fleet was dispersed by a violent freshwater current and disappeared without a trace. Ordaz sailed up the river as far as one of its tributaries, the Meta, but he was soon halted by the Atures Rapids. There he was informed of the existence of an extremely rich province, also called Meta. Unfortunately, his health did not permit him to continue, and he died before the rest of his flotilla could reach a Spanish port. The 300 soldiers who had disappeared would become the stuff of several legends, and many an explorer thought he had caught some sign of their survival or even claimed to have met them.

This initial failure in no way dampened the enthusiasm of the Spanish. In 1538, three armies set off in search of the 'New Land' without any prior consultation. The German Nicolas Federman wished to verify the information about the city of Meta; the *Adelantado* Gonzalo Jiménez de Quesada* looked for and found the fabulous temples of the Muiscas (formerly known as the Chibchas) and Sebastián de Benalcázar went in pursuit of the famous 'gilded chief'.[26] After having sacked the temples of Sogamoso and Tunja, Quesada reached the plateau of Bogotá, where he founded the future capital of the 'New Kingdom of Granada'. As fortune would have it, the armies of Federman and of Benalcázar converged on the new city at that moment. Tensions arose and war nearly broke out; but since each of the forces were about equal in size – about 160 men to each camp – the three leaders decided to go together to Spain to settle their disputes before the *Consejo de Indias* (Council of the Indies).

The conquistadors could not, however, content themselves with founding new cities, and waited impatiently for news of the fabulous realms. Quito, the most important Inca city after Cuzco, was then a meeting place for the Quechua civilization with the tribes of the Amazon. The city resounded with the echoes of impassioned debates about the 'realms of gold', debates that were fed by ancient Indian legends including that of the land of Cinnamon, believed to be situated east of the Equator.[27] This region owed its name to the cinnamon of Quijos, a flower much appreciated by the Incas, and it was said that Atahualpa had offered Pizarro a bouquet of the delicately perfumed cinnamon.

Impatient, Francisco Pizarro appointed his brother Gonzalo governor of Quito and entrusted him with the mission of finding in this 'land of Cinnamon' the source of the wealth of El Dorado.

*The title Adelantado was given in Spain to the military and political governors of border provinces. The title was transplanted to America in the early days of the conquest.

Gonzalo set out at the head of an impressive expedition made up of hundreds of Spaniards and thousands of Indians, accompanied by horses, hunting dogs and farm animals. But it soon proved impossible to advance through the Cordillera and the virgin forest with such a large army to feed. The main expeditionary force thus turned back without reaching its destination. Only lieutenant general Francisco Orellana continued the exploration with a small detachment, and would thus be the first European to cross South America from the Pacific to the Atlantic navigating along the Amazon River. This adventure would provide new information about the kingdom of the Omaguas and the land of the Amazons.

The mirage did not dissipate for all that, and in 1559, the famous expedition of Pedro de Ursua and Lope de Aguirre set off on a bloodied adventure that would be immortalized on screen by Werner Herzog and then by Carlos Saura. The first lines of the chronicle composed by the knight Francisco Vázquez recalled that the objective of this campaign had been to discover El Dorado:

> In the year 1559, while he was viceroy and president of Peru, the marquis of Cañete received information about certain provinces called

The arrest of Berrio, Spanish governor of Trinidad, by Sir Walter Raleigh. Berrio is said to be one of the initiators of the legend of El Dorado.

Amagua [sic] and El Dorado. Desiring to serve God and his King, he entrusted a great friend of his, the knight Pedro de Ursua, a native of Navarre, the task of discovering the aforesaid provinces. He bestowed very broad powers upon him, naming him governor of the provinces, and provided him with funds from the royal household. The information we have mentioned was collected and provided by Captain Orellana, and those who had left Peru with him descending the Marañón River (Peruvian part of the Amazon), where they were said to have found the said provinces.[28]

Like some of the other myths that of El Dorado underwent a significant metamorphosis: the Indian chief covered in gold was transformed into a legendary land that became the object of hopes and illusions. At the end of the sixteenth century, explorers were looking for a province or better yet an entire nation that the imagination placed on the map and gave it a capital, Manoa, built on the shores of a saltwater lake.

The decisive step towards the construction of El Dorado was taken by General Antonio de Berrio in the 1590s; while exploring the region of the Orinoco, he learned from the native people that 'an infinite amount of gold' was to be found only seven days away. The Indians had even specified that if the exploitation of the gold mines was reserved exclusively to the caciques and their wives, anyone at all could collect the gold that was in the rivers.

In reality, the information collected by Berrio came from a rather confused story: an account of the exploration was recorded by his lieutenant, Domingo Vera, who embellished it slightly in order to arouse the envy of his superior by including, along with his narrative, the alleged revelations of a certain Juan Martínez, an adventurer who had survived the expedition of Diego de Ordaz, and who was supposed to have lived in the capital of El Dorado. Details were not lacking: during the festivals of the Guyanese people – the pseudo-account of Martínez reported – 'the servants anoint the bodies of the notables with a white balm named "curcay" and cover them with gold powder by blowing it through hollow reeds until they shine from head to foot.' Gold was everywhere: in the cities, the temples, in the form of idols, plaques, arms and shields. It was for this reason that the region was called 'El Dorado'. Its capital was the famous city of Manoa, built on the edges of the no less fabulous Lake Parime.[29]

Be that as it may, what matters is that they believed it. This information crossed the boundaries of the Spanish Empire and reached the ears of the enemies of Philip II. An English military expedition seized Berrio's documents and passed them on to the British royal court. And so it was that the great Protestant nation would also succumb to the enchantment of the realms of gold.

It was at this point that Sir Walter Raleigh, one of the great Englishmen of his day, appeared on the scene. A soldier, navigator, poet, historian and statesman, he had in his youth fought alongside the French Huguenots. At Queen Elizabeth's court he held an enviable position thanks to his talent as a navigator and explorer, even if we may be justified in supposing that the attentions he showered on the queen did not fail to enhance his brilliant career. He, too, yielded to the fascination with the legendary mountains of gold and in 1595, he set sail from Plymouth headed for El Dorado with a fleet of five ships and 100 men. The expedition occupied a part of the island of Trinidad, where they captured Berrio, governor of the island at the time, along with his officers, before sailing up the Orinoco for about 110 leagues. The results were meagre, however: he returned to London with scarcely more than a few grains of gold.

Raleigh nevertheless followed the pattern of others before him: his first failure did not bring him back to reason but, on the contrary, only served to intensify the appeal of the myth. In London he published *The Discoverie of the large, rich and bewtiful Empyre of Guiana, with a Relation of the great and golden Citie of Manoa*, which the Spaniards call El Dorado.

His imagination, allied with the need to justify the costs of the voyage, showed itself at its peak. Raleigh began with an apology, imputing his failure to a flaw that was particularly shameful in his homeland: the lack of punctuality of one of his captains, who prevented him from reaching the city of Manoa:

> Captain Preston had not been persuaded that he should have come too late to Trinidad to have found us there (for the month was expired which I promised to tarry for him there ere he could recover the coast of Spain) but that it had pleased God he might have joined with us, and that we had entered the country but some ten days sooner ere the rivers were overflown, we had adventured either to have gone to the great city of Manoa, or at least taken so many of the other cities and towns nearer at hand, as would have made a royal return. But it pleased not God so much to favour me at this time. If it shall be my lot to prosecute the same, I shall willingly spend my life therein. And if anyone else shall be enabled thereunto, and conquer the same, I assure him thus much; he shall perform more than ever was done in Mexico by Cortes, or in Peru by Pizarro, whereof the one conquered the empire of Mutezuma,

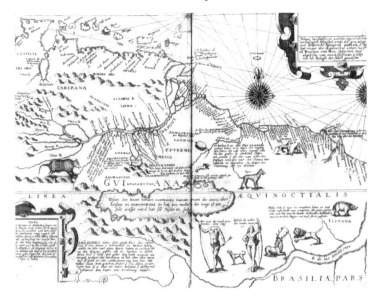

This engraving by Théodore de Bry shows a map of Guiana,
the region where El Dorado was believed to have been situated.
The legendary empire of Guiana, Lake Parime, the Amazons
and the Acephaloi of the Americas - referred to as
Ewaipanomas - are carefully depicted.

the other of Guascar and Atabalipa. And whatsoever prince shall
possess it, that prince shall be lord of more gold, and of a more beautiful
empire, and of more cities and people, than either the king of Spain or
the Great Turk.[30]

In his view, El Dorado and the kingdom founded by the Incas during
their exile were one and the same. What is more, in their new territories,
the latter were believed to have erected cities even more
grandiose than those of Peru. Raleigh's source? The famous account
by Juan Martínez, who had been charged with committing a serious
crime and condemned to death, but the sentence, was commuted
thanks to the collusion of his companions in having abandoned the
guilty man in a canoe:

But it pleased God that the canoe was carried down the stream, and
certain of the Guianians met it the same evening; and, having not at

any time seen any Christian nor any man of that colour, they carried Martinez into the land to be wondered at, and so from town to town, until he came to the great city of Manoa, the seat and residence of Inga the emperor. The emperor, after he had beheld him, knew him to be a Christian, for it was not long before that his brethren Guascar and Atabalipa were vanquished by the Spaniards in Peru: and caused him to be lodged in his palace, and well entertained.[31]

The English adventurer claimed to know that the city of Manoa enjoyed a delightful climate that never had winter, that the trees were bent under the weight of their leaves and fruits during all four seasons. Near Manoa he had heard that there was a mine called 'Mother of gold'.

The conquest of this nation was no easy matter. Its sovereign was indeed very powerful and – Raleigh noted – had he continued to advance with his small army he would only have succeeded in digging his own grave and that of his men. Even three times as many soldiers would have made no difference; he would have to rely on the help of the enemies of this great State in order to bring it to submission. He added that a few years earlier, 300 Spaniards (survivors of the shipwreck of the Ordaz expedition) had met a miserable end in the valley of Maccureguary, on the frontiers of El Dorado.

Temples, idols and tombs were all made of gold. There was even a mountain made of this precious metal; nearby lived the powerful Ewaipanomas, headless men whose eyes and mouths were in the middle of their chests, very much like the oriental acephali, with the only difference being that they had hair on their backs and were deft hands with bows that were three times the normal size.

Martínez was supposed to have spent seven months in Manoa. After that, the king of El Dorado allegedly permitted him to leave, laden with splendid gifts. He returned home enormously rich, though he was only a poor customs officer:

Martinez lived seven months in Manoa, but was not suffered to wander into the country anywhere. He was also brought thither all the way blindfold, led by the Indians, until he came to the entrance of Manoa itself, and was 14 or 15 days in the passage. He avowed at his death that he entered the city at noon, and then they uncovered his face; and that he travelled all that day till night through the city, and the next day from sun rising to sun setting, ere he came to the palace of Inga. After Martinez had lived seven months in Manoa, and began to understand the language of the country, Inga asked him whether he desired to return into his own country, or would willingly abide with him. But Martinez, not desirous to stay, obtained the favour of Inga to depart; with whom he sent divers Guianians to conduct him to the river of Orenoque, all loaden with as much gold as they could carry, which he gave to Martinez at his departure. But when he was arrived near the river's side, the borderers which are called Orenoqueponi (poni is a Carib postposition meaning "on") robbed him and his Guianians of all the treasure (the borderers being at that time at wars, which Inga had not conquered) save only of two great bottles of gourds, which were filled with beads of gold curiously wrought, which those Orenoqueponi thought had been no other thing than his drink or meat, or grain for food, with which Martinez had liberty.[32]

From the mouth of the Orinoco he apparently sailed to the island of Trinidad, and from there headed for San Juan de Portorico, where deathly ill, he is believed to have spent his last days. Having received the last rites, Raleigh continues, he called for his gold to be brought to him, along with the story of his adventures, and bequeathed his treasures to the Church in order that masses be said for the repose of his immortal soul. The Englishman concludes the story of Martínez saying: 'He was the first who, according to Berrio, discovered Manoa which he called El Dorado.'

These accounts would inspire other English expeditions to search – in vain – for these fantastic treasures. After 13 years spent locked up in the Tower of London for some obscure accusation of treason, and having taken advantage of the enforced retreat to write a remarkable History of the World, Raleigh was rehabilitated. He then succeeded in mounting a new expedition to Guyana, no longer in search of El Dorado but with the more modest objective of finding a gold mine. He lost his entire fortune, his illusions and one of his sons on the venture. The Spanish made him the object of their wrath, little inclined to lose the alleged gold mine to a rival explorer; thanks to the sordid diplomatic manoeuvres of the count of Godomar, Spanish ambassador in London, the brilliant English gentleman ended his days on the scaffold of Westminster in 1618.

In America, however, the legend continued to spread, and is still debated today between sceptics and true believers. In the end the myth came full circle, focusing attention on the enormous conical crater that, at an altitude of 3,200 m, contains the waters of Lake Guatavitá. The first licence to drain it was granted in 1580 to Antonio de Sepúlveda, a rich merchant from Bogotá, but the project was a failure: Sepúlveda received no more than 12,000 pesos in exchange for the few jewels he succeeded in finding, and he died of an illness contracted during these difficult and fruitless endeavours. Two further parties attempted the same operation; one in 1625 and the other in 1677, but both of them were ruined by the venture.

The French State also promoted the quest for El Dorado. Until 1720, the administration of French Guyana lent vigorous support to expeditions in search of the golden city. Governor Claude Guillouet d'Orvilliers sent a group of explorers financed by the colony, but the unfortunate men lost their lives in the process.[33]

At the beginning of the nineteenth century, Alexander von Humboldt carried out a five-year scientific exploration of America, during which he took a rational approach to finding El Dorado. He sailed up the Orinoco, passed its confluence with the Meta River and found himself on the Nero River, ending up at a settlement called Esmeralda. It was believed that Lake Parime and the great city of Manoa were to be found there. In fact, Lake Parime was none other than the Parima River, the name given to the Río Branco during the periods when the waters swell. As for Manoa, it was notable for its absence[34]. He continued on towards Lake Guatavitá and saw there the ancient breaches made by the Spanish. Rational but nevertheless fascinated, Humboldt inaugurated a new series of modern industrial prospects of Lake Guatavitá and of some of the nearby lakes.

The first English party that launched an assault on the legendary lake withdrew, requesting compensation from Humboldt for damages and losses sustained, a demand based on the disappointing results of his explorations. In 1870, two explorers died of asphyxiation in an 18 m gallery intended for use in draining the lake. In 1900, a Franco-English company was ruined by searching for the same treasures, and in 1912, an English firm finally succeeded in drying out most of the lake. The result was disastrous: the sun and the air hardened the mud, the sides of the crater solidified and the engineers could not remove the few gold objects they found. The proceeds from the sale did not cover even ten per cent of the costs. One of the few significant discoveries took place in 1856 when Tovar, París and Chacón uncovered a number of items in Lake Siecha near Guatavitá, including a magnificent piece of Muisca goldsmith work representing a raft carrying ten people, all in gold. Its design undoubtedly evokes the ceremony of the cacique covered in gold dust. It certainly suggests that there was a grain of truth in the most tenacious myth born in America.[35]

In recent years, a dam has been built on the crater of Guatavitá, and the resulting lake has flooded the old settlement: the new one, built a short distance away, tries to keep the memory of the myth alive and to satisfy the thousands of tourists who flock to the site.

In Search of the Great Paititi

An ever-active imagination eventually transposed its ghosts into the heart of the virgin forest, an exuberant and nearly impenetrable territory dominated by an unruly natural world. This landscape, unfamiliar to Europeans, could not help but awaken memories of medieval legends among the gold seekers.

Bearing in mind that finding gold was the only hope of enrichment for thousands of Spanish itinerant soldiers, it is understandable that the faintest rumour, the tiniest trail or the most minute information about the realms of gold served to nurture the illusions of these adventurers. During the seventeenth century, several expeditions thus set out from Peru and Paraguay in the hope of discovering the new and rich civilization called Sierra de la Plata or Noticia Rica, but which was most often referred to as the Gran Paititi, since it was believed to be the secret continuation of the fabulous empire of the Incas.

The first major expedition was organized by Domingo de Irala; in 1547, he set out from San Fernando sailing up the Paraná and then the Paraguay as far as Asunción, accompanied by 350 Spaniards and 2,000 Indians aboard dugout canoes and brigantines. At each stop he inquired after gold, and the Indians – perhaps out of malice – sent his party in several different directions. Exploring, warring, concluding alliances as well as committing massacres, he finally reached Peru after an enormous detour, but the golden realms did not reveal their mysteries to him.

Irala was followed by Nuflo de Chaves. The latter raised anchor in 1558 with 143 Spaniards and 2,000 Indians in order to go and found a village in the province of Xarayes in northwestern Paraguay. There he came across settlements with impressive fortifications whose inhabitants put up fierce resistance against the invaders.

Later a few Spanish soldiers affirmed that at that point they were on the verge of discovering a new empire. They convinced the viceroy of Peru of this, who in turn informed the king of Spain himself that Nuflo de Chaves had been given the mission of conquering the 'Mojos', another name for Paititi.[36]

The secret kingdom of the Incas now became an obsession among official circles. In 1568, the governor of Peru, Don Lope García de Castro*, granted Juan Álvarez Maldonado permission to discover

---

*Lope García de Castro was the successor of the count of Nieva, the fourth viceroy of Peru, assassinated in Lima following his love affair with a married woman. Lope was given the title of *Gobernador y Capitán General del Perú y Presidente de la Real Audiencia* (Governor and Captain of Peru and President of 'Royal Audience')

Paitití. If successful, he would be rewarded with the government of a province that would include all of central South America, from the Cordillera of the Andes to the limits of Portuguese territory along the demarcation line established by the Treaty of Tordesillas. Álvarez chose to follow the Madre de Dios River, a tributary to the Madeira that flows into the Amazon a little after Manaus. The 80 men who made up the bulk of the expeditionary party left the little port of Buenaventura on rafts and canoes. In the region referred to by the Indians as Toromonas, the cacique, Tarono, received them amicably. His apparent welcome turned out, however, to be no more than a stratagem to win him some time to organize his forces, and during one of Maldonado's absences the Indians launched a devastating attack that left only one survivor, a blacksmith, who would be obliged to put his art at the service of the victors.[37]

However, the thirst for discovery prevailed, as always, over the defeats endured. In 1617, Gonzalo de Solís Holguín signed a contract with the king of Spain and the prince of Esquilache to organize an expedition to Paitití, dubbed 'New Kingdom of Valencia'.[38]

Another known incursion was that of Benito Quiroga, who at the end of the seventeenth century would expend energy and a fortune on the quest for this gilded kingdom[39].

A curious commentary on American demography was the only interesting result of the investigations of a certain Juan Recio de León, who in 1620 found no city, gilded or otherwise, but nevertheless claimed – on the basis of the accounts of 'three or four leading Indians' – to have found the Paitití, a kingdom so important that 'the majority of the Indians who are missing from Peru had withdrawn to the aforesaid land.' He sent this enthusiastic news to the king of Spain. The Indians had probably told him that:

> Whether by sea or by land, in four days they reached a large "cocha", which is a big lake formed by all these rivers over the flatlands, and that there are numerous islands populated by an infinite number of people; and that they called the lord of all these islands the Great Paytití.

But Recio de León also sent more worrisome news: their English or Dutch enemies were selling knives, machetes, ropes and other tools to the inhabitants of this kingdom: 'The majority of them go to Paytite two or three times a year to try and trade, and that is how they have got hold of these utensils.'[40]

These writings bear interesting witness to the disappearance of a large number of the descendants of the Incas. The author considered that this was caused by their flight to the Paitití, but the reality of course was different: research on the historical demography of America during the sixteenth century, conducted by the California school, has shown that the continent's population was reduced to one-fifth, and in some regions to as little as one-tenth of preconquest levels as a result of epidemics, the destruction of indigenous societies, slavery and forced labour under atrocious conditions in the mines.[41]

The most complete list of the many expeditions launched in search of the Paitití was drawn up by the Peruvian diplomat Víctor Maurtua in 1906. In his treatise in 18 volumes entitled *Juicio de límites entre el Perú y Bolivia. Prueba peruana presentada al gobierno de la República Argentina* (Judgement regarding the boundary between Peru and Bolivia. A Peruvian proof presented to the government of the Republic of Argentina), he collected all available information on efforts to find the Paitití – those already mentioned here as well as others – along with testimonies and the routes taken by the conquistadors.

If belief in the Great Paitití was probably due to distorted information about the Inca civilization, it is equally plausible that there was at least a kernel of truth to the story. Thus, in 1782, when the Spanish Empire was beginning to decline, the mixed-blood Tupac Amaru II led a rebellion against the colonizers in the hope of restoring the Inca Empire, and he claimed for himself the titles of 'Inca, king of Peru, Santa Fe, Quito, Chile, Buenos Aires and of the continent of the South Seas, duke and lord of the Amazons and of the Great Paitití.'[42] Was this a reference to the Incas who had fled and remained hidden, or simply a revival of the legend spread by the Spanish? The question remains unresolved.

The most recent work we have found on the subject of the Paitití dates back to the 1970s. In it, the Argentine historian Roberto Levillier claims that this hidden kingdom was located on the territory that corresponds more or less to Rondonia, a region situated to the northwest of Mato Grasso in Brazil, and that 'their descendants were scattered among the neighbouring tribes whom they considered to be more peaceful than the Spanish or Portuguese invaders.'[43] No doubt there will be yet more echoes of these Incas who supposedly continued to live according to their customs, isolated from the rest of the world.

On the Road to the Enhanced City of the Caesars

The last outpost of the fabulous kingdoms was on the southern pampas (steppes) of Patagonia, vast plains and desolate plateaus, where a fierce wind twists the few trees that dare defy the monotony of the landscape.

The vista seems interminable and forbidding on these flatlands. The traveller can spend day after day crossing the plains, and nothing changes: sterile land, wind and snow in winter. They produce an optical illusion similar to the mirages of the deserts of the Old World, that the locals call *brillazón* (brilliance): the sun transforms the burned weeds into an oasis, and hallucination causes the sick, exhausted and starving travellers to see golden cupolas and shining towers of stone. Crossing this territory was no easy task, and the men and women who succeeded in adapting themselves to it defended it ferociously. It was in these regions that the myth of the enchanted city of the Caesars was born.

We could no doubt include this one with the three kingdoms of Cíbola, El Dorado and Paitití, but with one important distinction: the city of the Caesars did not take its roots in the legendary American civilizations, but rather is a projection of the great dream of the European conquerors: the belief that some of their predecessors had found fabulous riches and founded a city flowing with gold and silver. These inhabitants dressed elegantly, had numerous servants and strong defences; in other words, all that a bold adventurer might hope to acquire. The rumours were rapidly transformed into certainties, and the explorers, obsessed with far-flung riches, would not delay in setting out in search of the legendary Patagonian Caesars.

News from those shipwrecked in the Strait of Magellan had reached the leaders of the conquista. The first decades of the colonial era saw the launch of numerous official expeditions and religious missions intended to find the magical cities of the south. During the 1560s, while fighting a full-scale war against the Mapuche Indians, Francisco de Villagra, governor or Chile, charged Juan Jofré with repopulating Mendoza, founding San Juan de la Frontera and discovering, further south, the provinces of Duyo, Caesars, Telam, Trapalanda and Conlara. For its part, the *cabildo* (municipal council) of the city of Córdoba del Tucumán asked Governor Juan Ramírez de Velazco to set out in 'search of the great news of Trapalanda that is known as the (city of the) Caesars of which we have received information'.[44]

The number of expeditions was significant, as were the funds invested. There were at least 20 attempts, starting out from Buenos Aires or the cities of Chile, to conquer the city:

Expeditions to the city of the Caesars

1550	Jerónimo de Alderete
1553	Francisco de Villagra and Pedro de Villagra
1563	Gaspar de Zárate

1563	Juan Jofré (founder of Mendoza and San Juan)
1565	Juan Perez Zurita
1576	Domingo de Erazo
1579	Gonzalo Abreu
1604	Hernando Arias de Saavera (Hernandarias)
1617	Revs. Vieva, Toledo, Acuña and Fritz
1621	Diego de León (discoverer of Lake Nahuel Huapí)
1622	Jerónimo Luis de Cabrera
1643	Rev. Acuña
1646	Rev. Cardiel
1665–70–73	Diego Rosales
1670	Rev. Nicolás Mascardi
1740	Rev. Tomás Falkner
1776	Ignacio Pinuer (governor of Valdivia)
1780	Antonio de Viedma
1782	Basilio Villarino
1783–87–92	Rev. Francisco Menéndez[45]

Despite the uncertain results of the first efforts, the fable continued to spread. In 1604, the governor of Buenos Aires, Hernando Arias de Saavedra, known as Hernandarias, decided to organize a substantial expedition that was either to confirm the existence of the 'enchanted City' or disprove once and for all those who believed in it. He set out with 200 knights in search of the 'news of the so-called Caesars'. They spent two months crossing arid and uninhabited lands before reaching the Río Negro, but after three months and 18 days hunger and illness obliged them to turn back.[46]

Twenty years later, according to the chronicles, a party set out from the city of Córdoba, led by Jerónimo Luis de Cabrera with 400 men, livestock and carts laden with abundant provisions. This time the objective was not to find the survivors of the shipwrecks in the Strait of Magellan, but rather to search for those who had escaped the raids of the Mapuche Indians on the cities of southern Chile. Along the way they met a white fugitive who claimed that further east there was a city known as the 'City of the trees of the Caesars'. They headed in the direction the man had indicated, but found only a few vestiges of buildings and apple orchards, abandoned by the unfortunate colonists of Villarrica and Osorono. Once again the hostile environment and attacks by the native people forced them to turn back.[47]

The next person to attempt the journey was Nicolás Mascardi, an Italian Jesuit who had come to the island of Chiloé in the 1660s.

Shortly after he settled there, he witnessed an *entrada* (razzia) against the Puelche Indians organized by the governor of Chiloé, Juan Verdugo. Thousands of Indians were captured and immediately distributed among the notables of the region. Mascardi protested against the slavery and succeeded, after four years of endless efforts, to liberate the captives; this gesture gained him the confidence of the Indians, and in particular of a certain Estrella, the daughter of a cacique. Out of gratitude, they revealed to him the existence of a city inhabited by Spaniards. The Jesuit decided immediately to accompany them back to their lands in the hope finding these lost Christians.

Guided by Estrella, who had in the meantime converted to Christianity, Mascardi reached Lake Nahuel Huapi and from there sent messengers with missives written in Castilian, Latin, Greek, Italian, Mapuche, Puelche and Poya, addressed to 'the Spanish lords residing south of Lake Nahuel Huapi'. While he was waiting, two Indians appeared bearing knives, a piece of a spear and other objects belonging to white men, which suggested to him that the sought-after city was on an island. The objects had undoubtedly been abandoned by recent shipwreck survivors. Mascardi returned two years later to lake Nahuel Huapi, and then pushed on towards the southern steppes until he reached the Atlantic. Far from being discouraged, the indefatigable man of God made one more voyage, in the course of which he lost his life without having found the enchanted city.[48]

All these expeditions served only to stimulate further the imaginations of the Europeans, while providing them with new descriptions rich in details. Thus, it was that at the beginning of the eighteenth century, a certain Silvestre Antonio Roxas did not hesitate to describe the architecture and the way of life, complete with culinary habits, of the residents of the enchanted city.

Roxas appeared in Madrid in 1707, and introduced himself at Court as a former captive of the Pehuenches. He began the complex process of obtaining a commission to discover the city of the Caesars, but his efforts were unsuccessful. He then returned to Chile to propose his plan to the colonial administration there; Suddenly, he received an unexpected piece of news: he had inherited a large fortune in Spain. He, therefore, returned to the metropolis and used his inheritance to organize and outfit a company while waiting for the decision of the Council of the Indies regarding his proposal. The council summoned Roxas before the Chilean *Junta de poblaciones* (Assembly of the cities). He returned to Chile, but in the end the assembly's response was a negative one. In all, 12 years had passed!

Furious – understandably so – he published and diffused widely throughout the viceroyalty his 'Itinerary of a voyage from Buenos Aires to the Caesars, via Tandil and Volcán, towards the southwest, presented to the Court of Madrid in 1707, by Silvestre Antonio Roxas who spent many years living among the Pehuenche Indians*.' In it, he stated that the mysterious city was located on a plain; there are beautiful temples and houses of stonemasonry, as well as numerous Indian servants who had converted to Christianity. The inhabitants produced gold, silver and copper objects from the precious metals found in the Cordillera. The city abounded with cereals and garden produce but lacked wine and oil, which could not be produced at this latitude; however, the locals ate a great deal of fish and seafood.[49]

If these statements failed to convince the authorities, they nonetheless attracted the attention of others: Roxas's itinerary would be described a half-century later by the priest Tomás Falkner in his 'Itinerary from the city of Buenos Aires to the Caesars which are known also as the Enchanted City**'.[50]

In 1733, a renowned historian of the Río de la Plata, the Jesuit Pedro Lozano, published a *Descripción de Gran Chaco, Gualamba, y de los ritos y costumbres de la Naciones bárbaras e einfieles que le habitan* (Description of the Gran Chaco, Gualamba and the rites and customs of the barbarian and infidel nations who dwell therein). Though sceptical about the myth, he cited many letters and documents concerning the Caesars.

One of these missives alluded to the apparition at Chiloé of an unknown Spaniard during a season when it was impossible to cross the Cordillera of the Andes. It would not be long before it turned out – he claimed – that he was a citizen of the Caesars who had fled the city of Hoyos, the principal and most populous of the three cities of the kingdom of the Caesars, the other two being El Muelle and Los Sauces, situated barely ten leagues from Calbuco (on the mainland just across from Chiloé). The Chileans also add the city of Santa Mónica del Valle, near the Cahuelmo River. They are all – noted Lozano – defended and fortified against the cannibals, but also have commercial relations with some friendly tribes. They are very rich, although – contrary to what is usually stated – lacking in gold. Only silver is so

---

*Derrotero de un viaje desde Buenos Aires a los Césares, por el Tandil y el Volcán, rumbo al Sudoeste, comunicado a la corte de Madrid, en 1707, por Silvestre Antonio Roxas que vivió muchas años entre los indios Peguenches.
**Derrotero desde la ciudad de Buenos Aires hasta los Césares que por otro nombre llaman Ciudad Encantada.

abundant 'that their knives, pots, pitchers and even the receptacles intended for the vilest necessities are made of the finest silver'.[51]

The apogee of the belief in the Caesars came, however, a few years before the French Revolution. It was the work of a true specialist in the field, Don Ignacio Pinuer, governor of the Chilean city of Valdivia, who searched desperately for the secret kingdom in southern Chile. In 1774, two centuries after the first shipwrecks in the Strait of Magellan, he wrote *Relación de las notícias adquiridas sobre una ciudad grande de españoles, que hay entre los indios, al sud del Valdivia, e incognita hasta el presente* (Relation of information received concerning a great and hitherto unknown city of Spaniards located among the Indians south of Valdivia) that collected all the rumours that were making the rounds regarding the enchanted city. The information was still coming from the Indians, although it is very likely that in these final years of the Spanish Empire the native people were mainly repeating – and considerably expanding upon – the stories they had heard from the Spanish themselves. Be that as it may, Pinuer did not hesitate to provide countless details on the subject.

The city of the Caesars – he wrote – is fortified, surrounded by a moat, and accessible only by a drawbridge. Cannons fire rounds 'from time to time'. In their dwellings, the Caesars 'sit on golden and silver chairs…wear hats, jerkins, shirts, baggy trousers and very large shoes'. But the most extraordinary thing is that they are immortal, 'for in this land the Spanish never die', leading to serious demographic problems: 'Not knowing what to do with all the people, numerous families…moved to the other side of the lake, to the east, where they founded a new city.'

Pinuer organized an expedition of 80 soldiers. He left Valdivia for the Caesars in 1776. The Indian, who served as his guide led them to the shores of Lake Llanquihue; then, just as they thought they were only a short distance from their destination, the guide disappeared. Tireless, Pinuer led two other expeditions: one that would explore Lake Puyehue and another that would get as far as the magnificent Osorno volcano, relying on the directions provided by a resident of Valdivia who claimed to have heard artillery fire coming from the Caesars. Yet it was all in vain.

The last known expedition to the phantom city was launched in 1792 by Francisco Menéndez, a Franciscan from Asturias. On the shores of Lake Nahuel Huapi he discovered the ruins of an ancient mission; the Indians explained that the Caesars were living in a city named Chico Buenos Aires (Little Buenos Aires) on the edge of a great river that fed a lake that was much larger than the Nahuel Huapi, and which was governed by the cacique Basilio. In reality, the Indians had informed him, with considerable precision, of the colony of Carmen de Patagones, founded by Basilio Villarino at the mouth of the Río Negro on the Atlantic coast of Argentine Patagonia. However, since at this time the circulation of information among the different colonial administrations left much to be desired, the scorn of Menéndez was not surprising: having come from Chile and being a dependant of the viceroyalty of Peru, the Franciscan was not necessarily informed of the progress of colonization in the viceroyalty of the Río de la Plata to which Basilio Villarino belonged. Disappointed and under the threat of an Indian attack, Menéndez returned to Chile without having found the enchanted city, but continuing to dream of finding it.[52]

Belief in the existence of the enchanted city of the Caesars in Patagonia ended at the same time as the Spanish Empire, in the early nineteenth century. The legend would continue to exist in the world of letters, inspiring utopias and novels. Thus, in 1764, the Englishman James Burgh took it as the basis for a philosophical short story that, following the example of Thomas More's *Utopia* and Tommaso Campanella's *La Città del Sole* (City of the Sun), presented the model of an ideal society. His work, entitled *An Account of the First Settlement, Laws, Form of Government and Police of the Cesares: A People of South America, in Nine Letters*, situated the Caesars near the Cordillera of the Andes between Chile and Patagonia. He claimed that it had been founded by shipwrecked sailors of the bishop of Plasencia's fleet, and that it offered an alternative to English society in the eighteenth century. Its inhabitants, of the Protestant faith, had decided to build it in the form of a rectangle; the lands were distributed in equitable fashion and no one could accumulate wealth; neither begging nor idleness was permitted, nor was any other vice allowed, and trade in precious metals and alcoholic beverages was prohibited. Members of the 'papist sect' were tolerated, although they could not hold any public or political office.[53]

In modern South American literature there are several novels devoted to this myth: *Los Tesoros del rey blanco* (The treasures of the white king) and *Por qué no fue descubierta la Ciudad de los Césares* (Why the city of the Caesars was never found) by the Argentine Roberto Payró (1945), *La Ciudad de los Césares* by Manuel Rojas (1935), *Pacha Pulai* by Hugo Silva (1945)[54] and *Fuegana. La verdadera historia de la Ciudad de los Césares* (Fuegana. The true history of the city of the Caesars) by Juan Ricardo Muñoz (1983), a Chilean like the two previous authors mentioned. These works all describe the life of a unique city on the edges of the world.

It seems that, the more inaccessible they were, the more these realms of gold held a certain fascination. For Alexander von Humboldt, El Dorado constantly eluded the Spanish, even while continuing to hold an appeal. This aphorism can be applied equally to the cities of Cíbola, the Paitití and the Caesars.

The irresistible attraction of this illusion of reaching a magical place that contained great wealth and power, these focal points of human ambition, cost numerous lives and wiped out as many fortunes. The pursuit of these chimera did not yield the hoped-for mountains of gold, but did permit explorers to come to know better the American continent.

In the course of their peregrinations, the conquistadors thought they were discovering another extraordinary nation, populated and governed exclusively by superb warriors. This will be the subject of Chapter five.

CHAPTER 5:

The Indomitable Amazons

In the sixth century B.C., the Greek historian Herodotus recounted in his Histories a legend that would come down through the millennia and spread through several continents: on the banks of the Thermodon, near the Black Sea, there lived a tribe of warrior women, the Amazons, who had invaded a large portion of the Near East and captured Ephesus, Smyrna, Paphos and many other cities. Since that time, the image of a nation of warlike women has held pride of place in the collective imaginations of numerous people. The aquatic element is always present, manifesting itself in the form of a mighty river or inlet allegedly marking the frontier between the women's territory and that of men. When, in 1500s, the conquistadors succeeded with great difficulty in penetrating the equatorial forest, they thought, they would have to fight armies of Amazons, and gave that name to the greatest river system on earth.

> We live on the other side of the Amazon River and on an island in
> the middle of it. The perimeter of our land would take you a year to
> travel; the river has neither beginning nor end. Access to it is unique.

> *Letter from the Amazons to King Alexander, Pseudo-Callisthenes, III, 25.*

The origin of the Amazons is lost in the mists of time. If we are to
believe Herodotus, they were the ancestors of the Sauromatae (recent
research suggests this was a branch of the Sarmatians), a nomadic
people who lived on the steppes of the Volga, the Urals and north of
the Caspian Sea between the eighth and the fourth centuries before
our era. The 'Father of History' tells us that the Sauromatae, born of
the union of the Amazons and young men of Scythia (more or less
present-day Turkestan), granted a special place to women in their
society. Thus, a young Sauromat girl could not hope to marry before
she had killed an enemy. Be that as it may, archaeology has shown
that in Sauromat society, women had a very unusual and sometimes
dominant role: a woman's burial site might be at the centre of a cemetery and tombs of women often contained harnesses and weapons,
indicating a society that was, at least in part, matriarchal.[1]

As for the term 'Amazon', it may derive from the name of an
Iranian people, *Ha-mazan*, which means 'warriors'. In antiquity, however, the term was thought to derive from the privative prefix *a-* and
'mazos', or without a breast, because according to ancient tradition,
their right breasts were cut or burned off at an early age in order to
make it easier for them to draw the bow. According to still another
etymology, the prefix a- has an augmentative value, making the
Amazons, on the contrary, full-breasted women. Whatever the size of
their breasts, the important thing is that according to legend they had
set up an exclusively female society.

THE WARRIORS OF THE THERMODON

According to the descriptions of Hippocrates in the fifth century
B.C. and of Diodorus of Sicily in the first century of our era, these
women used men for the sole purpose of providing them with offspring. They saw the men once a year, during a brief 'season of love'.
If a son was born, he was handed over to his father; if it was a daughter, she remained with her mother and was taught to use a bow, an
axe, a shield, a javelin and to ride bareback or with a simple cover.
Graeco-Roman literature abounds with episodes, where warriors
from the Thermodon intervened. Thus, Virgil's *Aeneid*, for example,

tells how the Amazons entered the war of Troy alongside the Trojans. Under their queen, Penthesilea, they invaded Phrygia to rescue Priam and marched on the besieged city. After arriving at Troy:

> *Penthesilea there, with haughty grace,*
> *Leads to the wars an Amazonian race:*
> *In their right hands a pointed dart they wield,*
> *The left, forward, sustains the lunar shield.*
> *Athwart her breast a golden belt she throws,*
> *Amidst the press alone provokes a thousand foes,*
> *And dares her maiden arms to manly force oppose.*[2]

The Amazons killed many Greeks in the course of the battle, until the sword of Achilles inflicted a mortal wound on the queen. When the hero removed the armour of his adversary, he was moved by her beauty and fell in love with her.

The combat between Heracles and the Amazons has a key place in Greek mythology. Tradition has it that the demigod had to perform a series of twelve labours, of which the ninth consisted in acquiring the garter of Hippolyta, queen of the female nation. This object symbolized her power over her people. Without showing the least objection, the queen granted Heracles' request, but the Goddess Hera was indignant at such an easy victory and, assuming the appearance of an Amazon, stirred the warrior women up against the Greek. Surprised by this attack, Heracles accused Hippolyta of betraying him and killed her, stripping off her garter and returning home with the trophy. Later the Greek hero would wipe out another nation of Amazons, this time an African one led by queen Myrina. The latter had succeeded in conquering the Numidians, Ethiopians, Gorgons and Atlanteans.

Amazons can also be found in Pliny's *Natural History*, written in the first century of our era. In Book VI he notes the existence, beyond the Ganges, of a nation led by women:

> After these we come to the nation of the Pandæ, the only one throughout all India which is ruled by women. It is said that, Hercules had but one child of the female sex, for which reason she was his special favourite, and he bestowed upon her the principal one of these kingdoms. The sovereigns who derive their origin from this female, rule over three hundred towns, and have an army of one hundred and fifty thousand foot, and 500 elephants.

The myth acquired its full splendour, however, in the famous Alexander Romance, where we see Alexander the Great making the acquaintance of Candaules, son of the queen of Ethiopia. Candaules, accompanied by his wife and a small detachment, was on his way to celebrate some annual rite in the land of the Amazons[3]. The Macedonian king decided that he and his men would accompany them to the nation of women.

They crossed strange lands, where the mountains rose as high as the clouds and the trees were laden with fruit unknown in Greece: apples as shiny as gold, enormous bunches of grapes and nuts as large as melons. They saw monkeys the size of bears and countless other animals whose colours were as exotic as their shapes. [4] It was in this singular setting that a curious exchange of letters took place between Alexander and the Amazons.

To impress them, the king sent a long list of the nations and people he had conquered, occupied and even reduced to slavery. He specified, however, that his only wish was to visit their country, and exhorted them to receive him with joy so that war might be averted. The Amazons were not afraid, but replied to his missive point by point, describing their way of life and exalting their greatness in an extraordinary passage, a veritable catalogue of the main elements of the myth:

> The most powerful and important of the Amazons, to Alexander, greetings. We are writing to you so that you may know this before attacking our territories, lest you should later fail in a dishonourable manner. By these few lines we inform you of certain curiosities of our region and of our strict rule of life. We live on the other side of the Amazon River and on an island in the middle of it. The perimeter of our land would take you a year to cover; the river has neither beginning nor end. Access to it is unique. We are 270,000 armed young women who dwell here. There are no men among us. The men live on the other side of the river on the mainland. Every year, we celebrate a joint festival, where during 30 days, we sacrifice horses to Zeus, Poseidon, Hephaestos and Ares. All those among us who wish to lose their virginity stay with the men. Any girls that are born of these unions are entrusted to us from the age of seven. If enemies approach to attack our land, we mount an expedition of 120,000 on horseback, while the others guard the island. We go out to meet our enemies on our borders, while the men in combat formation follow us… If one of us returns with the corpse of an adversary, she is rewarded with gold and silver and will be looked after the rest of her days. This means that we fight for glory alone. If we defeat our enemies, or if the latter take flight, they are marked with the indelible stain of a

shameful confrontation; however, if they are victorious, they will only
have defeated a bunch of women.

Alexander replied with a reminder that he had subjugated all three
continents and that he did not seek anything but a gesture: that the
women show themselves to the Greeks. Then he would accept the
tribute they might wish to offer him. Furthermore, he requested that
they send him a few Amazons on horseback to enter his service.
Everything would be concluded to the mutual satisfaction of both
parties. The Amazons granted him the privilege of visiting their
country, promised to pay 100 golden talents per year, sent him a
detachment of 500 of their best warriors and agreed to obey
Alexander's commandment. Impressed, the emperor once again took
up the pen to write of his adventure to his mother, Olympias. The
Amazons, he wrote, live on the banks of the Thermodon and are
women who far surpass in stature all other women. They are highly
intelligent and clever, and are remarkable for their beauty and their
valour; they dress in floral colours, wear silver armour and wield bat-
tleaxes. But they have neither iron nor bronze. The river is wide,
impossible to cross and inhabited by a multitude of wild animals.[5]

These scenes and landscapes would remain latent in Europe's
cultural memory, and would come down through the centuries only
to resurface when a group of conquistadors undertook to navigate the
gigantic river that crosses the South American rainforest.

THE MEDIEVAL AMAZONS

Christian doctrine was ill at ease with this belief to which the Bible
does not even allude, and which exalted qualities in women that were
very different from those recommended by the Church. In the
Middle Ages, therefore, the Amazons came to be represented as a
sinister nation. Since tradition placed them near the Caspian Gates,
they could easily be taken to be one of the unclean races penned up by
Alexander beyond the bronze doors, where the future soldiers of
Satan were awaiting their appointed hour. In the fifteenth century, a
certain Breidenbach published a treatise in which he claimed that the
Amazons were messengers of the Evil One, and that their queen
would become the 'captain of the unclean people'. Once the Amazons
had entered the ranks of the Antichrist, the legend was adapted to
emphasize their repugnance; henceforth they did not simply leave
their male children with their fathers but executed them mercilessly,
in order that they might rear only daughters.[6]

Another solution consisted of domesticating the warrior women, transforming them into a group of women who were somewhat extravagant, living alone but unable to meet all their needs and thus, obliged to call upon the aid of their male neighbours. In certain versions they were turned in to good Christians, having even a bishop of their own.

It is within this tradition that we may situate Marco Polo's confirmation of the existence of the Amazon nation. In chapter XXXVII of his *Travels* he undertakes to describe the kingdom of Resmacoran, a province that marks the northwestern frontier of India. He tells of an island there that is inhabited exclusively by women, and another by men. The Venetian describes their customs, including those having to do with their sexual lives, as well as their trade relations with their neighbours. These Amazons were not very frightening; they even spent three months a year being good wives, and reared their sons until the age of 14. Their neighbours on the 'male' island worked to provide them with food, and all lived according to the Christian faith. Here he tells of the men and women of the islands:

The island indeed which is called Male is on the high sea quite 500 miles toward midday when one sets out from this realm of Resmacoran which is on the mainland. They are all baptized Christians and keep themselves to the faith and to the customs of the Old Testament. For I tell you that when his wife is pregnant he does not touch her afterwards until she has given birth, and from the time when she has given birth he leaves her again without touching her for 40 days. But from 40 days onward he touches her at his pleasure. But yet I tell you that their wives do not stay on this island, or any other ladies, but they all live in the other island which is called Female Island. On the island which they call Male stay all the men. And you may know that the women never come to the island of men, but when it comes to the month of March the men of the island go off to this island of Women and stay there for three months... And these three months the men go to that other island to stay with their wives, each man with his wife in his wife's house...and at the end of these three months they come back to this island and do their ploughing and their traffic and make their profit there all the other nine months of the year... And their children which are born, their mothers nourish in their island, and if it is a girl then the mother keeps here there till she is of the age to be married, and then at the season marries her to one of the men of the island. Yet it is true that as soon as they are weaned and the male child has 14 years, so soon does his mother send him to his father in their island. Yet it is true that their wives do nothing else but nourish their children, for the men supply them with what they need. When the men come to the women's island they sow grain, and then the women cultivate and reap it; and the women also gather any fruit, which they have of many kinds in that island... Moreover, I tell you that ambergris is produced in this island very fine and good and beautiful and in plenty, by reason of the whales of which many are taken in that sea. And they are very good fishers, for you may know that many very large good fish are caught in that sea of this island.[7]

It is possible that this description has some basis in reality. Marco Polo may have been in contact with groups of people endowed with what anthropologists call 'matrilineal systems of descent', very common in the Far East and in Africa. In these groups, the conjugal household is that of the maternal family; the husbands live with their wives but it is the mother's family that looks after rearing the children and taking all decisions that concern them. These kinship ties, unknown to the Venetian, no doubt awakened in his imagination the ancient myth of these androphobic women.

Belief in the Amazons endured for a long time. On the globe made by Martin Behaim in the same year as Columbus's first voyage to America, the following legend may be found next to a small group of islands in the Indian Ocean: 'Sconia is an island situated 300 Italian leagues from the Male and Female islands. Its inhabitants are Christians and they have an archbishop. Amber may be found there and good silk cloth is produced.' Columbus, too, had read attentively this passage in Marco Polo, for he noted in its margins 'two islands', 'Male Female' and 'where there is an abundance of amber'.[8] Even if it is now certain that Columbus would not receive the copy of Marco Polo's book that is now in the *Biblioteca colombiana* until after his first voyage, there is no doubt that his vision of the world prior to crossing the Atlantic was strongly influenced by the tales told by the Venetian, whom he must at least have heard of before then. Once he had reached the New World, which he took to be Asia, he would not fail to note the existence of an island, where only women were supposed to live, near another one inhabited only by men who at regular intervals paid visits to the aforesaid ladies.

The *Ymago mundi* likewise mentions the Amazons, but limits itself to a classic description of the myth, situating the nation in the region of Armenia:

Armenia has two sections, Upper and Lower... Cappadocia was named from one of its cities. Situated at the head of Syria it touches Armenia eastward, Asia Minor westward, and on the north the Cimmerian Sea and the Themiscyrian Plains (Themissorios), occupied by the Amazons.[9]

Niccolò de Conti, a compatriot of Marco Polo and like him a merchant seaman, repeated the legend of the parallel islands and situated them at less than 5,000 paces from the island of Socotra. In this version, it was sometimes the women who visited the men, and sometimes the other way around; but in each case the visitors were obliged to return home before the end of the 6 months that was allotted to them by destiny, otherwise they would die on the spot.[10]

Another word of warning concerning this 'information' came from a travelogue by a Bavarian, Hans Schiltberger. This strange person, captured by the Turks at the battle of Nicopolis in 1396, spent 32 years as a slave of the Sultan Bajazet I and of Tamerlane. Although he never travelled farther than Samarkand, he was able to observe the Turkish and Tartar worlds. Back in Europe he published his *Reisebuch*, in which he told juicy tales of his travels embellished with fanciful episodes. He gives considerable attention to a great military victory of the Tartar Amazons under the leadership of a princess thirsting for vengeance.[11]

These traditions may also be found in the so-called letter from Prester John, reproduced in the tales of John de Mandeville, whereas Portuguese sources claim to have received confirmation from the Arabs that the island of Socotra was formerly the island of the Amazons. Given this impressive number of writings and oral traditions, the existence of the nation of women could not be called into question. Like the legendary treasures and marvellous creatures, the Amazons were believed to live in the Far East, the final destination of Columbus's caravels.

Columbus Discovers the Island of Females

Scarcely, had the Admiral taken possession of the lands of the West, but he began avidly to interrogate the inhabitants, anxious to find some sign that would lead him to the treasures described in Pierre d'Ailly, Marco Polo and various theological authorities. He also enquired whether there was a colony of women without men, and sure enough, it was not long before he had found some trace of them. On Sunday 6 January 1493, he claimed for the first time to have learned 'that toward the east there was an island, where there were women only', and that 'it is said that many people know about it.'[12]

A week later, on 13 January, he prepared to leave the island of Hispaniola on an exploratory mission. His complete ignorance of the native languages did not represent an insurmountable obstacle for the impetuous explorer: he put his questions and interpreted the answers in accordance with his own fantasies. Thus, he confirmed the proximity of Cipango, of gold and of an island of women named Matininó: 'An Indian told him that the island of Matininó was inhabited exclusively by women without men, and that it contained great quantities of *tuob*, meaning gold or copper.'[13] It seems that this island was in fact present-day Martinique, and another, referred to as Carib, was Puerto Rico. Columbus decided to sail for these islands, but the disastrous state of his ships obliged him to turn back. On 16 January he noted that two of his caravels were taking on water and that 'there was no other remedy save that of God.' With a saddened heart he abandoned his quest for these isolated women in order to return to Europe, where people eagerly awaited news of his expedition. Nevertheless, on the last days of his first voyage the Admiral obtained further details about the island of Matininó:

> The Indians told him that on that route he would find the island of Matinino, which, he says, was inhabited by women without men, which the Admiral would have liked (to visit) so he could take five or six of them to the sovereigns; but he doubted that the Indians knew the route well, and he was unable to delay because of the danger from the water that the caravels were taking on. But he says it was certain that there were such women, and that at a certain time of year men came to them from the said island of Carib, which he says was 10 or 12 leagues from them; and that if they gave birth to a boy they sent him to the men's island and if to a girl they let her stay with them.[14]

Columbus was simply repeating what Marco Polo had written, but this information would revive the tradition of an island of women. In his letter to Luis de Santángel written on 15 February 1493, the first official document in which Columbus announced his discovery, he described the island of Matininó and referred to it as the easternmost part of the Indies:

> Thus I have not found, nor had any information of monsters, except of an island which is here the second in the approach to the Indies, which is inhabited by a people whom, in all the islands, they regard as very ferocious, who eat human flesh... These are they who have to do with the women of Matinino – which is the first island that is encountered in the passage from Spain to the Indies in which there are no men. Those women practise no female usages, but have bows and arrows of reed such as above mentioned; and they arm and cover themselves with plates of copper of which they have much.[15]

Three years later, at the end of his second voyage, Columbus decided to take a different route back to Spain by way of the lesser Antilles. When his little fleet lowered its anchors at the island of Guadeloupe in order to stock up on provisions, it was met by a volley of arrows from a group of women. The Spanish sent a few captive Indians ashore to tell the aggressors that all they wanted was some manioc bread. The women warriors then told them to go to the other side of the island, where the men were working the land. Columbus disregarded this suggestion, however, and sent a detachment of 40 men ashore. Bartolomé de Las Casas tells how one of the women, who happened to be the chief of the island, was pursued by a sailor and, feeling trapped, 'turned toward him like a mad dog, squeezed him and threw herself on the ground with him so that if some Christians had not come running, she would have strangled him.' The sailors returned to the ships with five women captives, whom they would release some time later. It was certainly in the Admiral's best interests to maintain good relations with the inhabitants of an island that lay en route to Spain and thus, might serve as a regular stopping off point for future Spanish convoys. The *cacique* and her daughter decided, however, to remain voluntarily with the Europeans, although Las Casas expressed his doubts about the freedom of their choice.[16]

It was not long before rumours of the existence of these islands inhabited by communities of women began to make the rounds of the metropolis. The 'reporter' of the discovery, Peter Martyr d'Anghiera, undertook to study the matter and sought to give a rational explanation of this episode. He claimed it was a group of 'Cenobite maidens who enjoy solitude'. If the men pay them occasional visits, this was 'not, however, for connubial purposes, but instead as moved by compassion, in order to tend to their fields and gardens'. In later writings, he would show greater scepticism with regard to these reports of bellicose Amazons who defended the shores of their islands with bows and arrows and who kept only the daughters born to them from their union with cannibals.[17]

Antonio Pigafetta, the chronicler of Magellan's expedition, also provided some information on an island of women. While the flotilla was passing through the waters of the Far East, one of the local pilots spoke to him of the Amazons. This paragraph in his chronicle seems to be a vestige of the ancient Egyptian belief that certain women could become pregnant from the wind:

> Our oldest pilot told us that in an island called Accloro, which lies below Java Major, there are found no persons but women, and that they

become pregnant from the wind. When they bring forth, if the offspring is a male, they kill it, but if it is a female, they rear it. If men go to that island of theirs, they kill them if they are able to do so. [18]

The reports of the first explorers did not diverge greatly from the descriptions of Marco Polo. It is certainly true that the Venetian's book was considered the indispensable instrument for the study of the Orient. However, a few decades later, when expeditions undertook to cross the virgin forests in search of El Dorado, of the Paitití or of some other fabulously rich kingdom, it was the Greek legend, almost in its original version, that would resurface.

The Amazons of America

Information about the existence of a nation of women arrived from various quarters of the New World and the rumours were gathered by prominent writers. Thus, Gonzalo Fernández de Oviedo, the first to try to give an overview of all of America in his *Historia General y Natural de las Indias* (General and Natural History of the Indies), a work completed in Seville in 1535, mentioned the existence of regions, where women 'were the absolute lords and governed their States…and practised the arts of war…like the queen known as Orocomay.' Earlier he had noted 'they may be called Amazons (if what I was told is true): but they do not cut off their right breast, as did those the ancients called Amazons in order not to impede them in pulling the bow.'[19]

Among all these tales of the kingdom of women, there is one that is truly exceptional. It is a direct testimony – perhaps the only one – of a man who claimed to have seen and fought the Amazons. A battle between the Spanish and the ferocious warriors is described by the Dominican friar Gaspar de Carvajal, who even lost an eye in the struggle. The events occurred during the expedition led by Francisco Orellana, who sailed down the 6,400 km of the greatest river on earth.

This prodigious feat began in Peru when Gonzalo Pizarro organized a major expedition to discover the Land of Cinnamon and the treasures of the Gilded King (El Dorado). Setting out from Quito, this veritable army made up of a main corps of 220 Spaniards accompanied by 4,000 Indians, 2,000 dogs, 200 horses as well as a few llamas and pigs, took the difficult route leading to the Napo River, a tributary of the Marañón. Francisco de Orellana took another route with a small team of 23 Spaniards and a few Indians in order to meet the others at Quijos, where he received the rank of lieutenant general. Both parties lost several weeks building a brigantine and, little by little, famine began to menace the troops. The expedition continued on its way, one group by water the other following the riverbank. But it soon became impossible to advance any further and keep so large an army supplied with food. Orellana decided to continue with a detachment of 60 men in search of provisions, while Pizarro was to wait a few days, and if by then he had heard no news of Orellana's party, his group would try to retrace their steps. The two men would never see each other again.

Orellana reached the place called Aparia, at the confluence of the Napo and the Marañón rivers. The Indians provided them with enough food for the little group, but had no other reserves, nor the means, nor perhaps the inclination to supply the entire army, and so Orellana realized that continuing up the Napo was beyond his capabilities. Yet the desire to find the gold of the Omaguas, the land of El Dorado and the domain of the Amazons was ever present. He and his troops thus, chose to go downriver and cross the South American continent to the Atlantic.[20]

Friar Gaspar de Carvajal noted day in and day out, the adventures of this group of men who were the first known explorers of the mighty river. They built a second brigantine, the San Pedro, and in April 1542 began the descent of the Marañón and then the river they would call the *río grande de las Amazonas* (the great river of the Amazons). They supplemented their meagre provisions by invading native villages and demanding food. They were not always successful in doing so, and during the first week, 18 Europeans were injured in combat, eight others fell ill and at least three died. Many a time they were forced to content themselves with a stew of monkey or with the flesh of some birds they had managed to catch, or even a soup of old shoe soles or other leather object. Their only hope of survival was to continue on their way through the thick forest.

When they approached the confluence of the Tefé and the Amazon, they received news of a nation of women: Carvajal noted that the Indians assured them that 'we would see the *amurianos* whom they called in their language *coniupuyara*, which means "grand ladies", and that we should be very careful for we were few and they very numerous, and that they would kill us; that we must not be found to be on their land.'[21] The amurianos or coniupuyara referred to towns of warrior women, the sign that they were approaching the land of the Amazons.

This region of strangely luxurious vegetation, filled with constant perils and supposed to be very close to the source of gold, undoubtedly

Medieval Amazons, BnF 2810, f. 181.

Engraving illustrating the Voyages en Afrique, Asie, Indes orientales et occidentales by Jean Mocquet (1685 edn). He explains that the Amazons do not burn off their breasts, but simply express the milk; thus, they are able to handle the bow with ease. Moreover, he claimed that they were of great height and combed their 'natural hair', which they wore very long.

called to mind the landscape, where Alexander the Great had encountered the Amazons. Many a conquistador had probably spent a deprived childhood in his native land listening to passionate sermons describing the Earthly Paradise and its surroundings, embellishing the account with one or other particularly colourful or terrifying detail. Nor could they fail to recall the tales of the minstrels and troubadours who had criss-crossed the villages and towns of their native Estremadura or Andalusia singing of the valiant deeds of King Alexander and other heroes of the past.

Was it not their turn to reach the lands that the Macedonian conqueror had crossed 2,000 years before? The Spanish adventurers imagined that they were contemplating the same vistas, facing the same threats and perhaps even meeting the same tribes of Amazons. Did the warrior women not live on the shores of a great and impassable river, inhabited with ferocious beasts that served as a natural frontier between them and the men? Everything in this new geography seemed to the Europeans to suggest that they were entering the fabulous realms, where myths became reality.

It was around Midsummer's Night, while they were sailing close to the shore in search of a place to drop anchor, that they met the Amazons. Catching sight of a village, Orellana gave the order to dock the brigantines in order to get some food from the native people. But the latter had apparently resolved not to allow the invaders to disembark, whereupon the Spanish crossbowmen and arquebusiers began to shoot. The Indians did not yield, but responded with so great a volley of arrows that the invaders could not defend themselves and row away at the same time. Before they had even set foot on land there were five wounded, including Carvajal himself. The battle would continue on shore in hand-to-hand combat for over an hour, the Indians stepping over their dead to continue the fight. Orellana, noticing that native reinforcements were on their way, ordered a quick retreat, and the Spanish only just managed to escape the flotilla of canoes that were hot in pursuit. Such great resistance – noted the friar – could only be explained by the presence of the Amazons:

I want you to know the reason why the Indians defended themselves in this manner. You should know that they are tributaries of the Amazons and, informed of our arrival, went to ask them for assistance. Ten or twelve of the warrior women arrived, and we ourselves saw these women fight so courageously that the Indian men did not dare to turn their backs, and anyone who did turn his back they killed with clubs right there before us, and this is the reason why the Indians kept up their defence for so long. These women are very white and tall, and have hair very long and braided and wound about the head, and they are very robust and go about naked, with their privy parts covered, with their bows and arrows in their hand, doing as much fighting as ten Indian men, and indeed, there was one woman among these who shot an arrow a span deep into one of the brigantines, and others less deep, so that our brigantines looked like porcupines...

But to return to the subject of the battle, it was Our Lord who gave strength and courage to our companions, who before our very eyes killed seven or eight of these Amazons; wherefore the Indians lost heart and were defeated and disconsolate due to the great damage inflicted on them; and it is only because other villagers sent numerous reinforcements...that the Captain ordered his men to board the ships posthaste, not wishing to imperil the lives of all. Thus, they embarked, not without great fear because the Indians began to fight again, and also sent a powerful fleet of canoes across the water, whereupon we set sail and headed away from the shore.[22]

After this battle, the Spanish, perplexed, avidly sought more information, and Orellana, using a lexicon of local languages that he himself had drawn up, interrogated an Indian prisoner. The latter's answers constitute a fine description of the land of women without husbands.

The cruelty of the Amazons, illustrating the account of André Thévet.
Engraving by Jean Cousin. Bibliothèque Royale de Belgique.

Amazon in her hammock waiting for the Indian, according to the ritual described by Cristóbal de Acuña, published in Voyages autour du Monde *by Captain Woodes Rogers, Amsterdam, 1717. Bibliothèque Royale de Belgique.*

He claimed to come from a domain that stretched over 150 leagues and belonged to a great lord named Couynco, who was a vassal of the Amazons. These Amazons lived in the interior seven days from the coast, and he himself claimed to have visited their lands several times in order to transport the tribute his lord was sending them. These women, he said, were numerous and lived in more than 70 villages built in stone, with gates that were closely guarded by sentries and linked together by a network of roads. Those whom the Christians had seen had come to help Couynco to protect the banks of the river.

When the desire comes to them, he added, they make war against a neighbouring lord and take male prisoners by force back to their own country. They keep them there for a time, and when they find themselves pregnant they send them away without harming them. If they give birth to a male child they kill it or send it to his father. If it is a girl, however, they rear them with great dignity and teach them the arts of war. There are innumerable riches in this land; the dishes of the most important ladies are made entirely of gold and silver, while the plebeians use wooden or earthenware dishes. All are subject to the rule of one sovereign, known as the *coñori*. In the capital city, where the sovereign resides there are five temples dedicated to the sun, called *caranaín*, which means 'Houses of the Sun'. Inside the ceilings are painted in many different colours and the temples contain many female idols of gold and silver as well as many vessels of the same metals consecrated to the service of the sun. The Amazons wear clothing of very fine wool, for there are in that region many 'Peruvian sheep' (llamas or alpacas). They wear tailored jackets from the chest down to their feet, and others that resemble shawls, tied in front with several strings. On their heads they wear large crowns two fingers thick.

This land, the Indian continued, is full of camels (llamas) that serve as beasts of burden, and contains two salt-water lakes. There is a rule that at sunset every man must withdraw from the towns. The Amazons rule over several provinces and have numerous vassals at their service who pay them tribute; however, there are other tribes with which they are at war.

Did Orellana understand the Indian's replies correctly? One might well wonder about the quality of the lexicon available to him for carrying on this conversation, as well as about the freedom of the captive, who was no doubt more interested in giving the answers he thought the conquistadors wanted to hear so that he might hope to regain his liberty than in providing accurate information about his land. Despite this, the answers show a certain coherence and seem to suggest that the Indian was referring to an actual civilization: the well maintained villages of stone, the dishes of gold and silver, the temples to the sun, the fine wool clothing, the presence of llamas and of tributary people are none other than descriptions of the Inca Empire, to which was added the very ancient tradition of the Amazons who only kept their female children.

Although the accounts of the battle and of the interrogation of the Indian are only a few pages apart, the descriptions are often contradictory. On one hand, we read of ferocious naked female warriors, and on the other of refined women, elegantly dressed and surrounded by fine objects. The first episode relies on first-hand testimony, while the second is of dubious veracity, the power of the myth being such that it did not for a moment occur to the Spaniards that the descriptions given by the Indian corresponded perfectly to the place of their origin, namely the civilization of the Andes.

In September 1542, the survivors of the expedition, having reached the Atlantic, found themselves at Cubaguá, a little island off Venezuela, where they were received with great honour. Gaspar de Carvajal returned to Lima by way of Panama, while Orellana left for Spain in the hope of obtaining royal support for a new expedition, this time armed with artillery. Death overtook him, however, in the midst of the preparations.

Two years later, in Seville, Sebastian Cabot drew the first map on which the entire river appeared, accompanied by the title 'River of the Amazons, discovered by Francysco de Orellana'. At the spot, where the aforementioned combat had taken place he sketched female Indians shooting arrows at the Spanish in full armour, helmets and bearing swords and shields: the Amazons had given the largest river of the planet its name.

The Great River of the Amazons

Almost 20 years later, in 1599, the army of Pedro de Ursúa, a native of Navarre, set out along the Marañón River in search of El Dorado and the riches of the land of the Omaguas. After Ursúa was assassinated, the adventure – now led by the villainous Lope de Aguirre – would be transformed into a sordid series of crimes that would meet a tragic end with the death of Aguirre at Barquisimeto.

Another half-century would go by before the Europeans decided to try once again to vanquish the Amazonian environment. This time, however, the motivation was political. In the early seventeenth century, when the kingdoms of Spain and Portugal were united under the same Crown, France, Holland and England strove to set up trading posts along the Brazilian coast and thus, to defy the new Spanish–Portuguese empire. At the same time, exploration of the Amazon River began anew. In 1617, a small expedition organized by the friars Brieva and Toleda in order to explore the possibility that there might be a link between the Andes and the Atlantic, went downriver. This journey, known as that of the two Franciscan lay brothers, did not meet with any opposition among the inhabitants of the banks of the Amazon, perhaps because they were not seen to pose any direct threat. On their way back, the friars were accompanied by a captain of Portuguese origin, Pedro Texeira; the group would be the first Europeans to go up the Amazon as far as San Francisco de Quito.

Texeira was a man of his time, having taken part in fighting against the English and the Dutch and participated in expeditions up the

Tapajós River in order to capture slaves from among the inhabitants of its shores. The arrival of two Franciscan friars on the Amazon delta gave him the opportunity to organize the return journey that would help intensify relations with the great Spanish cities of the viceroyalty of Peru. In the anonymous chronicle[23] of this voyage the Amazons reappear, though they are somewhat different from those described by Carvajal.

The Omagua Indians – the chronicle informs us – were engaged in conversation with a soldier who understood their language. They told him that once a year they went to the north shore to visit a group of women; they spent two months there and took back with them any sons born to them, while the daughters remained with their mothers. These concubines 'had only one breast, were very large and were related to a race of bearded men... These Indian women are commonly known as Amazons', the chronicler concludes.[24]

At Lima, the viceroy ordered Texeira to return to Brazil accompanied by two qualified persons in order to report to the Crown on all that they had seen and discovered on their journeys along the river. The men delegated to the task were a professor of theology from the University of Quito, Andrés de Artieda and the rector of the Jesuit College, Cristóbal de Acuña. The fleet set sail from Quito in February 1639, reaching Pará in December on the day before Portugal's liberation from the Spanish monarchy. Two years later, the Jesuit published the *Nuevo Descubrimiento del gran río de las Amazonas* (New Discovery of the Great River of the Amazons).

Acuña identified the shores of the Japurá, a tributary of the Amazon, as the site of the mythical Lake Parima: 'That lake of gold so greatly sought after and that, for so long, has been the principal preoccupation of all those living in Peru. I cannot guarantee that it is so, but perhaps one day God will free us from all doubt.'[25] A short distance away the Tupinamba Indians provided him with information about the Amazons and, although he never did see them, he became so convinced by his informants that all doubt was dispelled in his mind: 'But the proofs we have as to the existence of a province of the Amazons along the banks of this River are so great and so strong that we could not doubt it without renouncing all human belief.'

A century after Orellana, approximately in the same region, Acuña added some new details about a curious method of seduction practised by the Amazons during the visits of their male neighbours:

> These women have always supported themselves without the aid of men; and when their neighbours came to pay them a visit at the appointed time, they received them with arms at the ready, consisting of bows and arrows, in order not to be taken by surprise; but no sooner had they

recognized them but the descended en masse to their canoes, and each one grabbed the first hammock she could find, hung it up in her house, and there she would receive the one to whom the hammock belonged. After a few days, the new guests returned home, and they never failed to make this annual voyage during the same season.

The Jesuit insisted that he was transmitting information he had heard and that has been confirmed. Since people of many different nations had told him of their existence, and in many languages, he added, there was no risk of error. When Acuña enquired as to the location of the land of the Amazons, he was told that they lived in a mountainous region: 'They have their dwellings on mountains of prodigious height.'[26] The response was similar to the one that Orellana had received 97 years earlier from the Indian he had spoken with: perhaps this was yet another reference by the native people to the splendour of the former Inca Empire.

All the accounts of the first four expeditions up or down the 'Great River of the Amazons' claim to have seen them or at least to have heard reports about them. There would be many others, and a large number of the chronicles from the first two centuries of colonization confirm the legend.

Elsewhere in America

The Bavarian Ulrich Schmidl was likewise seduced by these inaccessible women. For some unknown reason he turned up in Seville, from where he enlisted as a solider in a fleet headed for the estuary of the Río de la Plata. For 20 years, between 1534 and 1554, he would participate in several expeditions into the heart of South America in pursuit of the realms of gold. En route he crossed the Argentine pampas, Paraguay and the Chaco as far as the Peruvian border. Back in his native village, he wrote a very crude historical account of his experiences, featuring massacres of innumerable Indians and recounting the sufferings endured by the conquistadors.

It was when his party had gone a considerable way up the Paraguay River that the natives of the region told them of the existence of the Amazons.

The king asked our captain what we desired, what our intentions were and where we were going. Our captain replied that we were looking for gold and silver, whereupon the king gave him a silver crown that weighed about a mark and a half, a gold plaque, a palm in length and one and a half in width, as well as a bracelet like a piece of armour and yet other silver objects, telling our captain that there was nothing more and that the aforesaid pieces had been won and taken as booty a long time ago in a war against the Amazon.

When he spoke to us of these Amazons and their great opulence we were very pleased, and our captain asked the king whether we could reach their lands by water and how far away they were. The latter replied that we could not get there by boat, but that we would have to go over-land and travel two months without stopping. Having listened to the king's account, we were absolutely determined to go and find the Amazons, as we shall tell below.

The rest of the text also sheds particular light on the strength of the myth. In fact, Schmidl never saw the Amazons but only heard a few more rumours, though that was enough to awaken in his mind the millennial myth. He understood from the reports that the Amazons lived in a place surrounded by water, burned their right breasts, bore children from visiting men and while keeping their daughters they sent their sons away, that they were rich warriors but that, in this version, their treasure was guarded by the men. Like many other Europeans, the Bavarian explorer thought he was on the verge of finding enchanted lands, where the fantasy mingled with reality.

These Amazons are women and their husbands only get to see them three or four times a year. If a wife finds herself pregnant with a male child, she sends him off to the man. If, however, her child turns out to be a girl, then she stays with the mother, who sears her right breast so that it cannot grow any further. The reason they do this is so that the girls can better employ their weapons, particularly the bows. This is because they are bellicose women who make incessant war against their (male) enemies. These women live upon an island that is completely surrounded by water, and theirs is a very large island. If you want to get to them, you must go by canoe. However, on this island the Amazons have neither gold nor silver; for that you must go to the mainland, which is where the men live. There, one will find many riches. The Amazons make up a great nation and they have a leader who must be called Iñis...[27]

The voyagers advanced, up to their knees or sometimes even their waists in water, Schmidl continued, and were ceaselessly tormented by tiny flies that made their lives impossible. They finally reached the land of the Orthueses, but this region was flooded and infested with grasshoppers that devoured the few provisions they had. The Christians received four golden plaques and silver earrings in exchange for some axes, knives, rosaries and scissors. However, as progress became more and more difficult and the food increasingly scarce, they had to give up the hope of finding the Amazons and make their way back.

In 1555, a French intellectual, the Franciscan André Thevet, cosmographer to the king, took up the legend of the Amazons while spending a ten-week period in Brazil. He was ill when he arrived, and would remain in bed till the day of his departure, though this did not prevent him from compiling numerous writings by other members of the expedition and publishing them in France under his own name. A chapter of his work was devoted to the Amazons. Lacking any first-hand witnesses, he was nonetheless so impressed by Orellana's travel account that he launched into great disquisitions on the origin of the warrior women. In his view, the women who fought the Spaniards were well and truly Amazons, 'since they lived exactly as the Amazons of Asia had done, as far as we know.' After the Trojan War they allegedly scattered throughout the world, or emigrated from Greece to Africa, from where a cruel king later expelled them. In America, Thévet continued, they may be found living on islands in small dwellings or caves. Constantly harassed by their enemies, they defend themselves with threats, fierce cries and gestures while shielding themselves with the shells of giant tortoises. The treatment they inflict on their prisoners is truly inhuman: in order to kill them they hang them by one leg from the branch of a tree. After a while they return and, if the unfortunate soul is still alive they shoot him with 'a thousand arrows' and light a fire under him until he is reduced to ashes.[28]

Thévet's successor as royal cosmographer of France, Jean Mocquet, repeated the usual clichés of the legend, but instead of the ritual amputation his Amazons simply expressed the milk from their right breasts.[29]

News about the Amazons continued to spread. The chroniclers repeated the core of the story: the Amazons were as rich as they were inaccessible. Juan de San Martín and Alonzo de Lebrija spoke of them in their *Relación del descubrimiento y conquista del Nuevo Reino de Granada* (Account of the Discovery and Conquest of the New Kingdom of Granada) dating from 1536 to 1539. In the Bogotá valley, rumours circulated of a nation of women who lived by themselves, without any men among them: the two Spaniards could not reach them on account of the endless mountains along the way, but they were able to learn that 'they possess endless quantities of gold'.

In 1543, Hernando de la Ribera declared at Asunción, Paraguay, that he had received reports of women who waged war against the Chiquito

Indians and who 'at certain times of the year united themselves with the neighbouring Indian men'.

Agustín de Zárate, in his *Historia del Perú* published in Antwerp in the second half of the sixteenth century, said that in front of [*sic*] Chile there reigned a great lord named Leuchengorma and that his vassals told the Spanish that 'fifty leagues further ahead there was, between two rivers, a great Province populated entirely by women who did not allow any men into their midst beyond a brief time necessary for procreation, and that if they gave birth to sons, they sent them to their fathers, while their daughters they reared themselves.' And he added that 'their queen is named Gaboymilla, which in their language means Golden Heaven, because in this land it is said that a great deal of gold is produced.'

In the same period, the cosmographer Juan López de Velasco reported in his *Noticia del Dorado o Nueva Extremadura* (News of El Dorado or New Estremadura) that near El Dorado lake there was 'a province of women known as Amazons who have no men.'[30]

The English buccaneer Walter Raleigh, famous for his description of El Dorado, managed to situate the land of the Amazons 'The nations of these women are on the south side of the river, in the provinces of Topago, and their chiefest strengths and retreats are in the islands situated on the south side of the entrance, some 60 leagues within the mouth of the said river.'[31]

And so the list continues. Nuño de Guzmán sought them in Mexico; the men of Jiménes de Quezada, in Colombia, came close to them but did not see them; and the women hid as well from Captain Hernando Ribera's party on the floodplains of Paraguay.[32]

INVESTIGATIONS BY DE LA CONDAMINE

The Frenchman Charles-Marie de La Condamine would attempt to endow the myth with a more plausible explanation. Part of a scientific expedition sent by the Academy of Sciences in Paris to measure the arc of the meridian near the equator, La Condamine would stay in America from 1735 to 1744. Like Orellana, he set out from Quito, went down the Amazon to its mouth and, besides carrying out important studies of rubber, also showed an interest in the kingdom of women. Upon his return to France, he published in 1745 his *Relation abrégée d'un voyage fait dans l'intérieur de l'Amérique méridionale* (Abridged Narrative of Travels Through the Interior of South America and Travels in all Parts of the World). La Condamine's writings reflect a new way of handling the information. Whereas a good number of his predecessors mixed what they had seen and heard with their own impressions and only rarely cited their sources, this time the explorers were no longer in search of finding gold or winning souls, but of acquiring scientific knowledge. Though the information La Condamine received was probably similar to that collected a century earlier by Acuña, his conclusions were much more prudent.

Having frequently questioned the Indians about the Amazons in the course of his travels, the Frenchman could not refrain from remarking that 'all this (information) tends to confirm that there was on this continent a Republic of women who lived alone without any men in their midst, and that they withdrew from the north shore towards the interior along the Black River (Río Negro) or one of those that flows on the same side into the Marañón.'[33] At Coari, 500 km west of Manaus, La Condamine spoke with an old Indian whose grandfather claimed to have seen a group of four Amazons heading for the Río Negro. Based on other testimonies gathered from various parts of the Amazon basin and Guyana, The scientist concluded that, according to the Indians, this nation of warriors apparently took refuge in a mountainous region in central Guyana, where neither the French nor the Portuguese had ever been.

The testimonies abounded, the Frenchman continued, but no concrete proofs were to be found, and he deemed it improbable that such a nation might still exist since none of the neighbouring native people who were in contact with the Europeans were aware of their presence. These women might have emigrated or lost their ancient customs, he speculated, considering the latter option the most plausible. He resolved the question by proposing a new hypothesis that integrated the basic belief in the existence of the Amazons with the realities of eighteenth-century America.

> I will limit myself to noting that if ever there were Amazons on earth, I believe it was in America, where the itinerant life style of women who often follow their husbands to war, and who are nonetheless satisfied with their domestic lives, must have given them the idea and provided them with frequent opportunities to rid themselves of the yoke of their tyrants by seeking to set up a settlement, where they could live independently, and at least avoid being reduced to the condition of slaves and beasts of burden. Undertaking and carrying out such a project would be no more extraordinary or more difficult than what happens every day in all of the European colonies of America, where all too often mistreated or dissatisfied slaves flee in bands into the woods and sometimes, if they find no community to associate themselves

with, they thus, spend many years and sometimes their whole lives on their own.[34]

A few years before the French Revolution, then, it seems that no one held out any more hope of finding the nation of women, but wished simply to ascertain whether they had indeed existed in the past.

Of all these accounts, that of Carvajal constitutes the sole direct testimony of someone who had seen and fought against a group of Indians that included a dozen women combatants. Nevertheless, the information about the Amazons was too numerous and spread out over time to make it likely that it was simply a product of the imagination.

It is impossible to review all the opinions and efforts on the part of the many historians, anthropologists and folklorists who have considered the subject. We shall limit ourselves to discussing a few of the more interesting hypotheses.

Efforts at Explanation

The Prussian naturalist, Alexander von Humboldt, who travelled through the tropical parts of America between 1799 and 1804, did not fail to show an interest in this unusual tradition. Back in Europe, he was frequently asked about the veracity of the affirmations by La Condamine, who claimed to have established that the Amazons had lived on the banks of the Río Negro in Brazil. The fascination with the marvellous, said Humboldt, and the desire to embellish the descriptions of the new continent with a few elements drawn from classical antiquity had led people to give undue credence to the first account by Orellana. Numerous authors thought that they had found among the recently discovered native people many of the traits and customs attributed by the Greeks to the barbarian people of the first age of humanity. Voyages through America seemed like travelling back into the past, since the American 'hordes', in their primitive simplicity, offered the Europeans a sort of antiquity contemporary to themselves.

In spite of this, Humboldt continued, the testimonies of La Condamine are admirable. But since he spoke none of the languages of the Oronoco or the Río Negro regions, the naturalist was unable to gain first-hand information about these exclusively female communities. Therefore, he called upon the testimony of Fatehr Gili, a highly educated missionary who had heard from an Indian that a nation of *Aikeam-Benanos* lived on the banks of the Cuchivero; the second of these terms meant in the Tamanaque language 'women who live alone'.

The Indian was said to have confirmed Gili's observation and added that they produced long sarbacans [blow-guns] and other instruments of war. They admitted men from the neighbouring nation of the *Vokearos* only once a year, and killed their sons in early childhood.

Humboldt reached the same conclusion as the one formulated 55 years earlier by La Condamine.

> What are we to conclude from this account by the old missionary of the Encaramada? Not that there are Amazons on the banks of the Cuchivero, but that, in various parts of America, women, tired of the state of slavery in which they are held by men, joined forces, like fugitive black slaves, in a *palenque*; that the desire to retain their independence turned them into warriors; that they had received visitors from some neighbouring and friendly tribe, perhaps somewhat less regularly than tradition would have it.[35]

During the 1920s, the Argentine historian Enrique de Gandía brought a new and fascinating perspective, albeit one that was far from complete. In his view, the Amazons interviewed by the conquistadors were the reflection, distorted over time, of the virgins of the Sun, the Houses of the Elect, and the social organization of the ancient civilization of Peru.

Indeed, in the Inca Empire government officials regularly visited the villages. Part of their mandate was to select the *acllacunas*, young women chosen to receive a careful education over a period of four years. These women were taught religion, the arts of weaving and household administration. Once a year the emperor selected his secondary wives from their midst, and bestowed some of the beautiful damsels upon members of the nobility, while the rest became *mamacunas* or 'virgins of the Sun' entrusted with religious functions. They were forbidden to marry and would spend the rest of their lives in a sort of convent, where among other activities they produced fine cloth for the nobility and the emperor himself.

For de Gandía, the testimonies of the Indian questioned by Orellana could this be interpreted as follows: when he spoke of temples, where they worshipped the sun, with their golden idols and multicoloured roofs, he was in fact referring to these 'elect women'. The Inca convents, larger than many a native village, were dispersed throughout the empire, including within the Amazon Forest, and as the Indians said, they were built in stone and kept in good order. The annual contact with men was none other than the annual distribution of the young women among the nobility, and the wars fought by the

Amazons corresponded to the incursions of the Incas into the interior of the forest. Moreover, when witnesses affirmed that the Amazons were very rich, they were no doubt alluding to the precious vessels that these mamacunas had for the temple cult.

The explanation is an attractive one, and undoubtedly sheds light on certain aspects of the myth. But how then to interpret the arrows shot by one such Amazon, that hit Gaspar de Carvajal in the eye?

The answer may be found in the studies of the Tupinamba Indians by the Brazilian historian Mario Maestri. The Tumpinambas, lords of the Brazilian coast before the European conquest, had a social structure that was spread throughout a large part of the Amazon basin: they lived in circular villages, organized around four to seven rectangular collective residences known as *malokas*, each of about 150 m^2 and able to house around 50 people. One of these malokas served as the collective residence, the 'great house', where the men deliberated over the affairs of the community.

The way in which the Tupinambas and, by extension, numerous other tribes lived their sexual lives was a great surprise to the Europeans, and caused more than one missionary to blush. Adolescents enjoyed great sexual freedom; a marriage alliance could be dissolved simply by the decision of one of the spouses; some forms of incest did not constitute a grave infraction against the norms of social behaviour. Moreover, homosexuality (both male and female) was accepted, and in that case a Tupinamba man or woman simply assumed the social role that corresponded to his or her sexual orientation. Homosexual men behaved like women and the others treated them as such, whereas lesbians were assimilated to groups of men and took on exclusively male prerogatives such as participating in the deliberations of the great house, keeping a wife and handling weapons for hunting and warfare.[36]

These clarifications allow us, with little risk of error, to explain the origins of the South American Amazons: homosexual women who had chosen the male social function and who, therefore, like any warrior, engaged in struggles against the enemy.

At least until the end of the nineteenth century, quite astonishing fables circulated about an exclusively female maloka, perhaps a distortion by the popular imagination of the myth of the warrior women. A French agent, Henri Coudreau, who visited the river in the 1880s, told a legend that circulated in the Amazon basin in Brazil. Near the border between the latter country and Guyana, where the sources of the Anauá or the Jauapiry met, there was a tribe of women who governed their own malokas. The origin of this nation was said to be a sort of association of extremely beautiful, passionate and provocative courtesans who were, moreover, lesbians. The women's maloka, Coudreau explained, was in fact a pleasure house, a convent of experts in sexual delights. They were uninterested in men, unless it was to lend some variation to their erotic games and to give birth to daughters, since they immolated any male offspring in the course of ritual ceremonies. They provided themselves with the services of men by taking prisoners of war from neighbouring tribes, and even accepted some volunteers. Most days, they went around naked, but if there was a festival they dressed in the manner of the Tupinambas. They made frequent use of aphrodisiacs. Around age 40, the men who had provided such good and faithful services, became irreversibly impotent from exhaustion, and although the women sometimes continued to use them for some secret pleasures, they simply assigned them some minor tasks in the garden or as fishermen. Only the women went out hunting and fought wars, and were notably very deft hands with their weapons, using subtle poisons on their arrows. During their many orgies, the Frenchman concluded, they entered into hysterical trances but never suffered from any nervous illnesses, quarrels or other violence: in fact, they were extremely well balanced.

Even though this legend circulated more in the form of an anecdote than as an actual belief, Coudreau thought or perhaps hoped that it might have a basis in truth.[37]

At present there are research projects under way to find some traces of American Amazons, in particular in the region, where the famous encounter between Orellana and the latter had taken place, near the confluence of the Nhamundá (sometimes spelled Iamundá or Yamundá) and the Amazon, not far from the town of Obidos. In the nineteenth century, the German naturalist Koch-Grünberg had noted that the Indians of the lower Amazon referred to the Nhamundá by the name of 'Uridxaniana', which in the Tupí language means a tribe or family of women. A local tradition has it that near the mouth of this river, at a lake known as Laciuaruá (House of the Moon), the Amazons organized an annual festival that coincided with the visit of their 'husbands', recruited temporarily from among the neighbouring tribes. Under a full moon they bathed in the lake and received from the aquatic spirits a special mud that the heat of the sun transformed into magnificent talismans, carved out of green stones: the *muiraquitás*. The Amazons offered these to the men who, the previous year, had succeeded in begetting a female child.

Although the efforts of a few naïve people to subject little mounds of mud to long exposure to the sun failed miserably, the muiraquitás were in fact perfectly real. Carved out of a sort of green jade, a stone almost as hard as diamonds, these talismans generally represent small animals, and local people believe they have protective and healing faculties against any number of illnesses.[38] Humboldt saw a few of these in the hands of the inhabitants of the banks of the Río Negro.[39] When La Condamine was on the right bank of the Amazon, across from Nhamundá, he asked the inhabitants about the origins of these strange jewels. They replied that they did not know how to make them and that their fathers' fathers had received them from women who had no husbands.[40]

The present-day Brazilian folklorist Antonio Saunier has undertaken to find definitive proof. He announced preparations for an excavation of a site near the lake of Laciuaruá, where there is an abandoned cemetery, where he hopes to find predominantly female skeletons. The results of his research are not yet known.

Let us end with this lovely Indian myth, told by the Portuguese photographer and traveller Luis Torres Fontes. Having gone up the Nhamundá for approximately 300 km, he met a chief of the Kaxuiana Indians who told him the story of the creation of the world: his tribe traced its origins to a group of women who had left their families in order to live alone in the mountains. They founded the tribe of the Kaxuianas who, after having dispersed, gave rise to all the tribes of Amazonia, and thus, by extension, to all of humanity.[41]

The vitality of the myth of the Amazons is astonishing. It has travelled through time from ancient Greece to the dawn of the French Revolution and to this day remains the subject of many a fictional tale. It is not found in the Scriptures nor is it part of the religious beliefs of the Jewish, Christian or Muslim worlds that issued from the biblical tradition. Nevertheless, it was present on all continents, in a variety of forms and at different times.

We can probably attribute its success to the fact that the Amazons represent the imaginary counterpoint to the male ascendancy in social and family organization. A symbol of the reversal of roles, the nation of women represents the antithesis of normality. In this utopian society, women reject their subordination to men and take on the attributes of virility par excellence: the right to wage war and kill their enemies.

In colonial America, the fate of Indian women at the hands of their new masters was far from enviable. At best they became servants, beasts of burden and concubines of some hidalgo. Others, less fortunate, were simply offered to the soldiers and colonists who did not have European wives. In this sordid context, even if it was only a dream, might the existence of a society of proud and free warrior women not have represented a desirable form of revenge for the victims, as well as a source of terror for their tormentors?

CHAPTER 6:

The Legendary Isles of the Ocean Sea

Between America and the Old World lay the Atlantic Ocean, rarely mentioned in biblical tradition or by the ancients, and yet it played a key role in the beliefs – often obscure in origin – that inspired the discoverers of America. The explorers were persuaded that they would one day be able to reach the islands with bizarre shapes and strange names that figured on the earliest maps of the Atlantic: Italian portolan charts drawn well before Columbus's historic crossing show the ocean dotted with known islands such as Madeira and the Canaries but also others, apparently imaginary, named Brazil, Antilia, Saint Brendan…

Also I believe that the earth is very vast, and that we who dwell in the region extending from the river Phasis to the Pillars of Heracles inhabit a small portion only about the sea, like ants or frogs about a marsh, and that there are other inhabitants of many other like places.[1]

Plato, Phaedo

The scientific exploration of America was begun by the Portuguese at the beginning of the fifteenth century. Filled with great enthusiasm and admirable determination, they nevertheless knew very little about the Ocean Sea. The kings urged their technicians to produce more precise navigational charts. Yet sources were lacking and, to make up for their lack of knowledge, the cartographers combined elements from the Greco-Roman tradition, the medieval imaginary world and the rumours of their day. The circumstances were propitious for the legendary isles of the Ocean Sea to gain a new lease of life and begin to appear on the portolan charts.

For the navigator, the islands were much more than bits of land drawn on maps; they were laden with unconscious expectations. As soon as he weighed anchor to set out for uncharted seas, he became an explorer ardently seeking a refuge and aspiring to discover a human community in the midst of the immense waters. The island was the incarnation of his hopes, but at the same time it was also the source of fear, especially if it was unknown. Isolated and hard to reach, the island constitutes a closed universe, a potential host for all manner of magic or sorcery. Did not Ulysses encounter the Cyclops Polyphemus, the Magician Circe and the Lestrigon giants on islands? Was it not on other distant islands that Sinbad, the sailor came across another Cyclops, enormous serpents and the giant Rokh bird?

WHAT WAS KNOWN ABOUT THE OCEAN SEA IN THE FIFTEENTH CENTURY?

The Ocean Sea

According to Herodotus, it was the Pharaoh Necho (609–564 B.C.) who was responsible for having armed the Phoenician fleet that allegedly completed the first circumnavigation of Africa. This legendary expedition set out from the Red Sea and three years later reached Gibraltar, having stopped during the winter to take time to sow and harvest. Herodotus also described the journey of the Carthaginian Hanno who, around 450 B.C., reached Cape Bojador, and on the way back visited the lush islands that he named the

'Fortunate Isles'. Moreover, there are references to an expedition by Pytheas, a Greek sailor from Marseilles, who visited Thule – probably Iceland – and Great Britain.

These explorations and others allowed people in antiquity to learn of the existence of a certain number of islands in the ocean. In his *Natural History*, written in the first century of our era, Pliny the Elder compiled a significant part of the scientific knowledge of his day. He had mentioned, notably, of four sets of islands: Atlantis, across from Mount Atlas at the far west of Mauritania; the Gorgades, two days by boat from the continent and formerly inhabited by the Gorgons*, where Hanno was supposed to have taken captive two women covered in hair; the Hesperides (isles of the setting sun), 40 days away by sea; and the Fortunate Isles, located near the coast of Mauritania (present-day Morocco), made up of: Ombrios, Junonia, Capraria, Nivaria, Canaria.[2] As for the more distant isles, says Pliny, we cannot situate them precisely.[3] During the same period, the Ibero-Roman Pomponius Mela noted in his Cartography that there were islands west of Great Britain, the Cassiteride Isles (Tin Islands).

There was, however, a fringe of the European population who, from the Gulf of Gascony to the North Sea, had lived for centuries facing the vast Atlantic Ocean. These people, ignorant of the learned sources of classical antiquity, nevertheless possessed an empirical knowledge accumulated by generations of humble fishermen and Basque, Breton, Irish, English and other sailors who did not hesitate to venture into vast stretches of the ocean in search of the precious cod, possibly reaching even the rich banks of Newfoundland, and in the process must have discovered numerous islands unknown to the Greeks or the Romans.

Among these sailors, the Irish monks occupy a particularly important place. It was in the course of the fifth century that Ireland was very rapidly converted to Christianity. The country then experienced a great wave of mysticism that moved certain monks to seek out far-flung and solitary lands, where they might set up communities of hermits. It was during these constant peregrinations by sea that the itinerant monks reached the northern islands, including Iceland.

Around the ninth century, the lack of arable land impelled the Scandinavians, commonly known as Norsemen (in France, as Normans) or Vikings, to cross their frontiers and seek to conquer new horizons. During these invasions they established the first Russian kingdom,

---

*The Gorgons were three sisters: Stheno, Euryale and Medusa, whose glance turned to stone anyone whom they gazed upon.

discovered Greenland and even reached North America during the astonishing adventure of Vinland, or 'land of vines', a name given to the territories west of Greenland, which is to say, present-day North America. The Scandinavians founded colonies there around the year 1000. However, the resistance of the native people and the difficulties in communication were such that the first European settlements disappeared a few decades later. For several centuries, southern Europe was unaware of these feats of Nordic navigation.[4]

It was not until the second millennium that southern navigators once again embarked on this mysterious exterior sea. In 1291, two galleys left Genoa under the command of the Vivaldi brothers; their objective was to 'reach the Indies by the Ocean Sea', but they never returned.[5] Lancelloto Maloccello had more luck than his compatriots, and re-discovered the Canary Islands in the early fourteenth century, giving his name to the island of Lanzarote.

In the fifteenth century, under the orders of the Infante Henry, Portuguese sailors undertook a systematic exploration of the ocean and its islands; in 1420 they landed at Porto Santo and Madeira, reached the Azores around 1427, and in 1455 arrived at the Cape Verde Islands.

This topographic knowledge was supplemented by legends. If the Atlantis of which Plato spoke in the *Timaeus* and the *Crito* did not mean much to the discoverers, other traditions, combining historical recollections, hagiography and popular beliefs, would inspire the efforts of numerous travellers. Thus a very ancient Irish saga celebrated the mystical peregrinations of Saint Brendan and was at the origin of the belief in a legendary isle. Another ancient tradition, this time from Iberia, was probably based on the island of the Irish monk, and praised the courage of seven bishops who, fleeing the Arab invasion, set out for the isle of Antilia along with their entire diocese.

Perhaps this legendary isle was known in Ireland as Brazil or *O'Brazil*, a name that might come either from *breasil*, meaning 'great island' in Gaelic, or from brasil, a tree used in dyeing known by that name since the beginning of the first millennium*. Another, quite convincing interpretation connects this toponym to the Irish expression *Hy Bressail* and *O'Brazil*, which apparently means 'Fortunate Isle', another name for St Brendan's Isle. The juxtaposition of St Brendan's Fortunate Isle and the isle of *O'Brazil* might be due to the southern mapmakers' misunderstanding of the Irish language.[6]

---

*Later the Portuguese gave this name to their colonies in America, which were originally called 'Santa Cruz'.

The confusion increases further if we recall that the ancients called the Canaries the Fortunate Isles.

HOW TO LOCATE THE ISLANDS?

Armed with new techniques and moved by new objectives, the cartographers of the fourteenth and fifteenth centuries began to draw maps of the Ocean Sea; their representations of the islands were based on the knowledge available at the time. They often copied from each other, sometimes making errors of translation; on other occasions, they sketched these lands on the basis of information provided by navigators who claimed or believed they had found them. In spite of these sources, however, tradition still prevailed in determining knowledge.

The Fortunate Isles of which the ancients spoke were soon identified as the Canary Islands, while the Greco-Roman Hesperides were mostly assimilated with the Azores and the Gorgades were identified with the Cape Verde archipelago.

What about the other islands? St Brendan's Isles, which first appeared in 1275 – on the Hereford map – soon proliferated on the maps. The same is true for the island of Antilia. On certain maps, the isle of Stockafixa also appears, a simple translation into Italian of the English word stockfish. Similarly, we find the island of Frislandia, the result of confusion between the Faroe Islands and the mysterious isle of Brazil.

After 1480, at least two expeditions would be organized by the merchants of Bristol to discover Brazil. John Jay affirmed in 1480 that he was but two fingers away from 'the isle of Brazil, west of Ireland'. The following year, it was Thomas Croft who went in search of the island. In 1494, thus after the discovery of America, the Spanish ambassador in London informed his sovereigns that 'each year, three or four caravels are outfitted at Bristol and sent in search of this island (Brazil), and of the island of the Seven Cities, at the instigation of the Genoese (John Cabot).'[7]

Scientists of the stature of Mercator (inventor of the method of projecting the globe onto a rectangle) felt obliged to include on their maps these legendary islands, of which they would even establish the contours and the cities that may be found on them. Even in the nineteenth century, many maritime charts and globes showed an Atlantic Ocean dotted with imaginary islands. They would appear even on the maps of the British Admiralty until 1873. [8]

Of all the legends concerning the islands, the saga of the Irish bishop and that of Antilia were the two most important.

The Navigation of Saint Brendan

Saint Brendan was an Irish bishop who took part in the evangelization of northern England during the sixth century, but the *Navigatio sancti Brendani*, a text that recounts the most important episode in the life of the saint, was written down only three centuries later by Irish monks who lived on the continent. This story enjoyed such great success that there are still 20 extant manuscripts in Gaelic, Saxon, Flemish, French and other languages, often adapted to the tastes of the day, with all that implies in terms of alterations or transformations.

The *Navigatio* tells how St Brendan one day received a visit from a messenger of God who informed him of the existence of a *terra repromissionis*, a land of redemption, inhabited by those who have merited eternal life, in other words Paradise. He and his disciples then proceeded to build a *curragh*, a traditional Irish boat, made of a wooden frame and covered with skin and coated with tar. Together they set out on an odyssey that would last seven years.

During the first year they reached Savage Isle, where Divine Providence had prepared an opulent feast for them. They then continued their voyage as far as Sheep's Island, where they captured a lamb to sacrifice at Easter. During Holy Week they reached a 'Naked Isle' but, having lit a fire, they realized that they were on the back of an enormous fish that was about to throw them into the sea. They finally landed on Birds' Island, where the songs of thousands of flying messengers of God announced that they would continue to sail for six more years.

The prophecy was fulfilled. They would return six times to the fish named Jasconius in order to celebrate Easter Mass, though henceforth, they would forgo lighting a fire. At the end of the voyage they would land on several more islands, and encounter a griffin, whom they would vanquish, a dragon, and then a giant whom they resurrected so that they might baptize him. While they were crossing a cold sea, they sailed before a crystal column, and then before an island spouting smoke and smelling of sulphur, where rivers of fire flowed into the sea. Later they discovered an island of black cliffs inhabited by the souls of the damned, and a rock, where Judas was eternally expiating his treachery.

They then set foot on a new island inhabited by a hermit named Paul, who wore nothing but his long hair and nourished himself with only the waters of a very pure spring. The hermit told them that their goal was near. One last time they celebrated Easter Mass on the back of the great fish Jasconius and, once the liturgy was over, the fish carried them beyond Birds' Island, from where they would sail for 40 more days before entering the zone of shadows that protects Paradise.

After emerging triumphant from the latter trial, a land of gold stretched before them, surrounded by a high wall decorated with precious stones, the door of which was guarded by two dragons and a sword of gold and diamonds that was perpetually twirling. With one gesture, the angel who was guiding them pushed the sword aside and opened the door.

> When they emerged from this dark mist and could see around them, they came on the finest land that could be upon earth; it was so clear and bright that there was great rejoicing. The trees were full of fruit, very thick on every branch. It was thickly planted with trees, and the trees bore heavily, the apples were all fully ripe, just as if it were autumn. They roamed about this land for 40 days; nowhere would they find any sign of limit to this land. It was always light, they experienced no darkness; they never found in any place so much brightness and light. The climate was always the same, neither too hot nor too cold – but the delight that they experienced there can never be recounted.

The angel then led them to a mountaintop so that they might contemplate Paradise and its marvels, and said to them:

> See, he said, here is that land for which you have sought far and wide, and for a long time, since our Lord wishes that you should long remain so that you should see his mysteries in this great ocean; load your ship with this fruit, since you may remain here no longer. For you must shortly return again to your own land, since you shall soon depart this world – your life is near the end.

Before Brendan and his disciples began their journey home, the angel suggested that they collect fruit and precious stones so that everyone in Hibernia (Ireland) might know that 'they had truly reached the land promised to the saints and the just.'[9]

HOW ARE WE TO INTERPRET THIS MIRACULOUS STORY?

Saint Brendan and the Church in Ireland

Ireland was never part of the Roman Empire. The arrival of Christianity, preached by St Patrick in the fifth century, brought with it some of the Greco-Roman cultural baggage that had hitherto been absent from this far-flung land. The new faith was adopted more rapidly here than elsewhere in Europe, and brought with it an extraordinary thirst for knowledge: ancient manuscripts were compiled and copied in monasteries, while at the same time – and without any sense of a conflict – the monks also recorded the Celtic oral traditions. This strange cultural amalgam composed of Christian fervour, Celtic imagination and classical rationality was spread throughout the West by Irish missionaries sent to evangelize or re-evangelize Europe. Their contribution constitutes one of the great cultural pillars of the Middle Ages. It was this context that gave birth to the story of St Brendan's voyage.

The influence of antiquity is quite evident in the story. The description of certain places, such as the Isle of Redemption surrounded by shadows or represented as a floating island, appear to have been inspired by the ubiquitous Pseudo-Callisthenes (Life of Alexander the Great).

It was no accident that St Brendan was looking for Paradise not in the Far East but in the midst of the immense ocean: the Irish were

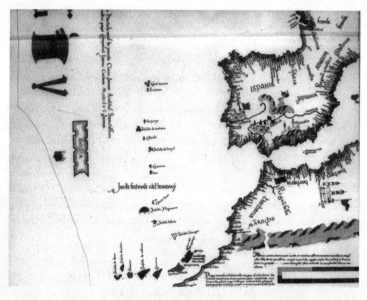

Map by Bartolomeo Pareto (detail), made at Genoa in 1455. The island of Brazil appears twice: to the west of Ireland and in the Azores. The legendary Insulle Fortunate Sct Brandany appear between this archipelago and that of Madeira. Farther west is the great Antilia shown in its traditional rectangular form.

good navigators and knew the sea so well that it became the privileged source of inspiration feeding their imaginations. In the Navigatio sancti Brendani there are episodes and descriptions comparable to those of the *Immrama* (sea voyages), sailors' epics written in Gaelic. It was to these very ancient sources that Christian elements soon came to be added.[10]

The mastery of the seas near Ireland is evident also in the scientific work of Dicuil, an Irish monk who belonged to the Carolingian court in the early ninth century. This scholar composed the *Liber de mensura orbis terrae*, a geographical compilation that revealed knowledge of the North Atlantic that far surpassed that of his masters Pliny, Solinus and Isidore, among others. Referring to the islands of this zone, he cited eyewitness accounts by Irish monks who had visited them:

Therefore, these authors were in error when they wrote that the sea was solid around Thule (Iceland) and that the white nights last the entire period from the spring equinox to the autumn and that, vice versa, the

Navigation of Saint Brendan. Fifteenth-century illustration.
Heidelberg, Universitätsbibliothek.

night endured from the autumn equinox to the spring; since these men (the Irish monks) have travelled during the period of great cold, entered the island and remained there, and saw that day and night alternated except during the period of the solstice. But one day's sailing to the north of there they found the sea to be frozen. There are many other islands north of Britain that may be reached in two days and two nights if travelled directly from the northern islands of the aforesaid Britain with favourable winds. A devout priest told me that he reached one of them in the summer by travelling for two days and the intervening night in a small boat with two benches. There are another group of small islands separated by narrow bodies of water; a group of hermits who sailed there from Ireland lived there for more than one hundred years. However, due to the Norman raiders, today these islands are as deserted as if they had been abandoned since the beginning of the world; there are no longer any anchorites living there, but only innumerable sheep and aquatic birds of many different species. I have never found these islands mentioned in the writings of the authorities. (Dicuil, Liber de mensura orbis terrae, p. 74–6).

In an extremely modern style, Dicuil refers to witnesses who had direct knowledge of the islands of the North Atlantic, and he himself had visited several of them. His description of the midnight sun, which shines only for a few days, corresponds to the phenomenon as it could be observed in Iceland. This is an important indication that the Irish monks lived there before the invasion of the Vikings in the ninth century.

The islands filled with sheep and sea birds that he mentions are probably the Faroe Islands, the name of which is related to *Faer-eyjar* which means 'Isle of Sheep' in Old Norse. This episode closely resembles those of the Isle of Sheep and Isle of Birds mentioned in the Navigatio sancti Brendani.

St Brendan's Isles in Cartography

Around the eighth century B.C., Homer situated the Elysian Fields beyond the ocean, in the Fortunate Isles; that is where the souls of heroes went to find their rest. The Romans, who knew the Canary Islands, called them the Fortunate Isles by reference to this tradition. At the end of the Middle Ages, some cartographers curiously mixed the traditions: since the ancients had located the Elysian Fields in the Fortunate Isles and Brendan had found Paradise on an island in the Atlantic, the Canary Islands and St Brendan's Isle or isles were presumed to be part of the same archipelago.

On the Hereford *mappamundi*, drawn in 1275, the following inscription appears: *Fortunatae insulae sex sunt insulae Sct Brendani* (six of the Fortunate Isles are those of St Brendan) and later, on the Pareto map (1455), the same islands are named *Insulle fortunate sancti Brandany*.[11] Until the end of the fifteenth century the islands were shown lying between the Canaries and Madeira.

Other cartographers simply made references to the saint's maritime peregrinations. On the map of Mecia de Viladestes (1413), we see a ship commanded by a bishop as well as a boat heading for a cetacean.[12] On the famous globe of Martin Behaim (1492)*, an island of San Borondon appears in the centre of the ocean that stretches from the coast of Spain to the island of Cipango (Japan) a few degrees north of the equator. On the no less famous map by the Ottoman admiral Piri Re'is (1513)**,[13] we see in the northern part of the ocean two people engaged in conversation sitting on the back of a whale, while three others are observing them from their boat.

In the fifteenth century, and for the first time in history, humanity succeeded in representing the surface of the planet in the form of continents: geography once again became a science, and distinguished scholars undertook complicated calculations to determine the dimensions of the seas and the continents. In spite of all this, the island of the Irish monk would continue to appear on famous maps: those of Desceliers in 1546, Sebastian Cabot in the early sixteenth century, Gerard Mercator in 1569 and Ortelius in 1570.

Even after Columbus' discovery, efforts to find the famous island did not abate. According to *Historia de las siete islas de la Gran Canaria* (History of the Seven Islands of Grand Canary) by Juan de Abreu Galindo in 1590, the most distant island of the archipelago is that of San Brandon, which Ptolemy had named *Aprositus* (hidden).[14]

---

*Martin Behaim's *mappamundi* is the oldest surviving globe. It was made in Portugal in 1492, when Columbus had already undertaken his expedition. Between the Spanish coast and that of Cipango (Japan) there is an ocean dotted with real and imaginary islands (the globe resides in the Germanisches Nationalmuseum in Nürnberg).

**The 1513 map by Piri Re'is is based on Portuguese and Arab sources. The recently discovered region of the world called *Littoral Antilya* seems to have been copied from a map drawn by Columbus himself. In one of the legends Piri Re'is alludes to a Spanish slave belonging to his uncle Kemal Re'is, who apparently accompanied Columbus three times on his voyage to America. The Admiral's map may have fallen into Turkish hands after the capture of a Spanish vessel on the Mediterranean around 1501.

St Brendan's isles continue to appear on many maps until at least 1759.[15] The captain general of the Canaries, Don Juan de Mur y Aguirre, set off in search of them in 1721;[16] other expeditions tried to locate them 100 miles west of Ireland, in the Caribbean Sea or even in the Indian Ocean[17] (map of Willem Blaeu, 1641). The modern scientific mindset would eventually carry the day, but the myth would have lasted for more than a thousand years.

The Island of Antilia or the Island of the Seven Cities

The Irish myth has a southern equivalent: the island of Antilia, the Iberian counterpart to St Brendan's Isle. The word 'Antilia' evokes the idea of an 'island on the other side', an 'anti-island', *Anti-ilha* in Portuguese, which can be pronounced Antilia. Its distant origin might lie in the tradition of a lost continent described by Plato, but it is more likely to be based on an important Spanish and Portuguese legend that Ferdinand Columbus would later mention.

During the 1530s, the latter, son of the Admiral and of Doña Beatriz Enríquez, found himself embroiled in the awkward affair of the famous *pleitos colombinos*. This complicated lawsuit over Columbus's heritage was initiated by the explorer's descendants against the Crown, a process that would continue for 50 years. Humiliated by the ingratitude that was shown to his father, Ferdinand decided to take up the pen to exalt his memory, and between 1537 and 1539 he wrote the first biography of the explorer, the *Historia del Almirante* (History of the Admiral), where he explained, among other things, how Columbus had collected the evidence that there were unknown islands in the ocean. Chapter IX begins:

> The third and last motive the Admiral had to undertake the discovery of the Indies was the hope of finding, before he arrived there, some island and land of great utility, whence he might the better pursue his principal design.[18]

He then listed the many signs that there were people living on lands on the far side of the Atlantic: a piece of wood ingeniously carved, large reeds and unfamiliar pine trees. He had even been told that the inhabitants of the Azores islands 'found on the shore two dead men whose face and appearance was different from those of the people of these shores.'

In 1484, Ferdinand explained, an inhabitant of the island of Madeira asked the king of Portugal for a caravel in order to 'discover a land…that people say they have seen from the Azores'; this land, he continued, was known because Aristotle affirmed in his book *On Marvellous Things Heard* that Carthaginian merchants sailing the Atlantic had landed on an extremely fertile island that some Portuguese navigators indicated on their maps by the name of *Anti-ilha*, knowing that this was the island of the Seven Cities settled by the Portuguese 'when the Moors captured Spain from King Rodrigo in 714 A.D.'

Ferdinand recounts the ancient legend:

> They say that at that time seven bishops embarked from Spain and came with their ships and people to this island, where each founded a city; and in order that their people might give up all thought of returning to Spain they burned their ships, riggings, and all else needed for navigation. Some Portuguese who speculated about this island conjectured that many of their nations had gone thither but were never able to return.

> In particular, they say that in the time of the Infante Dom Henrique of Portugal there arrived at this island of Antilia a Portuguese ship driven there by a storm. After coming ashore, the ship's people were conducted by the inhabitants of the island to their church to see if the visitors were Christian and observed the rites of the Catholic religion. Satisfied that they were Christians, the islanders prayed the ship's people not to leave before the return of their absent lord, whom they would immediately notify of the ship's arrival. They also said that their lord would do great honour to the visitors and give them many presents. But the ship's master and the sailors feared to be detained, reasoning that because these people did not wish to be known abroad they might burn their ships. So they left for Portugal with their news expecting to be rewarded by the Infante, who instead rebuked them severely and ordered them to return immediately to the island; but the master took fright and escaped from Portugal with his ship and crew. It is said that while the sailors were in the church on that island the ship's boys gathered sand for the firebox and found that it was one-third fine gold.[19]

The political climate at the time was marked by the reconquest of the Iberian Peninsula by Christians; the island of Antilia recalled ancient traditions of the refusal of the local population to submit to the Arab authorities and established that there were traces of the Christian faith in the lands to be conquered. On maps, this island was situated on the same parallel as southern Spain, and was represented in the form of a rectangle with irregular contours, oriented from north to south. As for the constant references to the number seven (seven bishops, seven islands, seven cities), this may be a recollection of ancient knowledge about the seven islands that formed the archipelago of the Canaries*. The number seven is of course also associated with certain magical symbols: the seven golden candelabra of the Apocalypse, the seven arms of the candelabra of the Tabernacle, the seven Churches of Asia and the seven planets known at the time.

The Portuguese historian Armando Cortesão found the first reference to the island on the 1369 map by the Venetian Pizzigani.[20] The island next appeared on the maps of Beccario (1435), Bianco (1436), Pareto (1455),[21] Fra Mauro (1460), Benincasa (1463) and yet others. In general, they show the island of Antilia together with three other islands: Roullo, which is square shaped and located 20 leagues to the west, Satanaxio or San Atanagio 60 leagues to the north and finally, still further north, the island of Tanmar or Danmar.[22] Benincasa, on the map he drew at Ancona, inscribed seven enigmatic names in the interior of Antilia: Anna, Antioul, Anselli, Anseto, Ansolli, Ansoldi and Cori, corresponding undoubtedly to the names of the seven bishops.[23]

Antilia begins to appear on maps at the same time as the discovery of the Azores (1427). From that point on, expeditions, whether authorized or clandestine, were organized in order to discover islands to the west.[24] Although the project would never be realized, the most significant expedition was the one planned by the Fleming Ferdinand Van Olm, also known as Fernão d'Ulmo or Duolmo. In 1486, he received from King João II of Portugal the patent letters authorizing him to set off 'to seek and find a large island or several islands or a continent, and to reconnoitre its shores at the spot, where we think the island of the Seven Cities is located, and all this at his own cost and expense.'[25] It is worth noting that at the time the king of Portugal was already aware of Columbus's plans. These ventures indicate that in the course of the fifteenth century, European navigators had some indication that there were islands in the Ocean Sea, and perhaps even some information, vague though it may have been, pointing to the existence of the American continent.

One of the arguments Columbus would adduce to justify his proposal to reach the Indies by way of the western seas was the map sent in 1474 by the Florentine astronomer Paolo del Pozzo Toscanelli to the confessor to the king of Portugal: it does indeed show the

---

*The seven Canary islands are: Grand Canary, Fuerteventura, Lanzarote, Tenerife, Gomera, Palma and Herro.

island of Antilia and that of Cipango (Japan) as being very near. The original map is no longer extant, but has been reconstructed with the help of the accompanying explanatory text.[26]

After his third voyage, the Admiral explained the decision he had taken to go further south than he had done on the previous expeditions. He wished, he wrote, to verify the statements of the king of Portugal when he spoke of lands situated on the other side of the ocean:

> The Admiral says again that he wishes to go to the south, because he intends with the aid of the Most Holy Trinity, to find islands and lands, that God may be served and their Highnesses and Christianity may have pleasure, and that he wishes to see what was the idea of King Don Juan of Portugal, who said that there was mainland to the south.[27]

This affirmation could be considered a serious indication that the Portuguese were aware of the existence of Brazil, or at least of a part of it, prior to its official discovery in 1500; but it may be that King João was referring instead to the island of Antilia. It is also possible that the two referred to one and the same thing: perhaps a navigator approaching the shores of Brazil at the time thought that he was nearing the legendary island.

In any event, recent news of the island was reaching Columbus from England. King Henry VII had given the Genoese John Cabot letters authorizing him to set out for China by way of the north. Cabot discovered hitherto unknown lands, most likely Newfoundland, and immediately after his return a certain John Day in Bristol sent Columbus a sketch of the Islands of the Seven Cities.[28]

In the same period, the Italian humanist Peter Martyr d'Anghiera in his *Decades de Orbo Novo* proposed that the island of Hispaniola was the same as the one known as Antilia;[29] his suggestion was adopted by Italian merchants including Amerigo Vespucci, who wrote that at the end of his second voyage he reached 'the island of Antiglia, being that which Christopher Columbus discovered a few years ago.'[30]

Following the discovery, the myth was curiously transposed: since the island, where gold and sand mix was not found in the ocean, it might well be located on mainland. Around 1526, only five years after the fall of the Aztec Empire, a rumour spread through the city of Mexico and stirred up its inhabitants: the Indians claimed that there were seven extremely rich cities located in the North, in a region called Cíbola or Sébola.

The first Spanish references to the latter region came from the writings of Alvar Núñez Cabeza de Vaca and his companions, who had embarked on the disastrous expedition of Pánfilo de Narváez to Florida in 1527. Abandoned by their fleet, they were forced to survive in strange lands, where the Indians tried to defeat them or reduce them to slavery: only four survivors would reach Mexico in 1534; among them was the Morisco* slave Estebanico de Orantes. They told of having seen 'the first houses that looked like houses', having met people dressed in 'cotton shirts', 'wearing shoes', and of having received turquoises and emeralds from them. They added that when Núñez asked them about the origins of these precious stones, the Indians replied 'that they brought them from some very high mountains to the North, where they traded them for plumes or parrot feathers. They said there were large towns and very large dwellings there.'[31]

The conquerors of Mexico could not resist the visions of turquoise and emerald, and inevitably they made the connection between what Alvar Núñez reported of having seen and the legend of the Seven Cities. Three years later, in 1537, Friar Juan de Olmedo, guided by Estebanico, set out on the adventure: they got as far as Casa Grande in southern Arizona.[32]

The same year, Friar Marcos de Niza travelled from Peru to Mexico, no doubt in the hope of discovering another city that could equal in splendour that of Cuzco. He obtained the necessary permissions and, on 7 March 1539, headed north with the intention of finding out about the wealthy cities. He was accompanied by another friar, a few Indians, and at the head of the party the indispensable Estebanico.[33] After several weeks on foot, they were informed by a messenger that 'in this province there are seven very great cities, all under the authority of one lord.' Further north, near the thirty-fifth parallel, Friar Marcos met an Indian from Cíbola who confirmed the existence of the Seven Cities and told him of the greatness of his own, which was, however, smaller than another one named Ahacus:

> I asked him for information and he told me that Cíbola is a big city with
> a large population, many streets and public squares, and that in certain
> parts there are very large buildings…where the notables gather on cer-
> tain days of the year. It is said that these buildings are made of stone and
> thatch…and that the portals and façades of the principal dwellings are

---

*Translator's note: the Moriscos were descendants of the Moors in Spain who, at the time of the Spanish reconquest, officially adopted the Christian faith in order to avoid expulsion, while often secretly remaining Muslims.

made of turquoise. He told me that the seven [*sic*] other cities are built
in the same manner as this one, and that some are even larger, and that
the most important one is called Ahacus. He also told me that to the
southeast, there is a kingdom called Marata.[34]

Beyond the Seven Cities, the Indian continued, there were three
other kingdoms: Marata, Acus and Totonteac. But Friar Marcos suddenly heard a sad piece of news: the inhabitants of Cíbola had killed
his guide Estebanico. He nevertheless continued his voyage to the
edges of Cíbola, of which he managed to get only a glimpse but
whose marvels he nevertheless confirmed: the population of Cíbola,
he said, is larger than that of Mexico. He took possession of the new
provinces on behalf of Emperor Charles V and in the name of the
viceroy Don Antonio de Mendoza, and erected a small cross to sig-
nify the event: 'There I declared that I am taking possession of the
Seven Cities and of the kingdoms of Tontonteac, Acus and Marata.'[35]
But he would never visit them, so anxious was he to return and report
quickly on what he had seen.

Having been informed of the expedition, the viceroy authorized
the governor of Mexico, Francisco Vázquez de Coronado, to lead an
expedition made up of 300 Christians and 800 native people who
were willing to repeat, on a larger scale, the achievements of Cortés
and Pizarro. They spent two years wandering through the region
before discovering the mouth of the Colorado. They went up the
Grand Canyon as far as Quivira (present-day Kansas), and were in a
terrible state when they discovered a small, insignificant village there.
Brother Marcos, who also took part in this second expedition, fled
the soldiers' rage and returned to Mexico, where he died from the
consequences of the cold and hardships he had endured during his
voyages. Vázquez de Coronado did not fare much better, for upon his
return he was charged with having undertaken explorations without
proper authorization.[36]

A few years later, in Florida, while unsuccessfully attempting to
colonize the area, the French recalled the myth and were excited by
the prospect of finding 'this kingdom and city of Sébola', where gold
and silver were abundant as well as precious stones and many other
riches. They claimed that the local Indians fitted their arrows not
with iron but with chiselled turquoise.[37]

By this time the island of Antilia had lost its magical aura, and gave
its name to the archipelago of the Antilles. But the Fortunate Isles, the
Seven Cities, Cíbola, St Brendan's Isle and others continued to evoke
forgotten worlds regularly revived by fresh fictions. The enigma of

the legendary isles of the Ocean Sea is summed up perfectly by the notice that may be found on the mappamundi of the Dutchman Johannes Ruysch (1508):

> This island of Antilia was formerly discovered by the Portuguese; now, if we look for it, we cannot find it*.

*'Ista insula Antilia aliquando a lusitâis est inventa modo qn queritur no invenitur invent…'

CHAPTER 7:

Wondrous Creatures

Both the writers of classical Antiquity and the medieval doctrinal authorities thought India and Ethiopia were home to the most wondrous creatures that human imagination could invent, but that experience proved unable to explain. The reports written by the few voyagers who had visited the Far East confirmed the existence of phenomena that would be transformed into fear or delight in the European imagination. Christopher Columbus himself took abundant notes on the wondrous creatures populating the Orient, and was so convinced of their existence that during his four voyages to the New World he claimed to have beheld or at least received first-hand information about six of them: sirens, sea serpents, griffins, Cynocephali (dog-headed men), Cyclops and men with tails.

> On none of the islands hitherto visited have I found any people of
> monstrous appearance, according to the expectation of some, but the
> inhabitants are all of very pleasing aspect.

Letter from Christopher Columbus to Luis de Santángel, February 1493.

The exploration of America would ultimately frustrate the hopes of
the conquistadors, who failed to find there any terrifying monsters or
even many very large animals. With no basis in reality, the belief in
such extraordinary beings faded within a few years of colonization.

The classification of flora and fauna according to objective criteria
did not begin until the Enlightenment. In 1735, Carl Linnaeus published his *Systema naturae*, a work based on anatomy, lists a scientific
description for 4,730 animal species, taking into account the internal
and external characteristics of the animals in order to divide them
into six classes: quadrupeds, birds, amphibians, fish, insects and
reptiles. No one before Linnaeus had undertaken a truly rational
investigation of the animal kingdom.

In Antiquity, Aristotle had inventoried 400 species in his *History of
Animals*, distinguishing two major categories: red-blooded animals
(vertebrates) and bloodless ones (invertebrates). Pliny's *Natural
History* did not add anything new to the classification of species; it
did, however, propose a list of monstrous people located beyond the
African deserts. There we may read that the Atlanteans, who lost all
their human qualities, contemplate the sun emitting terrible curses.
The Troglodytes, who live in caves, are mute and nourish themselves
with serpents. The Garamantes practice wife-sharing. It is said, Pliny
continued, that the Blemmyes, headless men, have their mouth and
eyes in the middle of their chest. The Himantopods have no feet, but
rather a type of belt with which they creep like snakes. In another part
of Africa we find people who eat human flesh and *Cynocephali*, men
with the heads of dogs.[1]

Medieval people did not feel the need to produce a systematic
classification of species. The chronological order in which the Creator
placed living beings in the waters, air and on the earth constituted a
division that was deemed adequate as far as the animals were concerned. According to Genesis, God created the world in seven days;
on the fifth, He created the fish of the seas and the birds of the air
and on the sixth the domestic animals, reptiles and wild animals.
Finally, before dawn, God created man to 'have dominion over the
fish of the sea and over the birds of the air and over every living thing
that moves upon the earth.' (Genesis 1.26) 'But the Scriptures also

provide another elementary classification, imposing a complex division into pure and impure animals that served as the basis for the dietary prohibitions of Judaism and Islam.' (Deuteronomy 14.3–21) These details provide some very basic guidelines as well as strict dietary doctrines, without adding any real knowledge about living species.

PORTRAITS OF HITHERTO UNSEEN CREATURES

The intellectuals of the Middle Ages imagined many other kinds of animals and men different from themselves, beyond their own horizons. St Augustine, for instance, mentions some in his *City of God*. He knew that in Africa and India there lived animals different from those of Europe. After the decline of Roman civilization, the crocodile, the elephant and even the lion were known mainly from literature; some illustrators drew them based more or less accurately on written accounts. The same is true for groups of human beings with exotic features: some Europeans who had visited distant continents had seen people with black skin or almond-shaped eyes. As well, descriptions of legendary people and animals found wide circulation.

In spite of the centuries that separated the compilations of Antiquity and the medieval bestiaries, information on distant lands came from the same types of sources: reports by ambassadors, travellers, merchants who had seen certain things but mainly had heard tell of strange beings; with a few exceptions, the writers had not observed them directly. For them, the description of a griffin was as credible as that of a gorilla. Both belonged to the same category of distant and unknown creatures. A document of Portuguese origin reports how the inhabitants of Rome in 1514 gathered together to gaze, flabbergasted, at an elephant from the Indies leading a procession of exotic gifts offered to the pope by the king of Portugal.[2] King Francis I of France even modified his itinerary on one of his journeys in order to pass through Marseilles and see a rhinoceros that was in transit between Portugal and Rome.[3]

The system nevertheless had logic of its own. The descriptions of seemingly incredible creatures had an air of reality. The human imagination can exaggerate traits, distort and recombine elements of different sorts, but to do so requires some foundation, no matter how distant, in the known world. When a monastic writer, copyist or illustrator received news of a great quadruped with a single horn on its forehead, he turned to the representation of an animal that was familiar to him – the horse – and added a horn to its forehead. In this

Miniature by Charles d'Angoulême, inspired by the Polyhistor, Containing the Noble Actions of Human Creatures, the Secrets and Providence of Nature by Solinus, painted around 1480. On it we see Acephali *(headless men), dragons, a snake charmer, a unicorn, an elephant and a serpent with a man's head.*

manner, the description of a rhinoceros planted in the human imagination gave rise to the unicorn.

In the Middle Ages, zoology followed a trajectory similar to that of cartography: the few bits of ancient knowledge that survived were reduced to a simple catalogue intended above all to provide hints of the designs of the Almighty. The observation of animal customs seemed useful only for the lessons they contained, reinforcing the Scriptures and the Passion of Christ.

The first known treatise that sought to associate episodes of the Old and New Testaments with animal allegories is the *Physiologus*, the work of an anonymous Alexandrian of the early centuries of our era. In the surviving copies we can read that the pelican resurrects its dead chicks, an allusion to the resurrection of Christ, and that the sexual union of elephants – as we shall see below – recalls the story of Adam and Eve.

The *Etymologies* of St Isidore of Seville, dating from the seventh century, devote several pages to descriptions of animals. The bishop established an even more ingenious nomenclature than his predecessors, not limiting himself to repeating the analogies of the *Physiologus*. He consulted other sources: Varro, Virgil, Ovid and Pliny's *Natural History* to establish a more complete schema in which animals are grouped into eight categories.

The first is made up of familiar domestic animals and livestock such as horses, cows and rabbits. Then come the wild animals that are very cruel with their jaws or claws, a category that combine the lion, the fox and the wolf with the griffin, the unicorn, the sphinx, the Cynocephalus and the satyr. Next, he lists the small animals: rats, mice, spiders, etc. The fourth group includes snakes that can twist and untwist themselves: to this group belongs the dragon, the largest animal on earth and the basilisk, considered to be the king of the reptiles because it can kill simply with its breath. Then comes the category of worms, born without sexual intercourse or laying eggs, which includes leeches, silkworms, lice, fleas and other bugs. Fish include all animals that swim in order to move, such as whales, dolphins, sardines, spider crabs, octopi, snails and frogs as well as amphibians such as the seal, the crocodile and the hippopotamus. The next group is made up of birds: eagles, vultures, crows, swans, bats and the mythical phoenix. In the last category are flying creatures that are much smaller than the preceding group: bees, wasps, butterflies, mosquitoes, etc.

A siren presenting a platter to a griffin. Roman wall painting, date unknown. Paris: Musée du Louvre.

Before describing the various species, St Isidore formulated a key question: why are there monsters and marvels that seem to be contrary to the laws of nature? He went on to give the following answer: 'In reality, they are not contrary to nature, because they come by the divine will, since the will of the Creator is the nature of each thing that is created.'[4]

Once the theological obstacle had been removed, the saint could take on the challenge, and he opened his repertoire of wondrous creatures with dwarfs and giants:

> There are large numbers of marvels and wondrous things; some on account of the enormous size of their bodies, which surpass the normal height of man, such as the Titan, whose body, according to Homer, measures nine yokes*; others on account of their small size, like that of a dwarf, or those whom the Greeks call Pygmies because their height is no greater than a cubit.[5]

Since monstrous beings may be found among every nation, St Isidore continued, the human race as a whole includes entire people made up of wondrous creatures. There are giants, who are ignorant of the Holy Scriptures can claim to be the offspring of a union between fallen angels and women born before the Flood. He then provides detailed descriptions of the Cynocephali, the Blemmyes (already described by Pliny), as well as the Panoti of Scythia, whose enormous ears cover their entire bodies** and the Ethiopian sciopods, endowed with a single foot of such enormous dimensions that they use it to give them shade in the summer.

St Isidore could also be sceptical at times: he declared that the story that sirens have the upper body of a beautiful young woman and the lower body of a bird (later replaced by the tail of a fish), and that they are virtuoso musicians endowed with voices of unparalleled beauty, was utter nonsense. 'What is certain is that they were loose women who brought ruin upon all passers-by, as a result of which the latter had no choice but to pretend they had been shipwrecked.' The same was true of the Gorgons: the saint noted that we cannot give credence to the story of their hair of serpents and their gaze that turned people to stone; in reality, they were three courtesans of such extraordinary beauty that one could say that their admirers 'turned to stone'.[6]

The *Etymologies* of St Isidore, the Bible, the *Physiologus* and theological writings are the sources behind the bestiaries, a new genre of

---

*1 yoke = 1 *iugerum*, a Roman unit of measurement equivalent to about 31 m.

**The Panoti, very common in medieval iconography, were not reported in America. Pigafetta described them as small men with long ears, 'no higher than a pail', living near Indonesia (p. 150).

zoological catalogue in the Middle Ages. These works were composed in order to help people come closer to God by contemplating the animal world and consisted of illustrated and descriptive repertories of real and imaginary animals. Reading them can shed light on the way medieval people viewed the world.

Bestiaries

The main precursor of the bestiaries was, in fact, the *Physiologus*. The original was written in Greek at Alexandria in the second century of our era. Over the centuries, through the many copies and successive translations, the text no doubt underwent repeated modifications. Unfortunately, the first versions have disappeared and we do not know whether they contained any illustrations. The first extant illustrated copies date from the Carolingian Era, in the ninth century. One of them, combining the classical text with extracts from the *Etymologies* by St Isidore, can be seen as the precursor of the bestiary.

At the time, only a very small part of the population was able to read, and every book was itself an object of great luxury. The bestiary was undoubtedly one of the most sophisticated forms of the art of the book. The manuscripts were prepared with great care at the best monastic *scriptoria*, where they were illuminated with fine drawings in lively colours. During the twelfth and thirteenth centuries, England produced a vast quantity of magnificent bestiaries.

Of these, manuscript Ashmole 1511 of Oxford's Bodleian Library contains one of the most famous and most beautiful medieval bestiaries. It constitutes an encyclopaedia of traditional zoological knowledge of the period, providing detailed descriptions of about 150 animals, as well as plants and minerals. It was also intended, however, as a work of Christian education, seeking to find in animal behaviour, whether real or imagined, a harmony between the Creator and the universe. The treatise begins with a description of the creation of the world according to the Bible, it devotes the central part of the work to entries on animals, and ends with a transcription of part of Book XI of the *Etymologies*: 'On man and his parts'.

We have summed up the description and symbolic interpretation of a couple of animals contained in the Ashmole text, translated into French by Marie-France Dupuis and Sylvain Louis*. These examples

*An English translation is forthcoming, edited by Christopher de Hamel, *A Spectacular Illustrated Medieval Bestiary: The Ashmole Bestiary* (Oakland, CA: Octavo Editions, forthcoming).

show how, in this period, descriptions of animal life was filled with elaborate conclusions. The first two show clearly how descriptions of the rhinoceros, unknown in Europe at the time, led people to imagine two different fantastic animals: the unicorn and the monocerus.

The unicorn, referred to as rhinoceros by the Greeks, resembles a particularly wild horse, and has a horn in the middle of its head. The only way to capture it is by the following ruse: the hunter must lead a young virgin into the woods, where the animal dwells, and leave her there alone. When the unicorn sees her, it runs toward her and lays its head on her bosom. 'Our Lord Jesus Christ is a heavenly unicorn, of whom it is said, "He was beloved like the sons of unicorns."' The fact that the unicorn has a single horn illustrates the words of Christ: 'My father and I are one.' The monocerus, on the other hand, is a veritable monster that roars ferociously. The size of a horse, it has feet like an elephant and the tail of a stag. On its forehead it has a horn four feet in length. Though it is possible to kill it, it is impossible to capture it.

The elephant knows no carnal lust. It eats with a trunk that resembles a serpent, and protects itself with its ivory tusks. It is impossible to find another animal of similar height. The Persians and the Indians place wooden towers on its shoulders, from whence they shoot at their enemies. Elephants live 300 years, are highly intelligent and have excellent memories. They move in herds, flee rats and mate back to back. The female carries its young for two years and can give birth only once. When the male wishes to mate, it goes off with the female towards the Orient, near Paradise, where the tree known as the mandrake grows. The female eats of the tree first, then with great urgency offers some to her male partner; the latter eats as well and then impregnates the female. When the time comes to give birth, the female wades into a pond while the male stands guard,protecting her from dragons; if a snake should appear, he tramples it to death. If an elephant falls, it is unable to get up again since it does not have knee joints. A large elephant will try to lift it up, then two, and then a dozen will try in vain to help him up; finally, a small elephant arrives and with its trunk sets the old elephant back on its feet. These animals represent Adam and Eve: before they had eaten of the fruit of the tree of knowledge (the mandrake) they did not mate, but after the dragon came to urge them to rebel against God, they were banished from Eden and, as the Scriptures say, 'Eve gave birth to Cain on the waters of

guilt.' The great elephant that appears to save them signifies the
king of the Jews, the twelve elephants that appear next are the
prophets, and finally, the small elephant naturally represents
Jesus Christ.

The beaver is endowed with testicles that are effective remedies
against numerous diseases. If a hunter pursues it, the beaver bites
them off and throws them at the hunter. But later, if the same
beaver is once again pursued, it stands on its hind legs and shows its
mutilated body so that he might be left in peace. Likewise, every
man who wishes to live in purity must rid himself of his vices and
flaws and throw them in the face of the devil. The animal is called
beaver (castor) because of the castration it inflicts upon itself.

The phoenix is a bird of Arabia, purple in colour, of which there is but
a single example in the whole world. It lives 500 years, and when it
feels old age coming on it gathers sweetly scented kindling and builds
a pyre; turning toward the sun, it flaps its wings to light the fire and
immolates itself. This bird symbolizes Jesus Christ, who said: 'I lay
down my life, that I may take it again.' In the Old as in the New
Testaments, the Saviour came down from heaven spreading his wings
with sweet perfumes and offered himself up for us to the God the
Father on the altar of the Cross, and then rose again on the third day*.

In spite of their lack of rigour, the bestiaries served as instruments
of knowledge about the animal kingdom during the twelfth, thirteenth and part of the fourteenth centuries. As the age of discovery
approached, new works on the earth and the creatures who dwell on
it set aside religious interpretations, but they continued to use the
same sources of information: the Greek, Latin and medieval texts.

Therefore, belief in wondrous animals and humans not only survived but in some cases was further reinforced.

THE ENDURING LEGACY OF WONDROUS CREATURES

Pierre d'Ailly, the eminent Chancellor of the Sorbonne and the
author of the *Ymago mundi*, accorded great importance to describing

---

*The legend of the phoenix reflects a cyclical view of world history. Responding to
a cosmic clock, the bird immolates itself and is reborn when the planets return to
their starting point to start anew their perpetual movement, and the ancients
believed that once the astronomical cycle was completed, history would repeat
itself, since the influence of the planets was repeated.

animals that lived in distant lands. His work consisted in bringing together in one volume the information that appeared in other books that were considered to be the summits of knowledge. The result was not some sort of crude exaltation of the divine, like the bestiaries, but a summary of the social, geographical, botanical and zoological knowledge available at the time.

Columbus considered this book an invaluable tool. Reading the authors who had provided information about the planet, such as Strabo, Ctesias, Pliny, Pomponius, Marinus of Tyre, Alfraganus, Aristotle, Seneca, Solinus, Plutarch, Eratosthenes, Marco Polo, Mandeville and Ptolemy, as well as saints Augustine, Ambrose, Isidore and Thomas Aquinas, represented a formidable task. We know that he had studied some of their writings, but he knew most of them through the compilations of d'Ailly and Pope Pius II. In these works, entries could be found on the wondrous creatures one could expect to encounter in the Orient.

Ymago Mundi	Notes by Columbus
Ethiopia…reaches from the Atlas mountains on the west to the confines the east. On of Egypt on the south, it is bounded by the ocean, on the north by the Nile River; having many tribes of diverse features, and monstrous appearance, and filled with multitudes of wild animals and serpents. In fact the rhinoceros beast, the camelopard (giraffe), the basilisk and huge dragons from whose heads gems are extracted, are found there. Also the hyacinth, the Chrysoprase (Crisoprallus) and the cinnamon tree.	*Atlas mountains* *The Nile* *Men with monstrous features and horrible appearance* *Land filled with wild animals and serpents* *The rhinoceros, the camelopard, the basilisk, the dragons from which gems are extracted.*[7]

d'Ailly mentioned other legendary beings: the Macrobians, giants of twelve cubits (5–6 m) who fought the griffins at the sources of the Ganges; people who live on nothing but the odour of fruit; women whogive birth only once in their lives to white children who become black as they grow older; others whose sons live only eight years. In the Hyperborean mountains, the temperature is so temperate and human life is so long that its inhabitants die only of suicide when they are tired of living. The extreme regions, with their great frost or extreme heat, are inhabited by human monsters with hideous features, feed on human flesh. All in all, it is difficult to determine whether these are men or beasts. The Admiral took note of all this.

This work and many others preserved the old, well-nigh universal myths such as those of the phoenix and dragon, the ancient representations of half-animal, half-human divinities such as harpies and sirens, and other beings composed of different animals, such as griffins, or with unusual features, such as the unicorn and the Cyclops. Basilisks and Cynocephali seemed to be based on the descriptions of real but largely unknown animals such as certain reptiles and monkeys.

IMAGINARY CREATURES IN THE AGE OF DISCOVERY

In America, these myths were short-lived. The conquistadors, having crossed the Atlantic Ocean, expected to see gigantic creatures, but with the sole exception of the large snakes of the Amazon basin, they did not encounter any animal that significantly exceeded in size those they were familiar with. They did find some new animals in the water, such as sea wolves and manatees; on land, such as the llama, the vicuna, the alpaca (a llama with a hump, also known as Peruvian sheep), the armadillo, the tapir and the iguana; and in the air, such as the quetzal, the hummingbird and the parrot; the latter became a veritable publicity tool with which Columbus would try to sell his discovery. None of these creatures, however, was either horrible or harmful. The inoffensive iguana was taken to be a dragon on account of its appearance, but it soon became a favoured dish in Creole cuisine.

Nonetheless, it was with a certain degree of frustration that Europeans acknowledged that the beings in which they had believed for centuries did not exist. The accounts of those who returned from the West Indies were expected to contain descriptions of marvels, in the absence of which the writings found only a scant audience. This tendency was noted and criticized by a most unusual person named Francisco de Enzinas (a name he would Hellenize as Dryander), a Spanish Protestant, friend of Melanchthon and renowned Hellenist. In a letter dated 1556 he wrote: 'The vagabonds with their foolishness and all their inventions of imaginary things are responsible for the fact that no one listens to the accounts even of people who are honest and have returned from distant lands.'[8]

Often imagination made up for the lack of monsters. In 1714, the work by the Frenchman Louis Feuillé that claimed to be scientific, an engraving shows the Monster of Buenos Aires, a robust bull of great size, with pointy ears, a small horn, almost feminine lips and the features of a Cyclops, since it had but one eye. The legend that accompanies the image reveals the true identity beneath the exaggeration: the creature was the foetus of a stillborn calf.[9]

The age of exploration saw the reconnaissance of hitherto unknown regions, places where the imagination had located extraordinary beings. Some of these were in the area that came to be known, through Columbus's error, as the 'West Indies', while others were discovered around India proper. What were these legendary creatures that haunted the imaginations of the conquistadors?

The Monsters of the Skies

Undoubtedly the most popular of the winged monsters was the griffin, believed to be half-lion, half-bird. Sir John de Mandeville describes it thus, in Chapter 85 of his fantastic voyages:

> In that country (Bacharia) be many griffins, more plenty than in any other country. Some men say that they have the body upward as an eagle and beneath as a lion; and truly they say sooth, that they be of that shape. But one griffin hath a body more great and is more strong than eight lions, of such lions as be on this half, and more great and stronger than an hundred eagles such as we have amongst us. For one griffin there will bear, flying to his nest, a great horse, if he may find him at the point, or two oxen yoked together as they go at the plough. For he hath his talons so long and so large and great upon his feet, as though they were horns of great oxen or of bugles or of kine, so that men make cups from them to drink of. And of their ribs and of the pens of their wings, men make bows, full strong, to shoot with arrows and quarrels.[10]

Representations of the griffin varied little among Mesopotamian, Egyptian, Classical and European artistic traditions. The great birds also appeared in some versions of the *Alexander Romance*. As guardians of the realms of gold and precious stone, they patrol the skies and swoop down on those who dare disturb the peace of these mysterious lands. According to Cardinal d'Ailly, a large part of the Scythians' lands was uninhabited 'because, although abounding in gold and precious stones, it is inaccessible to humans because of the griffins. There one may find emeralds in great quantities and the purest of crystals.' Columbus made note of the abundance of gold, diamonds, emeralds and pure crystal, but remained silent about the griffins.[11]

It was logical for the mythical guardian of treasures to protect the lands, where it was hoped there was gold in abundance. In 1494, a party that had set off to explore the interior of Cuba beat a hasty retreat, terrified at having encountered what they thought to be the traces of a griffin.[12] Eight years later, during Columbus's last voyage, his son noted that the expedition had put into a port in Cuba that the Indians called Huiva. 'When we went ashore, we found that the people here lived in the tops of trees, like birds... We could not learn the reason for this strange custom but judged that it was caused by their fear of the griffins that inhabit that country or of their enemies.'[13] A half-century later, in Mexico, Friar Toribio Motolinia recounted how he had been informed of the presence of griffins that lived at four or five leagues from Tehuacan and came down to a valley known as Auacatlan, which was gradually abandoned on account of their attacks. But all the friar himself could see was a wild cat, 'the griffins having disappeared in the last 80 years, so that no one remembers them any longer.'[14]

Oviedo, the first chronicler of the Indies, wrote of having seen a type of griffin in Peru, but without any of its terrifying characteristics. Its upper body was covered with grey feathers, while the other half was covered in bare skin, the colour of vermilion. It was very gentle and friendly, he affirmed, and a little larger than a pigeon. He speculated that it looked like the offspring of a bird that had mated with a cat, although it was more likely a natural species like that of the griffin.[15] A modest American epilogue to the horrifying wild animals that were believed to guard the treasures of Paradise!

Related to the Greek griffin as well as to the Iranian simurgh and the Indian garuda, the gigantic rokh bird owed its fame to an episode in the *Arabian Nights*. Sindbad, the sailor tied himself with his turban to the rokh's enormous leg, and the bird flew off and left him in a canyon inaccessible to human beings and filled with both diamonds and serpents. The merchants of the region managed to get hold of the jewels by means of the following strategy: from the edge of the canyon they threw large pieces of mutton, whereupon the rokh or a couple of white eagles descended, seized it with their talons and flew with them to the nearby high mountains. The men proceeded to frighten them by pelting them with stones, and in this way managed to catch a few diamonds encrusted in the remains of the pieces of meat.

Strangely enough, the same story figures in Marco Polo, who claims that on the island of Madagascar:

The (boats) come so fast (to this island) that it is a wonder...because the current goes all day toward midday...many very terrible grifon birds are found there… But I tell you that I Marco, when I first heard this told, thought that those birds were grifons, and asked those who said they had seen them, and those who had seen them asserted most constantly that they had no likeness of a beast in any part, but have only two feet like birds, and (they say) that it is made all exactly like an eagle in shape, but they say that it is immeasurably great… They say that it is so great and so strong that one of these birds, without the help of another bird, seizes the elephant with its talons and carries it off quite high in the air and kills it, and then it lets it drop to the ground so that the elephant is all broken to pieces, and then the grifon bird comes down upon the elephant and mounts up on it and tears it and eats it and feeds itself upon it at its will. Those who have seen them say also that some of them are so large that its wings open more than thirty paces from one side to the other and that its wing feathers are twelve paces long, and they are very thick as is suitable to their length.

The similarities between this description and that of the *Arabian Nights* do not end there. Chapter XXIX of Marco Polo's *Travels* is entitled 'On the kingdom of Murfili and how diamonds are found there'. In this land, the Venetian tells us, there is a valley filled with diamonds and surrounded by sharp rocks that make it impassable for human beings. Those who wish to collect the precious stones throw pieces of meat in the valley, and these often fall on the diamonds. A white eagle that lives in the area swoops down on the meat and takes it up to the rocky mountaintops or into the valley to devour. In the first case, the men chase the predator and find diamonds stuck to the pieces of meat; in the second, they collect the stones from the eagle's excrement.

This passage shows that Marco Polo knew of and believed in the legend that had inspired Sindbad's adventure. Three centuries later, Christopher Columbus would note in his copy of Marco Polo's book: 'birds', 'feathers about twelve paces long', 'seizing an elephant', 'where diamonds are found', 'white eagles'.[16]

Sindbad, the sailor was not the only human being, however, to enjoy the privilege of flying attached to the giant bird's feet; the same thing happened to a simple inhabitant of the Far East, if we are to believe the account of Antonio Pigafetta. He had been told that in Java or near the Gulf of China there is a colossal tree, where giant birds called garudas make their nests:

No junk or other boat can approach to within three or four leagues of the place of the tree, because of the great whirlpools in the water round about it. The first time that anything was learned of that tree was (from) a junk which was driven by the winds into the whirlpool. The junk having been beaten to pieces, all the crew were drowned except a little boy, who, having been tied to a plank, was miraculously driven near that tree. He climbed up the tree without being discovered, where he hid under the wing of one of those birds. Next day, the bird having gone ashore and having seized a buffalo, the boy came out from under the wing as best he could... The story was learned from him.[17]

The dragon appears as the king of the legendary animals, just as the lion is the king of the real ones. Its name comes from the Latin term *draco* (which in turn derives from the Greek *drakôn*) given to large serpents. It can also be used to designate imaginary animals that are both terrible and insatiable, against which legendary heroes or Gods have fought and that appear in all cultures of the world, from the Chinese civilization, where they are called lung, through the *Leviathan* of the Old Testament to the serpents *fafnir* and *midgard* of Germanic mythology. Generally speaking it is represented as a winged serpent, although its meaning is not always the same: the Chinese lung evokes the 'yang', the masculine forces of nature, and is associated with authority and knowledge; by contrast, the Leviathan is an image of the forces of evil opposed to the divine order.

In the West, it was the eloquent description of the biblical Leviathan that served as the archetype for the image of the dragon*.

---

*'His back is made of rows of shields, shut up closely as with a seal. One is so near to another that no air can come between them. They are joined one to another; they clasp each other and cannot be separated. His sneezings flash forth light, and his eyes are like the eyelids of the dawn. Out of his mouth go flaming torches; sparks of fire leap forth. Out of his nostrils comes forth smoke, as from a boiling pot and burning rushes. His breath kindles coals, and a flame comes forth from his mouth. In his neck abides strength, and terror dances before him. The folds of his flesh cleave together, firmly cast upon him and immovable. His heart is hard as a stone, hard as the nether millstone. When he raises himself up the mighty are afraid; at the crashing they are beside themselves. Though the sword reaches him, it does not avail; nor the spear, the dart, or the javelin. He counts iron as straw, and bronze as rotten wood. The arrow cannot make him flee; for him slingstones are turned to stubble. Clubs are counted as stubble; he laughs at the rattle of javelins. His underparts are like sharp potsherds; he spreads himself like a threshing sledge on the mire. He makes the deep boil like a pot; he makes the sea like a pot of ointment. Behind him he leaves a shining wake; one would think the deep to be hoary. Upon earth there is not his like, a creature without fear. He beholds everything that is high; he is king over all the sons of pride.' (Job 41.15–34)

The iconography of this monster was particularly prolific. The lower part of the body is often that of a serpent, complete with wings, claws, tongues of fire and often multiple heads. The animal can walk, swim and fly. Only a few chosen ones, such as St George, St Michael and romantic knights were able to defeat this symbol of absolute evil.

In America, the peaceful iguanas elicited an exalted lyricism on the part of their European observers. For Vespucci, these were serpents of terrifying appearance; Las Casas described its dorsal crest as like a hill running from its nose to its tail, while Oviedo compared it to dragons. They captured a few of them but refused to eat them. They noted with great astonishment that the Indians ate them roasted. Eventually, the iguanas lost their reputation as monsters and were gradually introduced into Spanish cuisine, which in turn gave rise to a different sort of problem: religious prohibitions required that they determine whether its flesh was meat or fish. Various answers were given, some identifying it with terrestrial animals and others with marine beasts, the latter being on the menu for fridays.[18]

There is another, fairly common monster of the air, the basilisk, generally represented with the feet of a chicken, the tail of a serpent and the head of a rooster with its crest. Its constant characteristics were a death-dealing breath and a murderous glance.[19] No one knew how it had crossed the ocean, but it appears in some popular American traditions.

Monsters of the Deep

The sailors who travelled in the newly discovered regions were prone to panic when they thought they saw giant monsters rise from the ocean that were capable of devouring entire crews. The Greeks had already feared the attacks of Charybdis and Scylla, which entrapped ships plying the Strait of Messina*.

For the Middle Ages and the age of exploration it is difficult to distinguish specific sea monsters with their own traditions and names, but the iconography is extremely rich in terrifying images. The fastitocalon is one exception: an Anglo-Saxon bestiary describes it as a powerful whale shaped like a rock as rough as if it were covered with sand. This made it very dangerous, for the sailors would tie up their ship to it and light a fire, mistaking it for an island; the

---

*Scylla was once a beautiful woman who, through the caprice of the Gods, was transformed into a monster 12 feet tall and endowed with six heads, each with three rows of teeth. Charybdis produced whirlpools three times a day.

fastitocalon then submerged itself underwater, dragging all the sailors who happened to be on its back down to the depths. This creature may be found in the *Arabian Nights* and resembles the great fish Jasconius from the story of St Brendan[20]

Moreover, Cardinal d'Ailly insisted that there were snakes so large that they could cross the ocean, such as eels 300 feet long (about 100 m), and crustaceans with feet so long that they could strangle an elephant*.[21]

All sea monsters were not equally terrifying, at least in appearance. Thus, the charming siren, harmless as it may appear to us today, was then considered a fearsome monster descended from the ghastly harpies. Both of these appear to be relics of the representation of the soul in ancient Egypt: a bird with the head of a woman. The harpies intervened in an episode of the legend of the Argonauts: having devastated Thrace, they were chased by two Argonauts and were forced to flee to a cave in Crete, where they and their pursuers ended up dying of hunger.

The Cuban novelist and historian Alejo Carpentier, in his story *The Road to Santiago*, includes a poem about the end of the last harpy. In the dazzling city of Seville, at the time when galleons were returning laden with gold, minstrels accompanying themselves on vihuelas** sang of the miraculous tale of the American harpy, a terrifying monster who returned to its land of origin to die there like its ancestors:

> *For an enormous sum*
> *A European bought her,*
> *With him she went to Europe,*
> *He landed her at Malta*
> *From there he went to Greece,*
> *Thence to Constantinople,*
> *The whole of Thrace exploring.*
> *Twas there she first refused*

*These examples, along with others, are found in the writings of a Swedish historian and geographer, Olaüs Magnus, entitled *Historia de gentibus septentrion-alibus* (History of the Northern People) (1555): it is illustrated with an engraving showing an enormous serpent holding in its mouth an unfortunate sailor, and another with a fish, equally large, is devouring a ship in one gulp. An assortment of impressive animals that gave the navigator's nightmares appear in *Cosmographia universalis* by Sebastian Münster (1554), where whales and giant crustaceans terrorise the poor sailors.

**A vihuela is a plucked string instrument like a guitar that was very popular in the sixteenth century.

The food they set before her,
And in a few brief weeks
She died raging and roaring.

CHORUS: That was the end of the Harpy
Monster most grim on earth
Oh that all such monsters
Might die at birth![22]

Originally, the sirens resembled harpies, but as time went by, their appearance changed. They lived on the island of Anthemoessa, where they sang such melodious songs that the navigators came closer to hear them better, until their ships capsized on the reefs. According to Greek tradition, only two heroes, Ulysses and Jason, succeeded in escaping this terrible fate*.

When Homer describes the episode of the sirens in the *Odyssey*, he does not mention their physical appearance. The medieval bestiaries describe them as bird-women, but also as mermaids or snake-women. This metamorphosis may be explained by confusion between sirens and the Greek Nereids, often represented as mermaids. In Europe, the latter model prevailed under the influence of local popular beliefs. In the Germanic legends, the terms *Meerweif, Meerfrau, Meermin, Seewaif, Wasserjungfer*, etc. referred to very beautiful women of the sea endowed with large bosoms. The chivalric romances exalted the image of the beautiful *Mélusine*, half-woman and half-serpent, the mother of great lineages of peasants and nobles, and guardian of the forest.[23]

On his first voyage to America, Christopher Columbus claimed to have seen the three sirens, but was a bit disappointed by their appearance: at the end of the day, as the Admiral was going towards the Río de Oro, 'he reported seeing three sirens, showing fully out of the sea, but they were not as beautiful as they are painted, and in some way they had manshaped faces.' He says, he has seen them on other occasions as well, for instance in Guinea on the shores of the Manegueta.[24] He is probably referring to manatees, a type of sea mammal that bears some resemblance to human beings, and the females of which have two teats on their chests.

---

*Ulysses made his oarsmen plug their ears with wax, while he attached himself to the mast in order to be able to listen with impunity to the songs of the sirens. As for Jason and the Argonauts, they were unaware of the fatal power of the sirens; when the sailors, enchanted by the marvellous melodies, were heading for perdition, Orpheus took out his lyre and began to intone even sweeter songs, thus, saving the navigators.

Monsters that Lurk on Land

The *Acephali*, having no heads but mouth and eyes in the middle of their chests, were among the favourite creatures of European imagination for more than a millennium. For Marc Bouyer, author of *América fantástica*, they were 'the symbol of spiritual functions that had sunk to the level of the belly, or the genitals.'[25] According to the popular beliefs of Northern Europe, they symbolized the return of the dead; in a sense they were living cadavers. Pliny called them Blemmyes and situated them in Africa. They received a place of honour in the medieval imagination when a work falsely attributed to the great St Augustine reported a strange piece of information: 'When I was bishop of Hippo I went to Ethiopia with some Christian slaves to teach the Gospel of Christ. We saw many men and women who had no heads, but their eyes were in the middle of their chests; otherwise, the rest of their bodies were like ours.' Such an affirmation by one of the greatest doctrinal authorities of the Christian Church constituted irrefutable 'proof' of the existence of the Acephali. Thenceforth, they became members of the earthly city.[26]

In *Alexander Romance*, they appear on the list of 22 unclean people. Medieval iconography produced several representations of the battles by Alexander's armies against the Acephali and the Cynocephali. St Isidore placed them in Libya. Cardinal d'Ailly tried to present them in a manner befitting their nefarious reputation: he wrote that they have eyes on their shoulders, a sort of nose and mouth consisting of two holes in their chests, and their bodies are covered in pigskin.[27]

Around 1600, the myth crossed the Atlantic: while old beliefs about the existence of headless people in Africa and Asia waned, the New World saw the appearance of the tribe of the Ewaipanomas. Walter Raleigh, in his prodigious account of the riches of El Dorado, claims to have heard of a nation of Acephali living in the vicinity of the empire of Guiana. He says, he learned that near the Orinoco there are two other rivers, the Atoica and the Caora:

> On that branch which is called Caura are a nation of people whose heads appear not above their shoulders; which though it may be thought a mere fable, yet for my own part I am resolved it is true, because every child in the provinces of Aromaia and Canuri affirm the same. They are called Ewaipanoma; they are reported to have their eyes in their shoulders, and their mouths in the middle of their breasts, and that a long train of hair growth backward between their shoulders. The son of Topiawari, which I brought with me to England, told me that they were the most mighty

men of all the land, and use bows, arrows and clubs thrice as big as any of
Guiana, or of the Orenoqueponi; and that one of the Iwarawaqueri took
a prisoner of them the year before our arrival there, and brought him into
the borders of Aromaia, his father's country. And farther, when I seemed
to doubt of it, he told me that it was no wonder among them; but that
they was as great a nation and as common as any other in all the
provinces, and had of late years slain many hundreds of his father's
people, and of other nations their neighbours. But there was no chance to
hear of them till I came; and if I had but spoken one word of it while I
was there I might have brought one of them with me to put the matter
out of doubt... When I came to Cumana in the West Indies, afterwards
by chance I spoke with a Spaniard dwelling not far from there, a man of
great travel. And, after he knew that I had been in Guiana, and so far
directly west as Caroli, the first question he asked me was, whether I had
seen any of the Ewaipanoma, which are those without heads.

If Raleigh's descriptions seem strange, so too are the comments of his
French editor in 1722, more than a century after the buccaneer's voyages. Though he did not call into question the existence of a nation of
headless men, he strove to find a rational explanation for the myth. In
a marginal note we read: 'It appears that these People have very short
necks, and perhaps also very high shoulders. Either nature made
them thus, or art and industry intervened in some way. The tastes of
these distant nations are very bizarre compared to ours; they often
consider beautiful that which to us seems horrible.'[28]
    As late as the beginning of the twentieth century, belief in these
headless people had not disappeared completely. Alexander von
Humboldt gathered testimonies of the existence of a race of Acephali.
    A few missionaries assured him that there was a nation of people
with 'their mouths in their navels' known as the Rayas, who lived in
the woods near the Sinapo River, a tributary of the Oronoco near the
border between Colombia and Venezuela. Moreover, an old cannibal
told him, he had seen these Acephali with his own eyes. Astonished,
Humboldt remarked that in these parts it was impossible to doubt the
truth of these stories. In fact, he said, even the strangest products of
the imagination have some analogy with the appearance and form of
nature's creations. Therefore, it was logical that the inventions of the
ancient geographers should shift from one hemisphere to the other.[29]
    His comments were judicious. The legend of the Acephali was
born before our era. Eminent Greek and Roman authors, and later
the theologians of the Middle Ages, confirmed their existence. They
immigrated to America and settled near El Dorado, and proofs of

their existence were being adduced until the last century. Hence they lived for more than two millennia in the human imagination.

Close relatives to the Acephali, the unipeds or sciopods were beings with only one leg and a foot so large that it could be used to provide shade when they were resting. Pliny, St Augustine and St Isidore attest to their existence.[30] They were said to be able to hop so high and so fast both on land and on water that no one can catch them. A strange uniped, perhaps the only one ever encountered in America, allegedly appeared during the Vikings' stay in Newfoundland: the saga of Eric, the Red recounts how one morning the uniped flung an arrow at Thorvald, son of Eric, who died of the wound shortly thereafter. His companions chased the uniped but were unable to catch it.[31]

Although probably based on distorted reports about very large monkeys, accounts of satyrs and other men with tails inspired the image of the devil in Christian iconography. Even Ptolemy had spoken of three islands populated by satyrs: creatures with baldheads, long, pointy ears and little horns. They had goats' feet and a little tail. Known for their lasciviousness, when they were not indulging in orgies they spent their time in pursuit of nymphs. They frightened the livestock and solitary travellers. According to Pliny, they walked sometimes on two and sometimes on four feet. Marco Polo said that on the island of Java Minor there were people whose tails were a palm in length.

These traditions no doubt influenced Columbus. In the account of his first voyage, he noted that there were two provinces on Hispaniola that remained unexplored, 'one of them called Auan, where people are born with tails.' Then, on his second voyage, he was told that in a region of Cuba 'all the inhabitants have tails'.[32] A century and a half later, an illustration published in *Historia del Reyno de Chile* (History of the Kingdom of Chile) by the Jesuit Alonso de Ovalle shows men with tails living in the southern regions.

As for the Cyclops and the Cynocephali, they were imaginary beings of the first order. Like the Acephali, they originated in Antiquity*, appeared in several medieval bestiaries, and after the conquest, were reportedly seen in America. According to the most recent

---

*It is possible that the myth comes from the name given to one of the most despised castes of India, who lived along the shores of the Indus. They hunted with the help of numerous dogs; for this reason, the Brahmins referred to them pejoratively as 'dog-men'. (This explanation is found in Gil, p. 30 and Mode, p. 230.). It is also possible that the Europeans' image of the Cynocephalus was based on a description of a type of monkey.

archaeological findings, the first known representation of a Cyclops was found in ancient Mesopotamia. In Greek mythology, the role of the Cyclops was to forge Zeus's thunderbolts.

The most famous Cyclops was the unfortunate Polyphemus, blinded by Ulysses. They were often represented as giants, with a single eye in the middle of their forehead, dog-like ears and hairy chest. The Cynocephali were sometimes shown with two of the important characteristics of the Cyclops: giant stature and a single eye. It was in this form that they were seen in the New World.

Claudius Elianus, a late second-century philosopher and the author of a treatise *De natura animalium* (On the Nature of Animals), provides perhaps the first compete description of the Cynocephali, calling them honest and harmless creatures:

> In the same region of India, where the scarabs dwell, we find beings known as "cynocephali", whose name comes from the appearance and nature of their heads, since the rest of their members appear human. They are covered with animal hair, are righteous and harm no one. They do not speak but emit guttural sounds, although they understand the native language. They eat the flesh of wild beasts, which they hunt with great ease, for they are quick and kill them when they get close. They do not roast their meat on a fire but cut it to slices and dry it in the heat of the sun. They raise goats and sheep. They also eat the flesh of repulsive animals and drink the milk of the livestock that they tend.[33]

Pliny located them in Ethiopia, but provided no further commentary.[34] The three itinerant monks who reached the edge of Paradise (see Chapter One) found there a nation of Cynocephali.[35] However, the general perception of the dog-headed men as harmless would not last. Their ferocious appearance suggested cannibalism. The *Alexander Romance* classified them, along with the Acephali, among the 22 unclean people.[36] The same Emperor Alexander, after having found the land of the Amazons, withdrew to the Red Sea, where there were 'men with the heads of dogs and others with no heads...'[37] In St Isidore's classification they figured among the 'wild animals'. The Ashmolean bestiary lists them as a species of monkey.[38]

The reputation of the 'dog-headed' creatures was such that they found their way into most of the travel narratives by those who had visited the Far East. The Franciscan missionary Juan de Pian de Carpino reported seeing them on his visit to the court of the Great Khan in 1246. The Arab geographer Ibn Batuta declared in 1356 that he had seen them in the land of the Barahnakar. Marco Polo situated them in the Andaman Islands (1298). Another itinerant Franciscan, Odorico de Pordenone placed them on the island of Nicuneman (1327). According to the fantasist John de Mandeville they dwelt on the island of Necumeran, where they were part of the retinue of the king of Ceylon, owner of a fabulous ruby.[39] Cardinal d'Ailly reported that in India there are people who 'have the heads of dogs and the skin of animals. They bark like dogs', while others 'have but one eye, and are called Carismaspi'.[40] Even Behaim, a contemporary of Columbus, notes on his globe: 'Island of Ceylon... Here John de Mandeville found an island whose inhabitants had the heads of dogs.' These reports could not escape the attention of the Admiral of the Ocean Sea. His sources of information were official: in the far corners of the Orient there were dog-headed creatures and Cyclops. He considered it not only possible but also probable that he would run into them in the territories he would discover. These two categories of monsters would blend into one when he began to hear reports of the cruel cannibals.

Less than a month after his arrival in the New World, while his three caravels were exploring the northeastern coast of Cuba, Columbus questioned the Indians about the nature of these territories and understood them to say that there were Cynocephali and Cyclops terrorizing the local Indians: 'Far from there lived a group of one-eyed people and others with dog-heads who ate human flesh, and who, having captured one (Indian), cut his throat, drank his blood and cut off his genitals.'[41]

Three weeks later, however, still in the same region, the Admiral would call into question his certainty about the Cynocephali and advance his own interpretation of the cannibals. 'Everyone I have met so far has said he is very frightened of the *Caniba* or *Canina* who live in this island of Bohío (Haiti), which is very extensive.' When the expedition headed in the direction of Bohío, he noted the terror among his Indian guides, 'who were so afraid of being eaten that they were speechless' and it was impossible to reassure them; moreover, they said that (the cannibals) 'had only one eye on the forehead and the head of a dog'.[42] According to this account, Cyclops, Cynocephali and cannibals evidently refer to one and the same people.

Columbus thought that they were exaggerating, however, and advanced a different explanation, one that allowed him to demonstrate the success of his venture. Indeed, he asserted, this story simply confirms that the empire of the Great Khan – the objective of his voyage – is very near. Naturally, the ships of that powerful empire would occasionally visit these peripheries and take a few prisoners.

A well-dressed sciopod.

Since no one saw them return, it was easy to imagine that they had been devoured. Phonetics and etymology also helped him make his case: how could the word *caniba* or *canina* (cannibal), used by the Indians to designated these people, be anything but a derivative of Can (Khan), the title of the great emperor of China?

The history of America would testify to still other extraordinary people. During one of his expeditions, Sarmiento de Gamboa – who also described the Paitití and was shipwrecked in the Strait of Magellan – captured an Indian who was so large that he was thought to be a Cyclops, if we are to believe Bartolomé Leonardo de Argensola, historian of the first, unsuccessful attempts to station a garrison in the southern part of the continent. The Patagonian giants would so inflame the imagination of Europe that they merit a chapter unto themselves.

CHAPTER 8:

The Patagonian Giants

Many nations have preserved traditions according to which, in some remote corner, there once lived people of colossal proportions, believed perhaps to be vestiges from the time when the gods created the world. This belief seemed to be confirmed when Magellan's ships discovered individuals of great stature on the southern pampas. For three centuries, Europe would be convinced that somewhere in America there was a race of giants.

> Just as in every nation there are some monstrous men, so in the
> entirety of the human race there are certain monstrous people such as
> the giants, the *Cynocephali*, the Cyclops and others.[1]
>
> *St Isidore of Seville, Etymologies*

GIANTS AT THE DAWN OF TIME

According to certain oriental myths, the first human beings were giants; this tradition also appears in some of the founding myths of the Hellenic world and in a few episodes of the Old Testament.

The Greeks believed that at the beginning of time the world was ruled by Titans, a race of people of gigantesque stature born of the union of Uranus and Gaia. Their reign was interrupted by a terrible war with the Gods on Olympus; the giants were defeated and hurled down to the unfathomable depths, where eternal darkness reigned. Only Atlas remained on the surface of the earth, but he was condemned to carry on his shoulders the weight of the heavens. Another famous giant was Antaeus, son of Poseidon and Gaia, who attacked anyone who tried to enter Libya until Heracles finally killed him.

Similar traditions are found in the Bible as well, where two races of giants appear: one that lived on the earth before the Flood, and the other that lived on the land destined for Moses' people. The antediluvian giants are mentioned in the first and last books of the Hebrew Bible: 'The Nephilim were on the earth in those days, and also afterward, when the sons of God came in to the daughters of men, and they bore children to them. These were the mighty men that were of old, the men of renown.' (Genesis 6.4) In the Book of Wisdom, we read: 'For even in the beginning, when arrogant giants were perishing, the hope of the world took refuge on a raft, and guided by thy hand left to the world the seed of a new generation.' (Wisdom 14.6)

Giants who were the enemies of the Hebrews appear frequently in the Old Testament: when Moses glimpsed the Promised Land, he hesitated to take possession of it, for 'there we saw the Nephilim (the sons of Anak, who come from the Nephilim; and we seemed to ourselves like grasshoppers, and so we seemed to them.' (Numbers 13.33) God Himself explained to Moses, shortly before the Israelites crossed the Jordan, that this land had been granted to the sons of Lot: 'That also is known as a land of Rephaim; Rephaim formerly lived there, but the Ammonites call them Zamzummim, a people great and many, and tall as the Anakim; but the Lord destroyed them before them, and they dispossessed them, and settled in their stead.' (Deuteronomy 2.20–1) The prophet Baruch also evokes this dispute: 'The giants were born there, who were famous of old, great in stature, expert in war. God did not choose them, nor give them the way to knowledge.' (Bar. 3.26–7) And let us not forget the famous giant Goliath, killed by the young David.

This tradition would spread far beyond the boundaries of biblical and Hellenic culture. Thus, Marco Polo spoke of an island of giants not far from that of the *Cynocephali*; they are tall – he tells us – but especially fat; they can lift the weight of four men and eat like five. The indigenous people of America prior to 1492 had similar myths. The chroniclers who described the Inca Empire noted the existence of a tradition that giants had arrived on rafts made of reeds: perhaps a recollection of ancient invasions by Polynesian navigators?[2]

The belief in the gigantesque stature of the first generation of humans had a certain logic. The creation of the earth, the sea, the sky and the beings who populated them must have been a gargantuan task; therefore, those who in some way or other participated in it, or who were simply alive at the time, must also have been enormous, endowed with great physical and spiritual strength and a stature worthy of the greatness of the era and of the works performed in those days.

This, at any rate, is how the matter was understood by a certain Henrion, who in 1718 presented to the French *Académie des Inscriptions et des Belles Lettres* a chronological table of the height of human beings through history, from the Creation to the birth of Christ. Adam was no less than 123 feet 9 ¾ inches tall, or nearly 40 m; Noah had lost 20 feet in comparison to his predecessor; Abraham was only 26 feet tall (8.40 m), Moses 13 (4.20 m), Heracles 10 (3.25 m), Alexander 6 (1.95 m) and Julius Caesar scarcely reached five feet. Fortunately, Henrion went on, Providence has halted this extraordinary shrinkage, otherwise we would soon have to be classified among the insects![3]

The discovery of fossilized skeletons of prehistoric animals – at a time when palaeontology did not yet exist – seemed to corroborate the existence of giants. Herodotus recalled that the skeleton of Orestes had been found to measure more than 12 feet; according to Plutarch, a certain Sertorius had the cadaver of the giant Antaeus exhumed at Tangiers, and found his height to be 60 cubits (approx. 30 m), while Pliny attributed 46 cubits (approx. 23 m) to the skeleton of Orion.[4]

In the imaginations of many Europeans, this idea that races of giants might still dwell in some distant corner of the planet survived in latent form. The discovery of America would awaken this reminiscence in spectacular fashion.

THE FIRST AMERICAN GIANTS

It is to Peter Martyr that we owe one of the first mentions of this type of human being, when he mentions, in his seventh *Decade*, the giant Datha, together with his wife and five children, who reigned over the province of Duhare in Florida.

The first contact with a population of unusually tall stature, however, would be made by Amerigo Vespucci. Like Columbus, he made four voyages: during the second of these he made landfall in the New World on the coast of Brazil, and from there sailed north. His meeting with 'giants' took place in 1499, on an island that might be present-day Curaçao, in the Netherlands Antilles. While the sailors were preparing to capture two large women, a group of armed giants appeared. The scene immediately called to mind the queen of the Amazons and Antaeus, the legendary giant. Under such circumstances, the Europeans preferred to retreat without carrying out their plans:

> We found a village of 12 houses, where we found only seven women so tall that not one of them was less than a palm and a half taller than I. And when they saw us they were very frightened of us, and the chief among them, who was certainly a prudent woman, led us, communicating by means of signs, to a house and gave us some refreshment. Seeing these large women, we decided to capture two of them, about 15 years of age, to make a present of them to the king and queen, for they were undoubtedly creatures who surpassed the height of any ordinary human being. While we were occupied with this task, however, 36 men arrived and entered the dwelling where we were having a drink. They were so large that each of them was taller when kneeling than I was standing upright; in sum, they were as tall as giants, their size and body proportions corresponding to their height. Every woman looked like Penthesilea, and every man like Antaeus. When the men entered, some of our party were so frightened that they have not yet fully regained their composure. The giants bore bows, arrows and very large sticks in the shape of swords, and as they saw that we were so small, they began to speak to us to find out who we were and where we came from. Remaining calm out of a desire for peace, we replied with gestures that we were peaceable men and that we were on a journey of discovery of the world. In conclusion, we judged it opportune to take our leave of them without any quarrel, and they accompanied us to the sea, where we boarded our ships.[5]

This meeting in fact set a precedent: the great height of the inhabitants of the island so impressed the conquistadors that they decided to swallow their pride, change their plans and become peaceful observers of the new world. The next contact with people of similarly impressive size would occur 20 years later, at the other end of the South American continent.

A NATION OF GIANTS IN PATAGONIA

The fleet that made the first voyage around the world would in fact realize the original project of Columbus: to navigate westward in order to reach the Spice Islands. But the venture was overshadowed by a significant question: no one knew whether America ended in the south, or whether it extended into a mythical southern continent known as *Terra australis incognita*. Sebastian Cabot and Díaz de Solís had already searched, to no avail, for an interoceanic passage. It was, therefore, essential to establish definitely whether or not there was a navigable passage between the Atlantic and the Pacific. The proposal was thus up for grabs, and various candidates were in the running. Emperor Charles V finally chose the Portuguese navigator Fernão de

Engraving by Théodore de Bry, based on the drawing by Stradanus (Jean Van der Straet), illustrating the discovery of the Strait of Magellan. We can see a rokh bird carrying an elephant, sirens and a giant who, as in Pigafetta's account, is thrusting an arrow down his throat to induce vomiting. Bibliothèque royale de Belgique.

Magalhães (Magellan), who was willing to sail to the southernmost latitudes in order to circumnavigate the immense American landmass.

In spite of the magnitude of the undertaking, the Crown provided him with only modest support: some old ships and a crew with little experience. The monarch had his own reasons for this: even if Magellan were to succeed in reaching the Spice Islands, how could he know whether these were located in the Spanish or the Portuguese zone, as defined by the Treaty of Tordesillas?

The task of recording every event of the voyage fell to the knight Antonio Pigafetta. Born in Vicenza around 1490, in his youth he had fought Suleyman the Magnificent on board galleys belonging to the order of the Knights of St John at Rhodes. He later settled in Barcelona, whereupon the Casa de Contratación* enrolled him on Magellan's expedition. His account would prove very valuable, for it records day by day the details of the first voyage around the world, providing descriptions of places, ethnographic and linguistic information about local populations, including the supposed giants of Patagonia.

On 10 August 1519, 237 men set out on board five ships: the *San Antonio*, the *Concepción*, the *Santiago*, the *Victoria* and the *Trinidad* on which Magellan raised his admiral's pennant. In search of an interoceanic passage, they explored the Bay of Rio de Janeiro and that of the Río de la Plata. They continued south until winter obliged them to stop at the bay of San Julián, in present-day Argentine Patagonia.

It was at this winter refuge that they first encountered a 'giant', a solitary man, almost bald and covered in paint, but so tall that the Spanish scarcely came up to his belt. A little later they saw other ones, accompanied by their wives:

> One day we suddenly saw a naked man of giant stature on the shore of the port, dancing, singing, and throwing dust on his head. The captain-general sent one of our men to the giant so that he might perform the same actions as a sign of peace. Having done that, the man led the giant to an islet into the presence of the captain-general. When the giant was in the captain-general's and our presence, he marvelled greatly, and made signs with one finger raised upward, believing that we had come

---

*Sometimes translated as the House of Trade, this was an office of inspectors set up by the Crown in 1503 to ensure that every expedition setting out for the New World was duly equipped with all that was necessary for navigation and for the survival of the crew.

from the sky. He was so tall that we reached only to his waist, and he was well proportioned. His face was large and painted red all over, while about his eyes he was painted yellow; and he had two hearts painted on the middle of his cheeks. His scanty hair was painted white. He was dressed in the skins of animals skilfully sewn together... His feet were shod with the same kind of skins which covered his feet in the manner of shoes. In his hand he carried a short, heavy bow, with a cord somewhat thicker than those of the lute, and made from the intestines of the same animal, and a bundle of rather short cane arrows feathered like ours... The captain-general had the giant given something to eat and drink, and among other things which were shown to him was a large steel mirror. When he saw his face, he was greatly terrified, and jumped back throwing three or four of our men to the ground. After that he was given some bells, a mirror, a comb and certain Pater Nosters. The captain-general sent him ashore with 4 armed men. When one of his companions, who would never come to the ships, saw him coming with our men, he ran to the place where the others were, who came (down to the shore) all naked one after the other. When our men reached them, they began to dance and sing, lifting one finger to the sky. They showed our men some white powder made from the roots of an herb, which they kept in earthen pots, and which they ate because they had nothing else. Our men made signs inviting them to the ships, and that they would help them carry their possessions. Thereupon, those men quickly took only their bows, while their women laden like asses carried everything. The latter are not so tall as the men but are very much fatter. When we saw them we were greatly surprised. Their breasts are one-half braza long, and they are painted and clothed like their husbands, except that before their privies they have a small skin which covers them.[6]

Six days later, another man of prodigious height appeared before the Europeans, and would spend a few days among them: they baptized him Juan. The encounter with the 'giants' made a profound and lasting impression on the navigators. Astonished by their size, Magellan decided to capture two of these men in order to exhibit them in Spain. After some time, a group of four Patagonians arrived, and the Spanish began to carry out their plan by taking advantage of the naïveté of the Indians:

The trick that he employed in keeping them was as follows. He gave them many knives, scissors, mirrors, bells, and glass beads; and those two having their hands filled with the said articles, the captain-general had two pairs of iron manacles brought, such as, are fastened on the feet. He made motions that he would give them to the giants, whereat they were very pleased, since those manacles were of iron, but they did not know how to carry them. They were grieved at leaving them behind, but they had no place to put those gifts; for they had to hold the skin wrapped about them with their hands. The other two giants wished to help them, but the captain refused. Seeing that they were loath to leave those manacles behind, the captain made them a sign that he would put them on their feet, and that they could carry them away. They nodded assent with the head. Immediately, the captain had the manacles put on both of them at the same time. When our men were driving home the cross bolt, the giants began to suspect something, but the captain assuring them, however, they stood still. When they saw later that they were tricked, they raged like bulls, calling loudly for *Setebos* to aid them.[7]

During the exasperating wait at San Julián, Magellan had to face his first mutiny. Although he succeeded in putting it down, the series of misfortunes would continue: the *Santiago* ran around off the coast of the South Atlantic, and while they were exploring the strait, the *San Antonio* deserted, taking with it one of the two Patagonians. The captive would not survive the passage across the equator.

After 38 days of difficult navigation through the Patagonia Channels, the group reached the immense open seas of the Pacific. On 28 November 1520, the three remaining ships began the first known crossing of the widest of all the oceans. The 3-month journey from the Strait of Magellan to the island of Guam constitutes one of the greatest achievements in the history of navigation.

On board, Pigafetta tried to communicate with the 'giant' – who by now had been baptized Pablo – to learn about his people's way of life. Their medicine struck him as strange: for stomach aches, they thrust an arrow down their throats to induce vomiting. They treated headaches by making a transversal incision across the forehead or in some other part of the body. Their custom was to cut their hair in the form of a great crown, like a monk's tonsure only longer, and held in place with a cotton string around the head. Their penises were attached between their legs. They made fire by rubbing two sticks together to produce sparks with which they lit another branch placed between the first two. They did not have real houses but rather shelters made of guanaco skins that they could carry with them from one place to another. When one of them died, 10 or 12 sorcerers, caked in paint, would begin a joyous dance around the body of the deceased until another, larger man appeared and began to shout even more

Map of the Strait of Magellan drawn by Hulsius in 1626. On it we see Patagonians giants – one of whom is practising the strange therapy with the arrow down the throat – and on the continental shore of the strait, a fortress named Philippopolis is dated 1582. This is a reference to Ciudad Real de San Felipe founded by the shipwrecked sailors of Sarmiento's party in 1584 who were, among others, at the origin of the myth of the City of the Caesars.

energetically. The first group of sorcerers was called *Cheleulle* and the other *Setebos*. The giants ate raw meat and a sweet root known as *chapae*. On board ship, they devoured rats without finding this the least bit disgusting.[8]

During the voyage, Pigafetta would draw up a brief dictionary for each of the languages of the people he had encountered: Brazilians, Philippines, Malays, Moluccans, and even produced a Patagonian vocabulary of 83 words. The latter included Patagonian terms for the various parts of the body, such as the head (*her*), the hand (*chene*) and the heart (*tol*). He would also translate a number of verbs such as to go (*rei*), to fight (*ohomagse*) and to eat (*mechiere*). Then came the colours, the stars and some natural phenomena.[9]

It was Magellan who gave these people the name of Patagons. It is very unlikely that this name came – as is often claimed – from their large feet (*patas* is often used in colloquial Spanish to mean feet) shod in guanaco skin, for there is no convincing semantic link between the 'patagon' and 'patas' either in Spanish or in Portuguese, Magellan's native tongue. It seems much more likely that its origin lies in the name of a character in a Spanish chivalric romance entitled *Primaleón*, derived from *Palmerín de Oliva*, which was very much in vogue in the early sixteenth century.

According to an English translation of the *Primaléon de Grecia*, dated 1596, used by the travel writer Bruce Chatwin, the knight Primaleón sailed to a distant isle, where he met a cruel and unfortunate people who ate raw meat and dressed in animal skins. In the island's interior there lived a creature known as the 'Great Patagon', who was as monstrous as he was clever. He had the head of a dog, ears that came down to his shoulders, sharp fangs and feet like a stag's. He was a very fast runner, very intelligent and fond of women. A struggle ensued, in the course of which Primaleón wounded the Patagon, causing the latter to produce ferocious roars. The knight captured him and decided to take him along to offer him as a gift to the king of Polonia.

Chatwin finds a certain symmetry between the characters in this episode of the romance and the native people described by Pigafetta: both eat raw meat, dress in animal skins, scream ferociously when captured, run very fast and are unusually large in stature. What is more, like the hero of the romance, Magellan also wished to capture these 'savages' to offer them to the king. Finally, another element lends support to this thesis: during the 1590s, the crew of a British ship commanded by Captain John Davis was attacked by a group of Tehuelche warriors; according to the description provided by Davis, their attackers threw dust into the air, leapt and ran like animals and their faces were covered with masks in the form of dogs' heads. This could not fail to evoke in the minds of the Europeans the 'Great Patagon' of the Spanish romance.[10]

As the weeks passed, living conditions on board deteriorated: the lack of water and fresh food gave rise to an outbreak of scurvy, the much feared disease that led to so horrible a death. The second 'giant' also perished. Pigafetta described the crossing of the Pacific and the death of the 'Patagon' as follows:

> We were three months and twenty days without getting any kind of fresh food. We ate biscuit, which was no longer biscuit, but powder of biscuits swarming with worms, for they had eaten the good. It stank strongly of the urine of rats. We drank yellow water that had been putrid for many days. We also ate some ox hides that covered the top of the mainyard to prevent the yard from chafing the shrouds, and which had become exceedingly hard because of the sun, rain and wind. We left them in the sea for four or five days, and then placed them for a few moments on top of the embers, and so ate them; and we ate sawdust from boards. Rats were sold for one-half ducat* piece, and even we could not get them. But above all the other misfortunes the following was the worst. The gums of both the lower and upper teeth of some of our men swelled, so that they could not eat under any circumstances and therefore, died. Nineteen men died from that sickness, and the giant together with an Indian from the country of Verzin. Twenty-five or thirty men fell sick (during that time), in the arms, legs, or in another place, so that but few remained well.[11]

It was in this state that they reached the island of Guam and then the Philippines, where Magellan was killed by the indigenous people. The losses had been so great that the new commander, Juan Sebastián El Cano, decided to destroy the *Concepción* and divide its crew between the *Victoria* and the *Trinidad*. The latter was in such a lamentable state that its captain decided to try to return to Spain by way of Panama, but unfavourable winds prevented him from doing so. The vessel was captured in the Moluccas by the Portuguese.

The *Victoria*, the only remaining ship, returned to Spain rounding the Cape of Good Hope and, with only 18 survivors on board, dropped anchor at San Lúcar de Barrameda on 8 September 1522. A few years later some of the crewmen who had been taken as prisoners by the Portuguese returned home, bringing to 35 the number of sailors who came back alive from the first voyage around the world. In spite of the many disasters, this was the first time in centuries that valuable merchandise, universally sought after, reached Spain by a direct route

---

*1 ducat = 3.5 g of gold, or 375 *maravedis* (1.5 kg of bread in Seville cost 16 *maravedis*).

without the duties imposed by eastern middlemen. Proceeds from the sale of spices transported in the hold of the *Victoria* were sufficient to cover all the costs of the tragic expedition.

But to return to our subject: what are we to think of the Patagonian 'giants'? As with that of the Amazons, the myth of the giants does not refer to a few individuals but to an entire group of people. In this case, it is based on the exaggeration of the difference in stature between Europeans and Patagonians. The average height of Europeans in the sixteenth century would have been between 1.50 and 1.60 m, whereas that of the Patagonians was in the neighbourhood of 1.80 m. Therefore, one of these 'giants' would have been about 30 cm taller than a European. There is an abundant bibliography on the tribes that inhabited Patagonia:[12] the Tehuelches and the Onas, nomadic people known to have been the tallest Indians in America.

The descriptions of Pigafetta have served as the starting point for a long-standing controversy about whether or not a nation of giants ever existed.

Information about the Patagonian 'Giants'

Given its highly strategic location, the Strait of Magellan soon aroused the interest of the great powers. Ships of various nationalities began to ply its waters in the hope of placing it under their domination, and many of their crew members described meeting 'giants'.

The French captain Jean Alfonse[13] affirmed in 1559 that the Patagonians were at least twice as tall as the tallest European; in 1572, John Jane insisted that he had seen giants throwing large stone blocks at the ships. Three years later, the French Franciscan André Thevet estimated that they were between 10 and 12 feet tall (3.05–3.66 m), while the Spanish chronicler Bartolomé Leonardo de Argensola thought they were related to the Cyclops.

Pedro Sarmiento de Gamboa told of having encountered giants in the course of his two expeditions in the Strait of Magellan (1579–80 and 1581–86). He claimed to have witnessed, on the second journey, a giant thrusting an arrow down its throat, a scene strongly reminiscent of the one described by Pigafetta.[14]

Then there were the accounts by Dutch travellers. Seebald de Weert, in 1599, claimed to have seen six or seven canoes filled with giants of between 10 and 14 feet. He said that they were so strong that, frightened by the arrows shot by the Dutch, they uprooted entire trees to defend themselves. Two years later, Olivier de Noort stated that they were 11 feet tall and had a terrifying appearance, long hair and painted faces, although there were some among them who were of normal height.

The information about the giants, coming from such varied sources, appeared convincing. Hence, during the sixteenth century and part of the seventeenth, Europe adopted the notion that in the southernmost part of the New World there was a nation of giants. But in subsequent decades, testimonies by Spanish navigators would reduce their proportions from that of 'giants' to standards closer to reality.

During the Enlightenment, detractors from the belief in the Patagonian giants gained ground over its partisans, who had not succeeded in proving their claims. The debate gradually subsided, until new testimonies by French and English sailors revived the controversy.

Thus Amédée Frézier, royal engineer, recounted that on his visit to the island of Chiloé around 1715, the Spanish governor Pedro Molina told him that the Patagonians were between nine and ten feet tall. The travel accounts of Frézier were published in 1716 in Paris, and were so popular that they were very soon translated into English, Dutch and German.

In 1767, it was the travel journal of the British officer John Byron, illustrated with engravings of the Patagonians, that found a wide audience. In it, Commodore Byron speaks of men of about nine feet tall. The legend thus gained new life for a few decades, but soon gave way to more realistic accounts.

In 1839, the Frenchman Alcide d'Orbigny, one of the principal players in the scientific revolution of the nineteenth century, spent eight months at the far south of the continent, during which time he measured hundreds of individuals. He informs us that he did not meat a single native person who was over 1.92 m tall, and that on average they measured 1.73 m. He also published a long list of voyages that had been made in the region, including a table of the height attributed to the Patagonians from Pigafetta to the French Bougainville in 1766.[15]

The same is true for George Musters, who spent a year travelling through Patagonia. Upon his return to England in 1870, he noted that the first thing everyone asked him was invariably about the height of the Patagonians.

The testimony of the North American Benjamin Franklin Bourne, held prisoner by an Indian tribe in the regions of the Strait in 1849, is free of all fantastical elements. Having only his own height of 1.65 m as a measuring stick, he observed that the Patagonians were all at least a head taller than him.

Finally, in 1901, a French anthropologist, Henry de La Vaulx, measured some skeletons found in ancient burial grounds of Patagonia: his investigation reveals that the height of the Tehuelches had not varied over the past few centuries, remaining constant at around 1.75 m on average.[16]

Like the belief in a nation of giants, so the Tehuelches and the Onas have died out. Decimated by illness, by the end of the nineteenth century their number had already been reduced to around 1,000 individuals. The southern pampas were then settled by powerful families, mainly of British origin, who carried out a systematic extermination of the indigenous people in order to turn Patagonia into a region suitable for sheep farming.

In spite of this sad conclusion, the legend of the Patagonian giants influenced several literary works of Utopian fiction, such as *La Découverte australe* (Discovery in the South) (1781) by Restif de la Bretonne, where Patagonia figures as an ideal land inhabited by *Megapatagons*, 'the largest and wisest of men'.[17] This was neither the first nor the last such work. The Patagonians inspired another Utopian project, rendering in concrete form the social ideals of the French Encyclopaedists of the eighteenth century. It seems appropriate to end this chapter with a summary of one of these idealized constructs that in certain respects evokes problems that remain highly relevant today.

The Patagonian Utopia

Gabriel-François Coyer was born in 1707 and entered the Society of Jesus as a young man, only to leave the order in 1736. A member of several scholarly societies, he soon gained a reputation for the accuracy of his studies and the literary quality of his writings. In a work entitled *Letter to Doctor Maty*, published in 1767, he conceived of a most attractive Utopia in which the Patagonians were the central characters. Under the influence of the theories of Rousseau and Montesquieu, Coyer described the education, urbanization, family life, social and political organization and laws of an ideal society based on some of the ideas that would lead to the French Revolution. Curiously, this work appeared three years after another Utopian work, that of the City of the Caesars, written in 1764 by James Burgh (see Chapter IV), and strongly suggested a French response to the rational but highly puritanical social ideal proposed by the Englishman.

The addressee of the *Letter* was Mathew Maty (1718–76), an English doctor and writer, librarian of the British Museum, who was a fervent advocate of smallpox inoculation, the ancestor of the smallpox vaccine.

*A Sailor giving a Patagonian Woman some Biscuit
for her Child.*

*An illustration from the narrative of John Byron (1767)
representing the meeting between the English
and the Patagonians. (BnF)*

Could there not be differences in height within the human race just as there is among certain animal species, Coyer wondered. The answer he proposed was that 'Our discoveries are insignificant compared to those yet to be made.' About this time, an English ship set out in search of the giants. Coyer decided to write the history of the Patagonians as he imagined it, and he did so even before any concrete information had reached Britain.

Childhood and Education

The Patagonian men's relations with women are based on honesty and the innocent feelings that once united human hearts in the Golden Age. Much attention is paid to pregnant women: care is taken to keep away anything that might sadden them, so that their hearts may be filled with joy; they are entertained with the sounds of musical instruments, and their every desire is catered for. Yet the future mothers need not avoid all physical activity: they can take long walks and continue to earn their living by doing some agricultural work. The mother alone nurses her baby but in such a way that her hands are free to continue to work.

The Patagonians do not like short or imperfect people. They believe that an unhealthy lifestyle can cause people to shrink in size. If this should happen to a family, they must seek refuge in the desert, where they sometimes found a weak race of people no more than five feet tall. To avoid this happening, they keep babies' heads bare in order to fortify the brain against inflammations. They dress them in loose, lightweight clothing without strings or anything that might obstruct circulation. Infants can crawl around to their heart's content in a room covered with rush mats out of harm's way. Some fruit or vegetable is left within their reach. They do not try to keep the little ones seated or lying down – when they want to move, they are helped to stand up. A hundred times a day, they are taken to the middle of a meadow so that they can breathe clean air and run around without any danger. Little by little, children grow accustomed to the rays of the sun, the rain and the frost. Their favourite food is placed in a basket hanging from a tree; to fetch it they have to throw a stone from a slingshot, shoot an arrow or climb the tree. Their preferred fruit is buried in the ground so that they have to dig it up with a spade.

The education of a Patagonian child is like a permanent physical education class. To reach their playmates, youngsters have to leap over a ditch filled with water, carry heavy loads and use levers. They are taught to use their right and left hands and feet without distinction.

Children compete in races, jumping, wrestling, archery and slingshot, weightlifting and fighting with wild animals.

The teaching of moral values also occupies a central place. Not satisfied with simply telling them what is right and wrong, the Patagonians oblige their children to practice the principles of justice daily. If a young person borrows something, he or she must return it on the agreed day; if someone is lacking something, it is considered an honour to share with that person what he or she needs. No one can take justice into his own hands, but if a stronger person mistreats a weaker one, he is punished with particular severity. Young people elect their judges own and a prince after the fashion of the ones that govern their nation.

The Patagonians have no tradition of ghosts, witches, portentous dreams, horoscopes, or unlucky numbers or days. Children's imaginations have, therefore, not been corrupted by fear. They are taught only about real dangers so that they might learn to avoid them.

City life

The capital of the Patagonians is a vast city, larger than the major European cities, but the population is much smaller. Everything is comfortable, if modest. The streets are wide, clean and straight and there are many markets, squares and fountains. Considering that cities, where people live packed together like sardines lead to the downfall of the human race, they have brought the countryside into the city. Each house is a single-storey detached dwelling made of wood, and has a park and a garden.

Their theatres are larger than the ones in Europe, and can hold about 30,000 spectators, which is approximately the number of the capital city's inhabitants. The architecture is rustic but majestic in appearance. Their operas are simple recitations: they celebrate nature, love, the heroic inventors of the plough, the mill, the art of construction, language, writing and navigation. Tragedies feature ancient giants who tried, unsuccessfully, to lord it over others. The favourite topic of their comedies is the inability of 'dwarfs', who are only five feet tall, to fend for themselves.

Customs

The Patagonians are the closest beings to the ideal of the noble savage. They do not have fixed mealtimes, but wait until they are hungry, since they eat only when they need nourishment. They prefer vegetables to animal flesh, and there is a season in the year when they eat only fish and vegetables in order to allow the other animals to reproduce. They practice agriculture and a few other useful activities. Idleness is condemned, but those who are too old to work are supported by the community without having to beg or be ashamed. Therefore, there are no beggars.

Their social activities are essentially centred around domestic life, for the family is one of their great sources of delight. Visits take place only for reasons of business, charity or friendship – courtesy calls are unknown. At public entertainments, young girls show off their charms in an innocent but forthright manner. They distribute the prizes at sporting events, and are free to choose their spouses, who must be at least 28 years of age. Social disparity between families is no obstacle to a marriage. Polygamy is forbidden, but divorce is permitted under the law.

The most highly honoured Patagonians are those who have served their land: those who played a key role in a victory, ploughed a large field, made stagnant waters flow, or advanced some agricultural technique or therapeutic method. The state then supports them at public expense.

Medicine

Patagonian medicine is quite simple and natural; they made no attempt to develop it into a science, but neither do they use bloodletting. Above all they value hygiene, temperance, exercise, a joyful disposition and common sense. No doubt they would be pleased to know that in this respect things have not changed very much over the past two millennia. It would never occur to them to put two patients in the same bed, much the less five or six. When a strange illness broke out and killed many people, they tried in vain to destroy the germs. So they decided to render it harmless by inoculating the people, after due preparation. The average lifespan of a Patagonian is about 200 years. They consider that the only certain proof of death is putrefaction. The highest court of the land prohibited the burial of the dead within the city limits.

The Organization of Society

The laws are made by the assemblies of the people. The prince of the Patagonians is obliged to see to the well-being of all, and must spend three months each year inspecting all the provinces of his country. Taxes are collected in kind during the harvest period, and are proportionate to the agricultural output of each family. They are used for the benefit of all of society, especially for the care of children. Patagonians only wage war for self-defence and do not have a standing army. In effect every Patagonian is a soldier trained to defend his own people, and in peacetime the soldiers maintain a more personal bond with their commander.

Their ancient laws, deemed too barbarian – in fact they are very much like French justice in the eighteenth century! – have been reformed and collected into a code entitled *On the common sense of laws*. This new legislation is simple and clear. Every city or village has its own court, judgements are without appeal except if capital punishment is involved, the latter being meted out only in cases of assassination. Every accused is to be judged within the lunar month, and has the right to a lawyer. Torture has been abolished. Patagonian prisons are quite comfortable, and the law has set down different degrees of punishment, which consist mainly of forms of community service. Finally, judicial office cannot be hereditary or undertaken for monetary gain, since the magistrates are paid out of the public purse.

Gabriel-François Coyer then interrupted his exposé, ending with the following words: 'When your ship brings back documents, I will be very pleased if there is nothing for me to correct.'

EPILOGUE

The conquistadors have left numerous traces in the continent's toponymy of the myths that once enticed Renaissance Europe. California was the name of a region situated near Paradise, according to the chivalric romance entitled *Amadís de Gaula*. Patagonia was the land of the Patagon, a character in the *Primaleón*, another romance. Guyana comes from the mythical empire of 'Guiana' where Lake Parime and Manoa, the capital of El Dorado, were to be found. The Solomon Islands owe their name to an expedition that reached them in search of the mines of the biblical king. The names Río de la Plata and Argentina are the incarnations of the desire of finding the rumoured source of precious metals and the Sierra de la Plata (Silver mountains). The archipelago of the Antilles evokes the mythical island of 'Antilia'. And the largest river on earth derives its name from the nation of warrior women, the Amazons.

For Europeans in the Renaissance, the social aspirations that we now call 'myths' were very real. The boundary between the real and the imaginary was a porous one. When the explorers gathered information about the dark side of the planet, the belief in imaginary worlds and beings, described in the Scriptures and in tradition, was often as important a source as their geographical discoveries and technological advances.

These two ways of perceiving reality coexisted in the men who undertook the exploration of the world. They made great efforts to learn about new seas and continents, measuring and mapping them, while at the same time identifying them as the sites of various imaginary lands. The discovery of America produced a curious and singular displacement of ideas. The myths that the European collective subconscious had placed in the practically inaccessible Far East were transferred to the New World, a land that was within the reach of the European ships. Perhaps for the first time in history, the Europeans thought they could reach the worlds of their dreams. It was enough to cross the ocean and undertake the conquest of new lands. There terrible dangers awaited them, but also the hope of the supreme reward: streams of the much-vaunted gold.

The association in the minds of the colonists between imaginary worlds and great riches would be a motor of the colonial enterprise. The first generation of discoverers, like Columbus and Vespucci, would seek above all for gold in mythical places that appear in the Scriptures, such as Paradise, King Solomon's mines, or in ancient beliefs such as in the Golden Chersonese. Their successors, on the other hand, continued obstinately to seek empires that were as rich or even richer than that of the Aztecs and the Incas that had been looted by Cortés and Pizarro.

Once colonization had begun, the mythology adapted itself to the fantasies of the conquistadors, coloured by American lore. During the sixteenth and part of the seventeenth centuries, hundreds of expeditions that dreamt of gilded cities and empires would travel the length and breadth of the continent in search of El Dorado, Cíbola, El Paitití and the Caesars. These products of the collective imagination would motivate the actions of the conquistadors and constitute one of the causes for the exploration and settlement of America by Europeans.

The quest for golden cities, for at least two centuries, shaped the conquistadors and their successors. Riches were not to be sought through labour, savings or accumulation. Their quest for wealth was something urgent, impetuous. This may account for their serious underestimation of the dangers that would face them along the road to the 'hidden city', their seizure of the treasures they found, and the inevitable pillaging that followed. The next generations would not find golden cities but, while searching for them, expropriated immense territories from their native inhabitants, institutionalized in the form of *encomiendas*. The conversion of adventurers into great land and slave-owners made them averse to an activity as vulgar as labour. The result was a sense of honour that was medieval in its arrogance and racism, generated as it was by wealth obtained through plunder. It was this system of values that shaped the personality of the lords of America and in some cases might help in explaining present-day attitudes and behaviours.

The behaviour of the Spanish and the Portuguese as regards these myths was somewhat different. For the Spanish, the discovery and appropriation of the American lands was the continuation of the wars of liberation waged by Iberian Christian kings against the Arab Muslim kingdoms and the Jewish population of Iberia. Although this was not part of their original intention, the Christian soldiers who reached the new continent in a sense were continuing the *Reconquista*.

This 'reconquest' had itself taken on almost mythic proportions. Sons of the main players in this 'holy war', the conquistadors were warriors and missionaries who fed on chivalric romances and religious literature, with reason playing only a small part in their actions.

The Portuguese, by contrast, had already completed their own Reconquista more than two centuries earlier. During the fifteenth century they systematically explored the African coasts in search of a route to the East. Their objectives were much more pragmatic: trading directly with the producers of spices and establishing productive colonies that would soon take the form of slave plantations. Their actions were guided by an extremely rational plan, and it was rare for them to set off in search of Paradise or golden empires. If the Spaniard took as his emblematic hero Don Quixote, it was the enthusiastic but prudent Henry the Navigator, who was the model for the Portuguese.

Myths are born, live, play their part and eventually are diluted and fall into oblivion. Although not completely. Our world is filled with messages that call for the return to an original innocence, or suggest that a certain natural substance can wipe out the ravages of time. The fear of the vast hordes of 'unclean people' who may invade the world from the East is sometimes subtly evoked, at times with discriminatory intentions. There is no lack of legends about unexplored regions – be they on earth, undersea, or in space – that might still be inhabited by monstrous beings such as giant sharks, the Loch Ness monster, the Yeti or Ridley Scott's *Alien*. These contemporary beings are, after all, not so very different from the terrible griffin or the armies of headless Ewaipanomas.

Human societies retain age-old fears and dreams that have not disappeared entirely. They are the guiding principle linking the biblical Paradise that Columbus thought he had glimpsed in the New World, with the Utopian projects of the age of Enlightenment and the myths of our own times: the dream that humanity might one day finally return to the Golden Age.

NOTES

FOREWORD AND INTRODUCTION

1. Abraham, p. 7.
2. Cortázar, p. 30. *In the *Phaedo, or A Dialogue of the Soul.* Phaedon was one of Socrates' favourite disciples, and was present at his death.
3. Sánchez-Albronoz, pp. 61–3.
4. Boorstin, pp. 108–9 and *Découvreurs & Conquérants,* no. 16, pp. 310–4.
5. Deluz, p. 3.
6. Heers, 1981, pp. 379–80.
7. Romano, pp. 37–9 and Duviols, p. 45.
8. Heers, 1981, p. 376.
9. La Roncière and Molat du Jardin, p. 20.
10. Carpentier, pp. 37–8.

1: IN SEARCH OF THE EARTHLY PARADISE

1. Varela, p. 311. English translation in Kadir, p. 202.
2. Plato, *Phaedo* (109a–b) in *Portrait of Socrates,* p. 183.
3. Boorstin, p. 101.
4. Heers, 1975, p. 120.
5. Meslin, pp. 79–80.
6. Van Beek, fasc. 43. See also Meslin, pp. 82–3, 162.
7. Isidore, *Etymologies,* Book XIV. 3.2, p. 158.
8. Boorstin, p. 102 and Duby, pp. 67–8.
9. For the maps we have consulted see Kupcik, La Roncière and Molat du Jardin, Bagrow and Skelton and *Los Beatos.*
10. These three examples are taken from Boorstin, pp. 103–4 and Graf, p. 8, pp. 55–66.
11. Duby, pp. 67–8.
12. *Libro del conosçimiento,* pp. 36–7.
13. d'Ailly, *Imago Mundi,* c. 7, p. 14, col. 1.
14. *Ibid,* c. 12, p. 17, col. 1.
15. *Ibid,* c. 55, p. 36, col. 1.
16. Madariaga, p. 326.
17. *The Four Voyages of Columbus,* vol. II, p. 30.

18. *The Four Voyages of Columbus*, vol. I, p. 38.
19. Varela, p. 264.
20. Vespucci, 'Letter to Lorenzo di Pierfrancesco de Medici', in Pohl, p. 78.
21. Vespucci, *The Letters*, p. 17, 24.
22. Vespucci, *The Letters*, p. 42.
23. Pigafetta, p. 222.
24. Duviols, p. 29.
25. Buarque de Holanda, pp. 18–19, 184–5.
26. *The World in Maps*.

2: ON THE THRESHOLD OF PARADISE

1. Pseudo-Callisthenes, III, p. 30.
2. Pliny the Elder, *Natural History*, Book VI, c. 30, p. 2072.
3. Cited by Slessarev, pp. 67–79.
4. Boorstin, p. 129.
5. Santaella, pp. 61–3.
6. Boorstin, pp. 104–5.
7. Gil, p. 220.
8. *Ibid*, p. 221.
9. Cuneo, *New of the Islands of the Hesperian Ocean*, 7.2.4, p. 52.
10. Vespucci, 'Letter on his first voyage', in *The Cosmographiae Introductio*, p. 92.
11. Gil, p. 223.
12. Buarque de Holanda, p. 152.
13. Mahn-Lot, pp. 87–8.
14. Nobrega, *Informação da terra do Brasil*, 1549, in D'Olwer, p. 629.
15. Buarque de Holanda, pp. 153–4.
16. *Ibid.*
17. Nobrega, in Duviols, p. 156.
18. In Duviols, p. 156.
19. Buarque de Holanda, pp. 158–73.
20. In Gil, p. 265 and Gandía, p. 50.
21. Buarque de Holanda, pp. 164–5.
22. Pseudo-Callisthenes, II, pp. 40–1.
23. *Travels of Sir John de Mandeville*, c. XVIII.
24. *The Four Voyages of Columbus*, vol. I, p. 6.
25. Gil, pp. 266–7.
26. On medicinal plants, see Gandía, pp. 51–4.
27. Vespucci, 'Letter to Lorenzo di Pierfrancesco de Medici', in Pohl, pp. 133–4.
28. Vespucci, *The Letters*, p. 47.
29. Duviols, pp. 30–1.
30. Gandía, p. 55.
31. Gil, p. 256.
32. Gandía, p. 56 and Gil, pp. 267–8.
33. Gil, pp. 269–78 and D'Olwer, pp. 117–23.

34. Gandía, p. 55.
35. Gil, p. 281.

3: KING SOLOMON'S MINES IN AMERICA

1. *The Four Voyages of Columbus*, vol. II, p. 104.
2. These three examples were taken from Heers, 1981, pp. 118–26.
3. Gil, p. 189.
4. Columbus, *Diario* (entry for 13 October 1482), p. 73.
5. d'Ailly, *Ymago mundi*, in Buron, p. 307.
6. Kupcik, pp. 21–2.
7. Columbus's copy of *Marco Polo*, fol. 57, cited by Morison, p. 237. Marco Polo cited from *The Description of the World*, c. 159, p. 361.
8. Heers, 1981, p. 126.
9. *Ibid.*
10. Madeira Santos, pp. 71–2.
11. *The Four Voyages of Christopher Columbus*, vol. II, p. 6.
12. Varela, p. 311.
13. Gil, pp. 176–7.
14. Varela, p. 319.
15. Gil, p. 176.
16. *The Four Voyages of Columbus*, vol. II, p. 104.
17. Gandía, pp. 158–9.
18. Sarmiento de Gamboa, 1947, pp. 23–8.
19. Gil, pp. 226–7.
20. *Ibid.*
21. *Ibid*, p. 234.
22. *Ibid*, p. 228.
23. *Ibid*, p. 247.
24. *Ibid*, pp. 229–30.
25. *Ibid*, pp. 232–7.
26. Mathieu, p. 152 and Gil, p. 250.

4: THE REALMS OF GOLD

1. Payro, 'Las Ciudades Quiméricas', p. 456.
2. Gandía, p. 137.
3. *Ibid*, p. 106.
4. *Ibid*, p. 108.
5. *Ibid*, pp. 111–2.
6. Rodrigues Fresle, *Conquista y descubrimiento del nuevo Reino de Granada de las Indias occidentales del mar Oceano*, cited by Gandía, p. 112.
7. Cited by Gandía, p. 113.
8. Gandía, p. 113.
9. Villanueva, p. 41 and Gandía, pp. 162–77.

10. Levillier, pp. 4–5.
11. Payro, 'Expediciones', p. 477.
12. Centenera, p. 74.
13. Sarmiento de Gamboa, 1947, pp. 224–5.
14. Cited by Levillier, p. 99.
15. *Ibid*, p. 270.
16. Gandía, p. 214.
17. *Ibid*.
18. According to Morales, p. 16, Francisco César's expedition lasted three months. According to Gandía, p. 250, the same expedition went on for 40 or 50 days.
19. Morales, p. 17.
20. Morales, pp. 24–30 and Gandía, pp. 244–75.
21. Morales, pp. 57–8.
22. Ainsa, pp. 23–7.
23. Morales, pp. 47–9.
24. Morales, pp. 58–9 and Gandía, p. 263.
25. Ortiz de la Tabla, p. 18.
26. Gandía, p. 128.
27. Díaz, p. 14.
28. Ortiz de la Tabla, p. 49.
29. Gandía, pp. 131–3 and Duivols, p. 210.
30. Raleigh, pp. 22–3.
31. *Ibid*, p. 30.
32. *Ibid*, p. 170–1.
33. Coudreau, pp. 4–5.
34. Humboldt, 1965, pp. 176–8.
35. Descola, pp. 38–9 and Gandía, pp. 116–7.
36. Levillier, p. 245.
37. *Ibid*, pp. 103–10.
38. Gandía, pp. 214–5.
39. *Ibid*, p. 222.
40. Cited by Levillier, pp. 272–4.
41. Sánchez-Albornoz, pp. 60–86.
42. Levillier, p. 281.
43. Levillier, p. 283.
44. Gandía, p. 261.
45. This list was made up based on information provided by Braun-Menéndez, p. 47 and Ainsa, p. 38.
46. Morales, pp. 68–70; Braun-Menéndez, p. 46 and Gandía, p. 262.
47. Morales, pp. 70–2 and Gandía, p. 262.
48. Morales, pp. 73–80; Payro, 'Expediciones', pp. 466–8 and Gandía, pp. 265–6.
49. Morales, pp. 59–60 and Gandía, p. 267.
50. Gandía, pp. 267–9.
51. Payro, pp. 461–3.
52. Gandía, pp. 269–73 and Morales, pp. 81–6.

53. Burgh, 1963.
54. Ainsa, pp. 86–102.

5: THE INDOMITABLE AMAZONS

1. Schiltz, p. 169.
2. Virgil, *Aeneid*, Book XI, p. 324.
3. Pseudo-Callisthenes, III, p. 20.
4. *Ibid*, III, p. 21.
5. *Ibid*, III, pp. 25–7.
6. Gil, p. 36.
7. Marco Polo, *The Description of the World*, c. 188–9, p. 424.
8. *Ibid*.
9. d'Ailly, *Imago Mundi*, c. 23, p. 23, col. 1.
10. Gil, p. 38.
11. Boorstin, pp. 140–1.
12. Columbus, *Diario* (entry for 6 January 1493), p. 315.
13. Varela, p. 115.
14. Columbus, *Diario* (entry for 16 January 1493), p. 343.
15. Columbus, 'Letter to Luis de Santángel', cited in Bourne and Olson, pp. 269–70.
16. Las Casas, cited in Madariaga, p. 292.
17. Peter Martyr, *Decades of the World*, 1.2.7; in *Selections from Peter Martyr*, p. 52.
18. Pigafetta, pp. 247–8.
19. Cited by Gandía, p. 76.
20. Levillier, pp. 115–27.
21. Díaz, p. 54.
22. Carvajal, p. 214.
23. Díaz, pp. 32–3. The account of Texeira's expedition was published for the first time in 1889 by the Spanish scholar Marcos Jiménez de La Espada. According to him, its author is the Jesuit Alonso de Rojas.
24. *Ibid*, p. 244.
25. Acuña, pp. 157–8.
26. *Ibid*, p. 183.
27. Schmidl, pp. 163–8; English translation cited in Moffitt, pp. 214–5.
28. Thevet, pp. 163–8.
29. Duviols, p. 49.
30. These citations are taken from Gandía, pp. 82–6.
31. Raleigh, p. 40.
32. D'Olwer, p. XV.
33. La Condamine, pp. 84–5.
34. *Ibid*, p. 88.
35. Humboldt, 1965, pp. 127–31.
36. Maestri, 1993.
37. Coudreau, pp. 230–2.

38. Torres Fuentes, pp. 104–6.
39. Humboldt, 1965, p. 124.
40. La Condamine, pp. 101–2.
41. Torres Fuentes, p. 106.

6: THE LEGENDARY ISLES OF THE OCEAN SEA

1. Plato, *Phaedo* (109a–114c), in *Portrait of Socrates*, pp. 183–4.
2. Pliny, Book VI, c. 36, p. 2106.
3. *Ibid*, c. 37, p. 2108.
4. Gravier, 1955.
5. Caddeo, p. 13.
6. Buarque de Holanda, pp. 223–5.
7. Mahn-Lot, p. 34.
8. Heers, 1981, p. 140.
9. Barron and Burgess, *The Voyage of Saint Brendan*, p. 319.
10. Orlandi, p. 75.
11. Kretschmer, 1892.
12. La Roncière and Molat du Jardin, p. 205.
13. *Ibid*, p. 218.
14. Heers, p. 139. For Heers, Saint Brendan's Isle and Antilia or the isle of the Seven Cities are parts of the same tradition.
15. Boortsin, p. 104.
16. Gandía, p. 7.
17. Draak and Aafjes, pp. 44–5.
18. Fernando Columbus, *History of the Life and Deeds of the Admiral Don Christopher Columbus*, p. 23.
19. *Ibid*, pp. 25–7.
20. Mahn-Lot, p. 32.
21. Babcock, pp. 152, 158, 179.
22. Gaffarel, 1881.
23. Gandía, p. 60.
24. *Ibid*, pp. 10–15.
25. Heers, pp. 138–9.
26. Madariaga, pp. 105–6.
27. *Narrative of the Third Voyage Columbus as Contained in Las Casas's History*, 1498, cited in Bourne and Olson, p. 326.
28. La Roncière and Molat du Jardin, pp. 30–1. The letters of John Day were discovered in 1954 by A Vigneras in the archives of Simancas (Mahn-Lot, p. 34).
29. Gil, pp. 81–3.
30. Vespucci, *The Letters*, p. 29.
31. Núñez Cabeza de Vaca, pp. 101–4.
32. D'Olwer, p. 311.
33. *Ibid*, pp. 311–2.
34. De Niza, published in D'Olwer, pp. 314–7.

35. *Ibid*, pp. 314–7.
36. Mahn-Lot, p. 90. See also Page p. 215 and Gandía, p. 67.
37. Ribault, 1958, *La Complète et Véridique Découverte de la Terra Florida*, 1563 (Les Français en Floride), Paris, PUF, cited by Duviols, p. 122.
38. Pliny, Book V, c. 8, p. 1405.

7: WONDROUS CREATURES

1. *Ibid*, p. 272.
2. Zapata Gollan, p. 9.
3. Mollat, p. 239.
4. Isidore, *Etymologies*, XI.3.1, p. 141.
5. *Ibid*, p. 49.
6. *Ibid*, p. 43.
7. d'Ailly, *Imago Mundi*, c. 37, p. 28, col. 1.
8. Cited by Zapata Gollan, pp. 9–10.
9. Duviols, pp. 14–15.
10. Mandeville, c. 8.
11. d'Ailly, *Ymago Mundi*, in Buron, p. 303.
12. Gil, p. 24.
13. Fernando Columbus, pp. 246–7.
14. Benavente, p. 150.
15. Zapata Gollan, p. 53.
16. Marco Polo, c. 191, p. 430.
17. Pigafetta, pp. 248–9.
18. Zapata Gollan, pp. 25–9.
19. Mode, p. 136; Ashmole, p. 147 and Page, p. 52.
20. Borges, pp. 90–1.
21. d'Ailly, in Buron, p. 267.
22. Alejo Carpentier, 'The Road to Santiago', in *Masterworks of Latin American Fiction*, pp. 236–7.
23. Mode, pp. 105–8.
24. Columbus, *Diario* (entry for 9 January 1493), cited by Madariaga, p. 228.
25. Bouyer, pp. 17–21.
26. Mode, pp. 232–3. On the attribution of the text, see John Friedman, 1986, 'The Marvels-of-the-East Tradition in Anglo-Saxon Art', *Sources of Anglo-Saxon Culture*, XX, *Studies in Medieval Culture*, Kalamazoo, Medieval Institute Publications, p. 320.
27. d'Ailly, in Buron, p. 267.
28. Raleigh, p. 69.
29. Humboldt, 1907, vol. 2, c. 2.20.
30. Mode, p. 219.
31. Gravier, p. 98. Prof. Gravier thinks that this passage might be a recent interpolation or that it might be an incorrect translation of *einfœtiger*, which may not mean uniped.
32. *The Four Voyages of Columbus*, vol. I, p. 12.

33. Cited by Gil, p. 30.
34. Pliny, Book VII, c. 2, p. 2134.
35. Graf, pp. 63–4.
36. Pseudo-Callisthenes, pp. 211–5.
37. *Ibid*, p. 207.
38. Ashmole, p. 68.
39. Gil, pp. 30–3.
40. d'Ailly, *Imago Mundi*, c. 16, p. 20, col. 1.
41. Varela, p. 51.
42. Columbus, *Diario* (entry for 23 November 1492), pp. 68–9.

8: THE PATAGONIAN GIANTS

1. Isidore of Seville, *Etymologies*, Book XI.3.12, p. 142.
2. Gandía, pp. 34–5.
3. Coyer, pp. 66–7.
4. *Ibid*, pp. 65–6.
5. Vespucci, *The Letters*, pp. 60–1.
6. Pigafetta, pp. 101–3.
7. *Ibid*, pp. 105–6.
8. *Ibid*, pp. 68–70, 75.
9. *Ibid*, pp. 165–6.
10. Chatwin, pp. 130–41 and Duviols, p. 59. Note that Braun-Menéndez leans towards the hypothesis of the 'big feet', pp. 37–8.
11. Pigafetta, pp. 122–3.
12. M. Guyot, 1968, *Les Mythes chez les Selknam et les Yamanas de la Terre de Feu*, Paris; Osvaldo Menghin, 1965, *Origen y desarrollo racial de la especie humana*, Buenos Aires, Nova and Salvador Canals-Frau, 1953, *Poblaciones indùigenas de la Argentina*, Buenos Aires, Sudamericana.
13. The list of references to Patagonian giants that follows has been taken from Duviols, pp. 60–9 and from the introduction as well as Coyer's *Sobre los Gigantes Patagones*, pp. 14–20.
14. Sarmiento de Gamboa, 1988. For the first voyage, see pp. 109–23; for the second, pp. 283–6.
15. Braun-Menéndez, pp. 40–1.
16. *Ibid*.
17. Cited by Duviols, p. 71

REFERENCES

Abraham, K, 1965, Rêve et mythe, contribution à l'étude de la psychologie collective, in *Psychoanalyse et Culture*, Paris, Payot.

Acuña C S J, 1716, Relation de la rivière des Amazones, in *Voyage autour du monde par le Capitaine Woodes Rogers*, vol. II, Amsterdam, translated by Clements, R M, 1859, A relation of the great river of Amazons in South America, in *Expeditions into the Valley of the Amazons*.

Ainsa, F, 1992, *Historia, utopía y ficción de la Ciudad de los Césares*, Madrid, Alianza Universidad.

Ashmole, M S, 1511, Bodleian Library, Oxford, translated by Dupuis M-F, and Louis S (eds), 1988, *Introduction and commentary by Xénia Muratova and Daniel Poirion*, France, Philippe Lebaud.

Babcock, W, 1922, *Legendary islands of the Atlantic: A Study in Medieval Geography*, Research series no. 8, New York, American Geographical Society.

Bagrow, L, and Skelton, R A, 1964, *History of Cartography*, London.

Barron, W R J, and Burgess, G S, 2002, *The Voyage of Saint Brendan*, Exeter, University of Exeter Press.

Benavente, T Fr, 1973, *Historia de los Indios de la Nueva España*, in O'Gorman, E (ed.), Mexico, Porrua.

Blaeu's The Grand Atlas of the 17th century world. Introduction, commentary and selection of maps by John Goss, 1990, London, Studio Editions.

Boorstin, D, 1986, *Les Découvreurs*, Paris, Robert Laffont.

Borges, J L, 1986, *El Libro de los seres imaginarios*, Barcelona, Brugera.

Bourne, E G, and Julius, E O (eds), 1906, *The Northmen, Columbus, and Cabot, 985–1503*, New York, C. Scribner's Sons.

Bouyer, M, 1974, América fantástica, in *Artes Visuales*, Mexico City, no. 4.

Braun-Menéndez, A, 1971, *Pequeña Historia Patagónica*, 4th edn., Buenos Aires, Santiago.

Buarque de Holanda, S, 1987, *Visión del Paraíso: motivos edénicos en el descubrimiento y colonización del Brasil*, Caracas, Ayacucho, translation corrected and augmented by the author in 1979.

Burgh, J, 1963, *Un relato de la colonización, de las leyes, formas de gobierno y costumbres de los Césares...*, Coll. Americana. Santiago de Chile, Ed. Universitaria.

Caddeo, R, 1927, *Le Navigazioni Atlantiche*, Milan, Alpes.

Cartes des Amériques dans les collections de la Bibliothèque royale Albert Ier:
   catalogue de l'exposition organisée du 13 novembre au 31 décembre 1992,
   Brussels, Bibliothèque Royale Albert Ier.

Carpentier, A, 1971, *El Camino de Santiago*, Santiago de Chile, Nascimento,
   translated by Canfield C (ed.), 1996, *Masterworks of Latin American
   Fiction: Eight Novellas*, New York, Westview Press.

Carvajal, G, 1934, *The Discovery of the Amazons According to the Account of
   Friar Gaspar de Carvajal and Other Documents*, in Medina J T (ed.), and
   Bertram, T L (trans.), New York, American Geographical Society.

Castellanos, J, 1589, *Elegías para varones ilustres de los Indias*.

Centenera, M B, 1965, *The Argentine and the Conquest of the River Plate*,
   Buenos Aires, Instituto Cultural Walter Owen.

Chatwin, B, 1977, *In Patagonia*, London, Cape.

Columbus, C, 1906, Letter to Luis de Santángel, in Bourne E G, and Olson
   J E (eds), *The Northmen, Columbus, and Cabot, 985-1503*, New York, C.
   Scribner's Sons, pp. 269-70.

Columbus, C, 1906, Narrative of The Third Voyage Columbus as Contained
   in Las Casas's History, May 30-August 31, 1498, in Bourne E G,
   and Olson J E (eds), *The Northmen, Columbus, and Cabot, 985-1503*,
   New York, C. Scribner's Sons.

Columbus, C, 1930–33, *The Four Voyages of Columbus*, in Jane, C, (trans. and
   ed.), vol. 2, London, Hakluyt Society, (reprint, 1988, New York, Dover
   Publications).

Columbus, F, 1984, *Historia del Almirante*, in Arranz L (ed.), Madrid,
   Historia 16, translated by Caraci, I L, 2004 (ed.), *History of the Life and
   Deeds of the Admiral Don Christopher Columbus*, Turnhout, Brepols.

Columbus, C, 1989, *The Diario of Christopher Columbus's First Voyage to
   America 1492–1493*, Dunn, O, and Kelley, J E, Norman, University of
   Oklahoma Press.

Columbus, C, 1992, Letter to Pope Alexander VI, February 1502, in Kadir,
   D (ed.), *Columbus and the Ends of the Earth: Europe's Prophetic Rhetoric as
   Conquering Ideology*, Berkeley, LA, University of California Press, p. 202.

Cortázar, J, 1984, *Ces mythes qui nous hantent…*, Document no. 9 of the Unité
   de didactique français, Radio-Télévision Belge Francophone and
   Université Catholique de Louvain.

Coudreau, H A, 1886, *La France équinoxiale*, Paris.

Coyer, G-F S J, 1767, *A Letter to Doctor Maty*, in Becket, T, and de Hondt, P A
   (eds), London, translated by Avila Martel, 1984, *Sobre los Gigantes
   Patagones. Carta del abate François-Gabriel Coyer al doctor Maty, secretario
   de la Royal Society de Londres*, Santiago, University of Chile.

Cuneo, M, 2002, News of the islands of the Hesperian Ocean discovered by
   Don Christopher Columbus of Genoa 1495, in Symcox, G (ed.), *Italian
   Reports on America 1493-1522, Accounts by Conteporary Observers*,
   Repertorium Columbianum, vol. XII, Turnhout, Brepols.

d'Ailly, P [Petrus Aliacus], 1930, *Ymago Mundi, Latin text and French translation of the four cosmographical treatises by d'Ailly with the marginal notes of*

Christopher Columbus, in Buron, E (ed.), Paris, Maisonneuve Frères Editeurs, translated by Edwin, F K, 1948, *Imago mundi by Petrus Ailliacus*, Wilmington, NC, British Library Latin photostat no. 40,582.

Découvreurs & Conquérants, 1980, Paris, Atlas.

Deluz, C, 1988, *Le Livre de Jehan de Mandeville, une géographie au XIVe siècle*, Louvain-la-Neuve.

Descola, J, 1976, Fabuleux Eldorado, in *Les Dernières Mystères du Monde*, Paris, Sélection du Reader's Digest.

Díaz, R, 1986, *G. de Carvahal, P. de Almestro y Alonso de Rojas. La Aventura del Amazonas*, Madrid, Historia 16.

Dicuil, 1967, *Liber de mensura orbis terrae*, Dublin, J J Tierney.

D'Olwer, L N, 1981, *Cronistas de las culturas precolombinas*, Mexico, Fondo de Cultura Económica.

Draak, M, and Aafjes, B, 1978, *De Reis van sinte Brandaan*, Amsterdam.

Duby, G, 1974, *L'An Mil*, Paris, Archives Gallimard/Julliard.

Duviols, J-P, 1985, *L'Amérique espagnole vue et rêvée*, Paris, Promodis.

Estorach, S, and Michel, L, 1984, *Christophe Colomb. La découverte de l'Amérique I, Journal de bord, 1492–93*, Paris, La Découverte.

Fernández de Oviedo, G, 1555, The historie of the Weste Indies, in Eden R (ed.), *The Deedes of the Newe Worlde,* London.

Friedman, J, 1986, The Marvels-of-the-East Tradition in Anglo-Saxon Art, in *Sources of Anglo-Saxon Culture. Studies in Medieval Culture, XX*, Kalamazoo, Medieval Institute Publications.

Gaffarel, P, 1881, *L'Ile des Sept Cités et l'île d'Antilia. Actes du congrès international d'américanistes, 4e réunion*, Madrid, Biblioteca nacional.

Gandía, E, 1929, *Historia crítica de los mitos de la conquista americana*, Buenos Aires, Juan Roldán y Cia.

Gil, J, 1989, *Mitos y Utopías del Descubrimiento*, vol. I, Madrid, Alianza Editorial.

Graf, A, 1925, *Miti, Leggende e Superstizioni del Medio Evo*, Turin, Giovanni Chiantore.

Grant, M, and John, H, 1988, *Dictionnaire de la mythologie*, Paris, Marabout.

Gravier, M, 1955, *La Saga d'Erik le Rouge. Le Récit des Groenlandais*, Paris, Ed. Montaigne, (Icelandic text with introduction, translation, notes and glossary by Maurice Gravier, professor at the Sorbonne).

Guerdon, J D, 1972, *Les Plus mystérieuses légendes de la mer*, France, Sélection du Reader's Digest.

Hale, J R, 1967, *L'Age des découvertes*, Paris, Time-Life collection.

Heers, J, 1975, *Le Travail au Moyen Age*, Paris, PUF.

Heers, J, 1981, *Christophe Colomb*, Paris, Hachette.

Humboldt, A, 1965, *L'Amérique espagnole en 1800 vue par un savant allemand*, in Tulard, J (ed.), Paris, Calman-Lévy, translated by Ross T (ed.), 1907, *Personal Narrative of Travels to the Equinoctial Regions of America During the Years 1799–804*, London, George Bell & Sons.

Isidore of Seville, 1983, *Etimologías*, Madrid, Biblioteca de los autores cristianos, translated by Brehaut E, 1912, *An Encyclopedist of the Dark Ages: Isidore of Seville*, New York, Columbia University.

Jomard, E-F, 1862, *Les Monuments de la géographie, ou recueil d'anciennes cartes européennes et orientales*, Paris.

Julien, N, 1992, *Le Dictionnnaire des mythes*, Alleur, Belgium, Marabout.

Kadir, D, 1992, *Columbus and the Ends of the Earth: Europe's Prophetic Rhetoric as Conquering Ideology*, Berkeley, LA, University of California Press.

Kretschmer, K, 1892, *Die Entdeckung Amerikas in ihrer Bedeutung für die Geschichte des Weltbildes*, Berlin.

Kupcik, I, 1984, *Cartes géographiques anciennes*, Paris, Grün.

La Condamine, C-M, 1981, *Voyage sur l'Amazone*, Paris, François Maspero, translated by Pinkerton, J, 1808, Abridged narrative of travels through the interior of South America and travels in all parts of the world, in *A General Collection of the Best and Most Interesting Voyages*, vol. 14, London.

La Roncière, M, and Michel, M J, 1984, *Les Portulans*, Fribourg, Office du livre.

Levillier, R, 1976, *El Paitití, el Dorado y las Amazonas*, Buenos Aires, Emecé.

Libro del conosçimiento, 1912, Jiménez de la Espada first published this book in volume VII of the *Colección de libros españoles raros o curiosos* in Madrid in 1874. It was then published in the appendix of volume II of the *Boletín de la Sociedad geográfica* in Madrid in 1877 under the title *Libro del conosçimiento de todos los reynos y tierra y señoríos que son por el mondo y de las señales y armas que han cada tierra y señorío por sy y de los reyes y señores que los proven, escrito por un franciscano español a mediado del siglo XIV*. It was then translated into English under the title *Book of Knowledge of all the Kingdoms, Lands, and Lordships that are in the World*, London, Hakluyt Society.

Los Beatos, 1985, *Catalogue de l'exposition réalisée en 1985 dans le cadre d'Europalia 85 España à la Bibliothèque Royale Albert Ier*, Brussels.

Madariaga, S, 1940, *Christopher Columbus: Being the Life of the Very Magnificent Lord Don Cristóbal Colón*, London, Macmillan.

Madeira Santos, M E, 1988, *Viagens de exploracão terrestre dos Portugueses em Africa*, Lisbon, Centro de estudos de História e Cartografía Antigua.

Maestri, M, 1993, *I Signori del littorale*, Typescript.

Mahn-Lot, M, 1964, *La Découverte de l'Amérique*, Paris, Flammarion.

Mandeville, J, 1900, *Travels of Sir John de Mandeville*, in Pollard, A W (ed.), New York, Macmillan.

Mathieu, J, 1977, *Drakkars sur l'Amazone*, Paris, Copernic.

Meslin, M, 1984, *Le Merveilleux*, Paris, Bordas.

Mode, H, 1977, *Démons et Animaux fantastiques*, Paris, Librairie G. Kogan.

Moffitt, J F, 1996, *O Brave New People: The European Invention of the American Indian*, Santiago Sebastián, University of New Mexico Press.

Mollat, M, 1984, *Les Explorateurs du XIIIe au XVIe siècle*, Paris, J-C Lattès.

Morales, E, 1944, *La Ciudad encantada de la Patagonia*, Buenos Aires, Emece.

Morison, S E, 1983, *Admiral of the Ocean Sea: a Life of Christopher Columbus*, Boston,MA, Northeastern University Press.

Núñez Cabeza de Vaca, Á, 1987, *Naufragios y Comentarios*, in Morales, J G (ed.), Madrid, Aguilar, translated by Favato, M A, and Fernández, J B,

1993, *The Account: Alvar Núñez Cabeza de Vaca's Relación*, Houston, Arte Pública Press.

Orlandi, I, 1968, *Navigatio sancti Brendani*, vol. I, Milan, Varese.

Ortiz de la Tabla, J, 1987, *Introducción y notas a Francisco Vázquez: El Dorado: Crónica de la expedición de Pedro de Ursúa y Lope de Aguirre*, Madrid, Alianza Editorial.

Page, M, 1985, *Encyclopédie des mondes qui n'existent plus*, Paris, Gallimard.

Payro, R J, 1927, 'Las Ciudades Quiméricas', and 'Expediciones en busca del Dorado y la Ciudad de los Césares, desde 1513 hasta 1800, según los datos que he podido compulsar', in *Nosotros*, Argentina, no. 218.

Peter, M, 1998, *Selections from Peter Martyr*, in Eatough G (ed.), Brepols, Repertorium Columbianum V, Turnhout.

Pigafetta, A, 1985, *Primer Viaje alrededor del mundo*, in Leoncio, C (ed.), Madrid, Historia 16, Crónicas de Amérida, no. 12, translated by Charles, E N, 1962, *First Voyage around the World* in *Magellan's Voyage around the World: Three Contemporary Accounts*, Evanston, IL, Northwestern University.

Plato, 1938, *Phaedo*, in *Portrait of Socrates: Being the Apology, Crito, and Phaedo of Plato in English Translation*, in Livinstone, R W (ed.), Oxford, Clarendon Press.

Pliny the Elder, 1855, *Natural History*, Bostock J, and Riley H T (trans.), London, Henry G. Bohn.

Pohl, F J, 1944, *Amerigo Vespucci Pilot Major*, New York, Columbia University Press.

Polo, M, 1938, *The Description of the World*, Moule A C, and Pelliot P (trans.), London, George Routledge and Sons.

Pseudo-Callisthenes, 1977, *Vida y Hazañas de Alejandro de Macedonia*, in Carlos, G (ed.), Madrid, Gredos, translated by Ernest, A W B, 1889, *The History of Alexander the Great, Being the Syriac Version, Edited from Five Manuscripts of the Pseudo-Callisthenes with an English Translation*, Amsterdam, APA, Philo Press, (English translation and reprint, 1976, Cambridge University Press).

Raleigh, W, 1887, *The Discovery of Guiana and the Journal of the Second Voyage Thereto*, London, Cassell and Company.

Romano, R, 1972, *Les Mécanismes de la conquête coloniale: les conquistadores*, Coll. 'Questions d'Histoire', Paris, Flammarion.

Sánchez-Albornoz, N, 1977, *La Población de América latina, desde los tiempos precolombinos al año 2000*, Madrid, Alianza Universidad.

San Martín, J, and de Lebrija, A, 1536–39, *Relación del descubrimiento y conquista del nuevo Reino de Granada*.

Santaella, R (ed.), 1987, *El libro de Marco Polo*, Madrid, Alianza Editorial.

Sarmiento de Gamboa, P, 1947, *Historia de los Incas*, Buenos Aires, Emecé, translated by Clements, R M, 1907, *History of the Incas*, Cambridge, The Hakluyt Society.

Sarmiento de Gamboa, P, 1988, *Viajes al Estrecho de Magallanes*, Madrid, Alianza Editorial.

208 *America Magica*

Schiltz, V, 1975, 'La Civilisation des Sauromates', in *L'Or des Scythes. Catalogue de l'exposition*, Paris, Ed. des Musées nationaux.

Schmidl, U, 1986, *Relatos de la conquista del Río de la Plata y Paraguay 1534–54, Introduction and notes by Klaus Wagner*, Madrid, Alianza Editorial.

Slessarev, V, 1959, *Prester John: The Letter and the Legend*, Minneapolis, University of Minnesota Press.

Thevet, A, 1983, *Les Singularités de la France Antartique*, Paris, La Découverte/Maspero, in *The New Found Worlde or Antarctike*, 1568, London, (reprint 1971, Amsterdam, The True Orbis Terrarum).

Torres Fuentes, L, 1989, A Lenda das Amazonas, *Océanos of the Comissão nacional para as comemoracões dos descobrimentos portugueses, Lisbon*, vol. 2.

Van Beek, C, 1938, *Florilegium patristicum*, fasc. 43, Bonn.

Varela, C, 1984, *Cristóbal Colón. Textos y documentos completes*, Madrid, Alianza Editorial.

Vespucci, A, 1907, Letter on his first voyage, in *The Cosmographiae Introductio by Martin Waldseemüller followed by the Four Voyages of Amerigo Vespucci*, translated by Joseph, F, and von Wieser, F, in Charles, G H (ed.), New York, US Catholic Historical Society.

Vespucci, A, 1986, *Cartas de viaje, Introduction and notes by Luciano Formisano*, Madrid, Alianza Editorial, translated by Clements, R M (ed.), 1894, *The Letters of Amerigo Vespucci*, London, Hakluyt Society, first series no. 90, (reprint, 1964, New York, Burt Franklin).

Villanueva, H, 1984, *Vida y pasión del Río de la Plata*, Buenos Aires, Plus Ultra.

Virgil, 1951, *The Aeneid of Virgil: A Verse Translation*, in Humphries, R (ed.), New York, C. Scribner's Sons.

World in Maps, 1990, The Documentary broadcast on Granada Television International.

Zapata Gollan, A, 1963, *Mito y Superstición en la conquista de América*, Buenos Aires, Ed. Universitaria de Buenos Aires.

INDEX